James Bald

T0243851

"Finally, the James Baldwin we've been waiting for: the revolutionary, fierce internationalist, queer theorist, anti-imperialist, anti-Zionist, and perhaps the most dangerous thinker of the twentieth century. If you want to know the real Baldwin, this is the book to read."

—Robin D.G. Kelley, author of *Thelonious Monk:*
The Life and Times of an American Original

"A fresh, incisive, and uplifting biography."

—*Kirkus*

"A clear, incisive writer, Mullen succeeds with providing a fresh perspective on an author he so obviously admires. Recommended for readers seeking a broader understanding of the opinions of one of the great writers of the twentieth century."

—*Library Journal*

"A smart, concise introduction."

—*Guardian*

"A remarkable biography."

—*Le Monde Diplomatique*

"One of the most important publishing events of this political age. Lucidly and compellingly written, it updates and recontextualizes our knowledge of the complex, humane brilliance of Baldwin, drawing out his importance not only for the ages, but most urgently for our present day. It is a book that angers, moves, and inspires. An indispensable weapon for any activist fighting today's raging fires."

—David Palumbo-Liu, Louise Hewlett Nixon Professor
and Professor of Comparative Literature at Stanford
University and author of *The Deliverance of Others*

"A welcome contribution to a portrait of the radical Baldwin, untamed by liberal platitudes."

—*Jacobin*

James Baldwin

Living in Fire

Bill V. Mullen

PLUTO PRESS

For Max and Shayari

First published 2019 by Pluto Press
New Wing, Somerset House, Strand, London WC2R 1LA
and Pluto Press, Inc.
1930 Village Center Circle, 3-834, Las Vegas, NV 89134

New edition published 2024

www.plutobooks.com

British Library Cataloguing in Publication Data
A catalogue record for this book is available from the British Library

ISBN 978 0 7453 3853 8   Paperback
ISBN 978 0 7453 3854 5   Hardback
ISBN 978 1 7868 0496 9   PDF eBook
ISBN 978 1 7868 0497 6   EPUB eBook
ISBN 978 0 7453 4034 0   Audio

This book is printed on paper suitable for recycling and made from fully
managed and sustained forest sources. Logging, pulping and manufacturing
processes are expected to conform to the environmental standards of the
country of origin.

Typeset by Stanford DTP Services, Northampton, England

Simultaneously printed in the United Kingdom and United States of America

Contents

Illustrations

1. James Baldwin in 1955, the year of publication of his essay collection *Notes of a Native Son*.

2. Baldwin with his friend, actor Marlon Brando, at the 1963 March on Washington.

3. Baldwin lecturing in Amsterdam, 1984.

4. Baldwin in Hyde Park, London, 1968.

5. Baldwin on a 1974 speaking tour in Amsterdam, here promoting a Dutch translation of his novel *If Beale Street Could Talk*. In 2018 Director Barry Jenkins (*Moonlight*) adopted the novel for film.

6. Baldwin demonstrated an interest in anarchism in the 1940s. He subscribed to both *Why?*, a U.S.-based anarchist periodical, and *War Commentary*, an anarchist publication produced in the United Kingdom. He likely attended anarchist meetings in New York before leaving the U.S. for Paris in 1948.

7. Baldwin described himself as a "socialist" and a "Trotskyite" for a brief time during the 1940s. He subscribed at least temporarily to *Challenge!*, the newspaper of the Young People's Socialist League, which he claimed to have joined. This issue from his personal archive is dated 1944.

8. Baldwin struggled to make ends meet after graduating high school. In 1944, he worked temporarily for both the U.S. Postal Service, and the Office of War Information. These 1944 government tax forms show him earning

a total of $47.25 in the former job and $125.00 in the latter.

9. Baldwin's dear friend, mentor and muse Beauford Delaney, a model for Baldwin of what the Black artist could be, painted this portrait of Baldwin around 1957.

10. Letter sent to Mary Painter by Baldwin, from the A.G. Gaston Motel, one of the few Black-owned hotels in the South, and thus something of a refuge.

11. A page from the manuscript for *Another Country* including the handwritten inscription, "Mary's Copy."

12. 81 Horatio Street in Greenwich Village. Baldwin wrote parts of his novel *Another Country* here.

13. In 2015, the Greenwich Village Society for Historic Preservation dedicated this plaque to Baldwin's time lived at this Horatio Street address.

14. Baldwin in Hyde Park, London.

15. In 2014, New York designated 128th Street between Madison Avenue and Fifth Avenue "James Baldwin place."

16. Public school, P.S. 124, on 128th street in Harlem, attended by Baldwin.

17. The house in St. Paul de Vence in southern France Baldwin purchased in 1971. Baldwin spent much of his later years there, and died there in 1987.

18. Tombstone of James Baldwin and his mother, Berdis. In Ferncliffe Cemetery and Mausoleum, Westchester County, New York.

Preface to the Paperback Edition

I'm optimistic about the future, but not about the future of this civilization.

I'm optimistic about the civilization which will replace this one.

James Baldwin, Interview, *Transatlantic Review*, 1970

James Baldwin: Living in Fire was first published by Pluto Press in September 2019. The first edition underscored Baldwin's long history of writing and organizing against U.S. racism and capitalism, his support for decolonial liberation, his radical queer politics, and his lifetime of unheralded political work on behalf of the oppressed. It was for these reasons that after the 2012 shooting of Trayvon Martin helped to launch the world-wide Black Lives Matter movement Baldwin became a symbol of that moment. Writers from Ta-Nehesi Coates to Teju Cole, internet activists like Robert Jones, Jr. (son of Baldwin), and filmmakers like Raoul Peck rushed to document and revive Baldwin's record as an activist, especially against police brutality. Suddenly, Baldwin's famous 1966 essay "A Report From Occupied Territory," which called the police the main oppressive force against Black people, took on the weight of prophecy.

Nine months after the book was published, on May 25, 2020, history repeated itself when George Floyd was murdered by Minneapolis police. Literally millions of people again took to the street. In Minneapolis, protesters set the third police precinct on fire. In Portland, protesters occupied the city center. Rebellions raged across American cities large and small. It was as if Baldwin's words were again echoing in the ears of a new generation of protesters. The only way to reform racism, poverty and police brutality, Baldwin wrote, was "out of existence."

This new paperback edition of *Living in Fire* coincides with and commemorates not just these events but an even more important one to a biography: 2024 marks the 100th anniversary of James Baldwin's birth. In the five years since the original hardback edition of this book was published, the centennial of Baldwin's appearance in the world has become even more timely for our present. Baldwin's predictions about the rise of fascism in the United States took on an urgent register with the 2021 January 6th white supremacist riot in Washington, an event preceded by attacks on Black citizens of that city. Baldwin's warning that, "The truth is that the bulk of white people in America never had any interest in educating black people, except as this could serve white purposes" has been starkly realized in the revival of book banning, attacks on critical race theory, and the demonization of so-called "wokeness" across the United States. Baldwin's classic works, such as *The Fire Next Time*, have themselves come under renewed fire by the Far Right,[1] just as his radical and groundbreaking first novel, *Go Tell It On the Mountain*[2], has frequently been banned by reactionaries for its rendering of gay male sexual desire.

The fact that James Baldwin and his writings remain dangerous 100 years after his birth tells us several things. First, that the structures of power—racism, sexism, homophobia, transphobia, nationalism, capitalism—that Baldwin railed against are still in need of dismantling. Second, that to be Black and queer and left in America (or anyplace in the world) is still a position of extreme vulnerability—something the leadership of the Black Lives Matter movement helped us further understand. Third, that words are dangerous in the best possible way, because until full fascism does come, they can be read, and used, to dismantle what Audre Lorde once called the "master's house." Indeed, since 2019 there has been further eruption and discovery of things unseen about Baldwin's magnificent life: for example, a trio of documentary films about his years as an expatriate,[3] and a theatrical recreation of Baldwin's 1984 dialogue with Audre Lorde, a life-changing moment for them both discussed in this book.[4] Other Baldwin scholars like William Maxwell are at work on new studies of Baldwin, and there are plans to make a feature film of David Leeming's 1994 biography of Baldwin.

The persistence of our desire to know and understand James Baldwin is a mirror up to his own radical impulses. Baldwin was a master of historical analysis who knew that the past is prologue to the present, and that understanding both is a precondition for making a revolution. This new edition of James Baldwin's life on his 100th birthday is a gift that can let us see and feel once again how to realize his dream of a better world.

January 2024

Introduction

James Baldwin—A Revolutionary for Our Time

You are talking to a man who lives in fire. What you have to understand is that people who are living in fire, have no sympathy with them who are afraid of the fire.

> James Baldwin, television interview, 1972[1]

[L]ove between men predicates not only the inevitable suffering but the very real possibility of becoming absolutely bankrupt.

> James Baldwin, letter to Mary Garin-Painter, 1956[2]

The only hope this country has is to turn overnight into a revolutionary country, and I say "revolutionary" in the most serious sense of that word: to undermine the standards by which the middle-class American lives.

> James Baldwin, speech at the Liberation Committee for Africa, 1961[3]

James Baldwin was born in Harlem, New York's vital, turbulent black Mecca, in 1924. His school teacher, Orilla Miller, said the Baldwin family home embodied the "worst poverty" that she ever saw.[4] Baldwin was born five years before the 1929 stock market crash, but Harlem was already in a state of depression: his first memories were of ghetto detritus—rats and broken glass, heroin needles, and abusive landlords. Baldwin later referred to the area of his birth, 135th Street and

Lenox Avenue, as "Junkie's Hollow."[5] His father, David, a Pentecostal storefront preacher, was an angry working-class man, a worker at a soda bottling plant in Long Island, New York, just across the Harlem River. He hated most white people, a fact Baldwin only later in life understood as a by-product of the fact that he couldn't feed his nine children on a salary of $27.50 per week.[6] His mother, a migrant single mother from the American South, felt love for her son James matched only by the hardship she endured raising him—and later—his eight siblings.

In many ways Baldwin's life was an attempt to both transcend this fire, and carry it with him. His first of seven novels, *Go Tell It On the Mountain*, is based closely on events in his Harlem youth. One of his first major essays, "The Harlem Ghetto," published in 1948 when he was all of 24, was a searing dissection of the grotesque social conditions that produced himself, and many, many African-Americans like him. Baldwin knew that escaping Harlem made him an exception—for every one of me, he wrote, there were thousands of young black boys dead, in prison, or "on the needle"—and created two roles for him as an American writer: as survivor and witness. In this Baldwin conjoined himself to a long history of African-American protest writing dating to the American slave narrative, which seeks to describe oppression and economic subjugation for readers in a world outside that system. This capacity, which Baldwin called "truth-telling," or "disturbing the peace," was also fundamental to the development of a political self that showed no patience for oppression or the oppressor, and compelled him to turn rage into resistance. In a famous 1970 letter to his political sister, the revolutionary Angela Davis as she awaited trial in Marin County on false charges of murder, Baldwin wrote:

We know that we, the blacks, and not only we, the blacks, have been, and are, the victims of a system whose only fuel is greed, whose only god is profit. We know that the fruits of this system have been ignorance, despair, and death, and we know that the system is doomed because the world can no longer afford it—if, indeed, it ever could have. And we know that, for the perpetuation of this system, we have all been mercilessly brutalized, and have been told nothing but lies, lies about ourselves and our kinsmen and our past, and about love, life, and death, so that both soul and body have been bound in hell.

The enormous revolution in black consciousness which has occurred in your generation, my dear sister, means the beginning or the end of America. Some of us, white and black, know how great a price has already been paid to bring into existence a new consciousness, a new people, an unprecedented nation. If we know, and do nothing, we are worse than the murderers hired in our name.[7]

This passage encapsulates for Baldwin what it means to "live in fire," and to relentlessly rage against those who made him burn. It is no accident that his most famous work of social protest is titled *The Fire Next Time*, and his most famous metaphor for America a "burning house."

The second epigraph above points us to another dimension of Baldwin's radical life: as a Black, queer, working-class man coming of age in Cold War, homophobic America. Baldwin noted in his diary while in high school that he believed he might be gay. Yet his introduction to queer life in America was indirect, covert, and violent in ways characteristic of the homophobic hegemony of the world of his youth and young adulthood. He recalled being seduced into an alleyway by a desirous man as an adolescent, an encounter that left him confused, and given his religious upbringing, ashamed. Baldwin was forced to live on the "down-low" as a boy in Harlem, closeting his sexuality from his family, especially his mother. John Grimes, the protagonist of *Go Tell It On the Mountain*, is Baldwin's avatar of this life experience. Once Baldwin graduated from school, he moved immediately to Greenwich Village in New York, then, as now, a partial port for gay men. He meandered between confused heterosexual attraction—nearly marrying—and chance queer encounters in public places, like movie theaters.

His move to Paris in 1948 was, in part, an effort to reconcile what he called the "mystery" of his sexuality. As he later told an interviewer of his state of mind before leaving the U.S., "I no longer felt who I really was, whether I was really black or really white, really male or really female."[8] Once in Paris, Baldwin began to imagine his breakthrough queer novel of the 1950s—*Giovanni's Room*, set in France and published in 1956. The bold experiment of writing the novel, and threats of censorship, terrified him. Its publication, however, allowed him incrementally to include more and more of his gay private life—lovers from Paris, and later Istanbul—into his fictional representations of the 1960s and 1970s. Yet throughout this period, Baldwin remained a vilified, stigmatized figure: his mentor Richard Wright gay-baited his "unmanly weeping" as part of their private feud; a popular slur of the civil rights era referred to him as "Martin Luther Queen;" Black Panther Party leader Eldridge Cleaver accused Baldwin in his real life and fiction of giving himself up to political sodomy from the white man. Public homophobic acrimony was the price Baldwin paid for his sexuality, a cost he understood as literal and figurative "bankruptcy" for those for whom queer life could mean literally forfeiting chances at a normative life. The metaphor of bankruptcy was a reminder too that despite an extraordinary publishing career that included bestselling novels (*Another Country*), several successful books of essays, a pair of well-received plays, and numerous high-profile magazine articles, Baldwin lived perpetually on the meanest margins of capitalist society, fending off poverty as a constant, even as he battled to provide materially for those he loved and supported, like his family, from whom ironically he was forced to shield elements of his life.

Baldwin navigated these predicaments and assaults skillfully, though often internalizing debilitating depression, even suicidal thoughts. By the 1980s, Baldwin was "out" enough to publically identify as gay, though he disliked the term, a point to which we will return. More importantly, though, Baldwin spent his life challenging heteronormative black and white sexuality on its own terms, ridiculing the fetishizing of straight bodies and straight lives as part of a culture of reaction, repression, and gay panic in the United States. It was in part in conversation with black feminists of the 1970s that Baldwin began to further prise open this space of critique: both defending black men like his father from assault by the capitalist system, while recognizing in black feminism a parallel struggle to his own to disrupt and dispel white, middle-class hegemony in both the women's movement and the gay and lesbian movement (this was before transgender rights were attached to those two, and before the common self-designation "queer.") Yet if Baldwin's "truth-telling" was to be both witness and survivor, his life is also a bracing testimonial to being the first African-American radical to make his sexuality an integral aspect of his public attack of racism, sexism, homophobia, and more generally, the matrix of repressive American power both domestically and internationally. Indeed, Baldwin's famous and long periods of exile from the U.S. were also platforms to literally live and write a queer life—an "erotics of exile," as Magdalena

Zaborowska has dubbed it—and to dissect his homeland as a place that functioned to repress, depress, or destroy young black men like himself.[9]

Yet rather than succumb, Baldwin developed a capacious, revolutionary theory and practice of lived resistance to capitalism, imperialism, and oppression fueled by a lifetime of study, engagement, and creative tension with the most dissident political movements in the U.S. and around the world. In 1961, at the age of 37, Baldwin named this dissidence "revolution," to reference our third quotation above, inspired by the worldwide sweep of anti-colonial movements across Africa and Asia, and by the sudden emergence in the United States of more militant wings of black civil rights struggle: the Student Nonviolent Coordinating Committee, and the Nation of Islam. But Baldwin was also no political neophyte to the idea of "revolution" in 1961; the word and idea had come to him in prior forms that this book will also mine, interrogate, and discuss. Baldwin was exposed to Communist school teachers as a child, and to socialist and anarchist political organizations in 1940s New York; he was recruited by the Trotskyist left, and described himself in the 1940s as a socialist. His poetry appeared in the Communist *Daily Worker*, and his essays in journals, like *Partisan Review* and *Commentary*, both influenced by the anti-Stalinist left. Even before the Cold War began formally, Baldwin had discerned the Stalinist nature of the U.S. Communist Party, which during World War II had retrenched on questions of racial justice in order to support the Soviet Union, and betrayed personal friends, in Baldwin's estimation, like Richard Wright. Baldwin also claims that for a brief time he was a member of the Young People's Socialist League, convinced to join by his friend Eugene Worth. Finally, Baldwin's personal archives indicate he read the newspapers of both the Socialist Workers Party and its offshoot, the Workers

Party, both Trotskyist organizations. They also indicate—
something heretofore not noted by scholars—a close interest
in anarchist politics during the war years. As Baldwin later
put it in a letter to his teacher Orilla Winfield, "After my
father died (1943) I ... made it all the way from the Stalinists
to the Anarchists in what I think must be record time."[10] For
Baldwin, the 1930s and 1940s, the years of his adolescence and
young adulthood, was a period of exploration and experiment
that this book will argue gave direct shape to many of the later
more radical political decisions of his life, such as his support
for Palestinian liberation, his embrace of "Third World"
non-aligned politics during the Cold War, and his relentless
critique of anti-Communist repression in the United States,
a tendency on evidence in his letter to Communist Angela
Davis, cited earlier.

Indeed, as critical as his endeavor to build an "indigenous"
radical American politics—what Baldwin called, sympathetically in 1971, a "Yankee Doodle" form of socialism—was,
Baldwin's embrace of global anti-imperialist politics themselves nurtured by a sympathetic exposure to and engagement
with anti-colonial, subaltern, anti-racist struggles. The first
example beyond U.S. shores was Baldwin's attention to the
plight of North African refugees and residents of France
after his exile there in 1948. Baldwin was in Paris when the
Algerian Revolution began in 1954. Even prior to it, he had
noted the disproportionate number of North Africans in
French prisons, their tenuous economic existence on the
fringes of French society, and the unsubtle French racism
that made him assert, in later writings, that Algerians were
the "niggers" of France. Baldwin's decisions to leave France
to go to the U.S. to cover the civil rights struggle (in 1957)
and to go to Turkey (in 1961, where he lived on and off
more than ten years) should be seen as dialectical moments

in his political education: especially after reporting on the 1956 *Présence Africaine* anti-colonial conference in Paris and listening to speakers like Frantz Fanon, Baldwin knew, despite early resistance to the idea, that the African-American, the Turk, the Arab, the Muslim, the African, the colonized everywhere, were one unified "wretched of the earth." His 1961 call for "revolution" at a meeting for African liberation was thus a suturing together of nascent political understandings of global political relations. The emergence of the Nation of Islam in the U.S.—the subject of his classic manifesto *The Fire Next Time*—also allowed Baldwin to think analogously, as a Pan-African, beyond America, across the time and space of anti-colonial and anti-imperialist movements: the Nation of Islam and its representative voice, Malcolm X, conjoined the African and Asian decolonization struggle, the plight of the Palestinians in a still new Israel, the end of the French war against Vietnam, and the beginnings of the American one.

By the end of the 1960s, and in all of these sites of contestation, Baldwin was a transfigured, committed, street-fighting intellectual, as comfortable debating conservative William Buckley at Cambridge, as marching with forces of the Student Nonviolent Coordinating Committee in Selma, Alabama, and defending Black Panthers from political attack in the U.S. This element of Baldwin's life—his willingness to organize, march, contribute money, write letters, sign petitions, and, where necessary, lead campaigns for social justice—has been under-appreciated by scholars, but will be a significant dimension of this book. Baldwin should be understood as a literary "revolutionary" in the way we have come to know the great twentieth-century writers of the Global South: Fanon, Gabriel García Márquez, Léopold Senghor, Carmen Lyra, Assata Shakur. Indeed, many of Baldwin's most important political books, including *The Fire Next Time* and the incendiary *No*

Name in the Street, were written largely outside of America, or about events in Asia and Africa, and were postmarked to the entire world. The closing dateline for *No Name in the Street* is "New York, San Francisco, Hollywood, London, Istanbul, St. Paul de Vence, 1967–1971."[11] Ironically, in a way, this self-consciously radicalized Baldwin, friends by the end of the 1960s with Malcolm X, Martin Luther King, Jr., Angela Davis, Huey Newton, Bobby Seale—and the world of Black Power and global decolonization that drew him close to its radical flame—was still catching up with the most radical, itinerant visions of his own youth. After all, it was in his 1953 *Harpers Magazine* essay "Stranger in the village," a personal reminiscence about his relationship to European civilization prompted by being the only Negro in a small Swiss Village, that ended with the stentorian claim, "The world is white no longer, and it will never be white again."[12] Understanding the prophetic valence of Baldwin's words, their capacity to run ahead of history, predict it, and live it, is one of the true hallmarks of his mind and vision. Baldwin's revolutionary insights, in other words, really were the result of ruthlessly criticizing, matching the present to its past, and craving a means not simply to study the world, but to change it.

*   *   *

A singular argument for a new biography of James Baldwin is his reemergence in public discourse as an icon of the global Black Lives Matter movement. Since its inception in 2012 after the brutal killing of 17-year-old Trayvon Martin in the U.S. by George Zimmerman, Baldwin, writes scholar Eddie Glaude in 2016, "is everywhere. To account for the latest disasters around race in this country—grief over the death of another black person at the hands of police; the fact that we have vomited up the likes of Donald Trump—activists often reach for him."[13] Baldwin's resurrection as a popular symbol of Black Lives Matter and black radicalism was concretized when best-selling African-American public intellectual Ta-Nehisi Coates published his own book on racist police violence, *Between the World and Me*, in 2015. Coates modeled the book after Baldwin's most famous political text, *The Fire Next Time* (1963), implicitly comparing Baldwin's book on rising Black civil rights struggle to our time.[14]

Since then, Baldwin has been the focus of a new documentary film linking him to Black Lives Matter, Raoul Peck's 2016 *I Am Not Your Negro*, and has been the inspiration for a book of essays on Black Lives Matter by young African-American writers and activists, *The Fire This Time: A New Generation Speaks About Race*. African-American writer Teju Cole's 2016 book *Known and Strange Things* also paid tribute to Baldwin, especially his important 1953 essay "Stranger in the Village," in which Baldwin describes his liminal relationship to Western culture and society. More recently, Michael Eric Dyson revisits Baldwin's role in a 1963 White House meeting to discuss the civil rights movement with U.S. Attorney General Robert Kennedy as a cautionary tale of ignored, prophetic warnings about the state of racism in America in his book *What Truth Sounds Like: Robert F. Kennedy, James Baldwin and Our Unfinished Discussion About Race in America*. Alice Mikal Craven and William E. Dow have recently published a striking new edited collection of essays on Baldwin, *Of Latitudes Unknown: James Baldwin's Radical Imagination*. Also important to Baldwin studies has been the launch of the *James Baldwin Review*, an open access, online peer-reviewed journal.

More recently still, acclaimed filmmaker Barry Jenkins has adapted Baldwin's 1974 novel *If Beale Street Could Talk* to the screen. Finally, Baldwin exists for a rising generation of black writers and activists as a popular culture touchstone: the political blog *Son of Baldwin* draws its name from him, and black queer and transgender activists within and without the Black Lives Matter movement (which is headed in the U.S. by queer black women) typically invoke Baldwin as a forerunner of their own quests to merge identity with political activism.[15]

In many ways, Baldwin's life has been recovered by a new generation of black radicals for its paradigmatic qualities. By his own account Baldwin's "biography" of racial dissent began at the age of ten, when he was beaten and pushed to the ground by New York police. His 1966 essay "A Report from Occupied Territory" could itself serve as a prefigurative manifesto of the Black Lives Matter movement. Baldwin writes of the police presence in black neighborhoods in cities like New York, Chicago, and Detroit, "the police are simply the hired enemies of this population. They are present to keep the Negro in his place and to protect white business interests, and they have no other function.

This is why those pious calls to 'respect the law,' always to be heard from prominent citizens each time the ghetto explodes, are so obscene."[16]

In more recent years, Baldwin has also been recovered as a forerunner and model subject of the explosion of black queer studies in the academy, and more widely among LGBTQ writers. Beginning in the late 1990s, well after publication of the last of the "major" Baldwin biographies by David Leeming, Baldwin became an avatar of the rise of academic analysis of the history of black gay male sexuality in the U.S. Groundbreaking scholarship has followed in recent years by scholars like Marlon Ross, Dwight McBride, E. Patrick Johnson, Roderick Ferguson, Maurice Wallace, Robert Reid-Pharr, and Matt Brim.[17] A signal moment in the recovery of Baldwin's "queerness" was Dwight McBride's 1999 edited critical anthology *James Baldwin Now*, which included essays on Baldwin's sexuality by Wallace, Ferguson, Ross, and others. Baldwin's recovery also helped to trigger, or anticipate, groundbreaking public critical assessments of black gay life, like Marlon Riggs's 1994 autoethnographic film *Black Is, Black Ain't*. Scholars of late have begun to focus attention on Baldwin's relationship to queer public history—like the AIDS crisis of the 1980s, which he lived through, as in Joseph Vogel's book *James Baldwin and the 1980s: Witnessing the Reagan Era*.[18] As Vogel argues, Baldwin saw in Ronald Reagan a consummation of cowboy culture masculinity, a political incarnation of the "Gary Cooper" figure of the American Western who, he had remarked years earlier at Cambridge, taught him that when he was watching Cowboy and Indian films as a child, little did he know that *he* was the Indian. Recently, too, Ed Pavlić has examined in depth the role of music in Baldwin's work as an aesthetic, political, and spiritual trope.[19]

Baldwin's capacity to tether white masculinity, state power, and U.S. domestic and international political power allows us then to see him as a prefigurative black "queer" way of reading American culture and popular culture. Baldwin, we know now, anticipated not just writers like Coates, but cultural studies scholars like Paul Gilroy, Stuart Hall, Audre Lorde, and bell hooks, with their exceptional analyses of intersecting "modalities" of race, class, gender, and sexuality, of cinematic "black looks," of the contours of what Gilroy calls the Black Atlantic. Indeed, it wasn't until Magdalena Zaborowska's superb study *James Baldwin's Turkish Decade: The Erotics of Exile*, on Baldwin's ten-year period living in Istanbul, that scholars began also to grapple with Baldwin's peregrinations beyond his popularly discussed period of exile in France: Israel, Palestine, Turkey, Africa, to take some examples. Baldwin, in other words, was laying down transnational and transatlantic "roots and routes," doing so as a black gay man in exile in part from his own sexual habitus, well before the vogue of contemporary scholarship on the black diaspora.[20]

This study will also foreground a political dimension of Baldwin's diasporic wanderings that has been underappreciated: namely his self-conscious black internationalism, particularly as it relates to Western imperial power in the Middle East. The Black Lives Matter movement in the U.S. and globally has resurrected a tradition of Afro-Arab and Afro-Palestinian solidarity to which James Baldwin made a significant, unheralded contribution. Recall for example the 2013 "Black for Palestine" statement signed by more than 1,000 black intellectuals in the wake of Michael Brown's murder by police in Ferguson, Missouri.[21] The statement was prompted by Palestinians in the West Bank and Gaza "tweeting" out solidarity instructions to Ferguson demonstrators about how to respond to live tear gas attacks by Missouri National Guard—the very same tear gas used against them by Israeli Defense Forces in their protests against the 2014 massacres in Gaza. The itinerant solidarity was part of a wider trend of interracial anti-racist unity between African-Americans and Arabs nurtured by the Palestinian Boycott, Divestment, Sanctions movement against Israel, a movement rooted, as many African-Americans still recall, in the model used to bring down apartheid in South Africa. In recent years, scholars like Keith Feldman and Alex Lubin have recognized Baldwin's role in the 1970s as a vocal advocate for Palestinian self-determination.[22] Particularly after the 1967 "Six-Day War," and encouraged, and mentored, by comrades on the black left like the Student Nonviolent Coordinating Committee and the Black Panthers, Baldwin came to understand the state of Israel as a placeholder for Western imperial interests, literally the U.S. "watchdog in the Middle East," and Palestinians as the unrepresented victims of this history (indeed, Edward Said once cited Baldwin as an inspiration for his own anti-colonial writing). This insight was part of Baldwin's longer arc of understanding of North African Muslims as subalterns within Europe, and an "Arabized" form of rejection of Judeo-Christian political hegemony that had dogged his own queer, secular revolutionary spirituality his whole life. At the same time, Baldwin's sympathies for Palestinian dispossession allowed him to carefully delineate over time distinctions between Zionism—which he outright opposed—and Judaism, which provided him with both salient histories of oppression, and Jewish comrades who were lifelong friends and allies.

Finally, Baldwin has rightly been recovered by a generation of living radicals today because his life in the "fire" of dissidence included abrupt and persistent challenges to the capitalist state he opposed. Baldwin was, in the contemporary parlance, super woke. Indeed, because of his numerous public acts of opposition to the U.S. state—its policies of racism, segregation, repression, arrest, militarization, war, imperialism—Baldwin was surveilled by the Federal Bureau of Investigation (FBI). His FBI file, recently republished in part by scholar William Maxwell, runs to more than 1,700 pages.[23] FBI Director J. Edgar Hoover, himself a closeted gay man, pursued Baldwin in part because the FBI suspected he was gay: "Isn't is true that Baldwin is a well-known pervert?" the director wrote in a 1963 internal memo. Baldwin in response publically threatened to write a book exposing the machinations of the FBI, which had long tracked, trailed, badgered, and even forced out of the country black radical writers and intellectuals, Baldwin's intimates, like Richard Wright, a former Communist. Baldwin, in other words, had nothing but contempt for the same U.S. state that despised him. Baldwin, then, should be considered a victim of the "literary" arm of the U.S. state's vicious COINTELPRO (Counterintelligence

Program) which in the 1960s policed, surveilled, and infiltrated virtually every radical black political formation in the
U.S., including the Black Panthers, and resulted in the assassination of Panther leaders like Chicago's Fred Hampton. The
life of "fire" Baldwin lived in, in other words, was quite real,
and included living in the crosshairs of a U.S. government that
conceived of him as an enemy of the state, a mantle he came
to wear proudly.

*   *   *

This book offers a chronological account of Baldwin's political
life and development. Baldwin's life was an arc of change,
reflection, and evolution. Past, present, and future were
embedded for Baldwin in his literary life and his political
practice.

Chapter 1, "Baptism by Fire: Childhood and Youth,
1924–42," recounts the key personal, sexual, and political
moments of Baldwin's childhood and youth. It argues that
many of his literary and political themes from his mature life
can be found here.

Chapter 2, "Dissidence, Disillusionment, Resistance:
1942–48," conveys Baldwin's turn to political and sexual independence after leaving his familial home and launching as an
itinerant worker and aspiring writer into a wartime world.

Chapter 3, "Political Exile and Survival: 1948–57," shows
how racism and economic desperation drove Baldwin to
Paris, where his life as a writer, and anti-colonialist, began
after exposure to the beginnings of the Algerian war for independence.

Chapter 4, "Paying His Dues: 1957–63," charts Baldwin's
dramatic decision to return to the American South to both
write about—and give support to—a burgeoning U.S. civil
rights movement.

Chapter 5, "Baldwin and Black Power: 1963–68," details Baldwin's political evolution from radical race liberal into an independent voice for black self-determination as recorded in seminal books and journalism from the period.

Chapter 6, "Morbid Symptoms and Optimism of the Will: 1968–79," shows the effects of the end of the Black Power era on Baldwin's deepening anti-imperialist politics in response to the Black Panther Party, Vietnam War, and Palestinian liberation struggle.

Chapter 7, "Final Acts, Death, and Baldwin's Queer Legacies," charts Baldwin's sharp political criticisms of the Reagan era and his grappling with emergent black feminist and LGBTQ struggle related to the crisis of HIV/AIDS. The chapter concludes by looking at Baldwin's multiple, ongoing legacies for the politics of our time.

1
Baptism by Fire:
Childhood and Youth, 1924–42

I know, in any case, that the most crucial time in my own development came when I was forced to recognize that I was a kind of bastard of the West.

James Baldwin, "Autobiographical Notes," 1955[1]

I see myself ... not as I am, which is, I suppose, to see simply a rather odd looking black boy with a certain excess of nervous energy, with great uneasiness, a certain charm, and much panic and dishonesty and foolishness—but as a man—or often as a women—in another situation entirely.

James Baldwin, early unpublished essay[2]

A ghetto can be improved in one way only: out of existence.

James Baldwin, "Fifth Avenue: Uptown," 1960[3]

James Baldwin's birth, childhood, and upbringing embody enduring themes of African-American history that animate his writing in intimate and personal ways. Baldwin was born James Arthur Jones on August 2, 1924, in New York's Harlem Hospital on 135th Street, the heart of Harlem. His mother, Emma Berdis Jones, arrived impoverished in New York City in the early 1920s from Deal Island, Maryland, once a slave-holding state. Baldwin would use her life as the model for the character Elizabeth in his first novel, *Go Tell It On the Mountain.* The book dramatized the plight of southern black migrants to the North during what historians call the "Great African-American Migration" during World War I, a momentous event in American history which created black Meccas like Harlem.

Baldwin's paternity provided him with another deeply personal theme. He never knew his birth father nor his name. For Baldwin, this was symbolic of problems of African-American identity descending from slavery, a system which hid or masked family ancestry, and tore black children from both their parents and homeland. This theme would resonate in later symbolic book titles by Baldwin like *Nobody Knows My Name* and *No Name in the Street*. When Baldwin was three, Emma married David Baldwin, a factory worker whose mother had been a slave. David was once before married, with a son, Samuel, about twelve at the time. James Baldwin took his name from the stepfather, but as a child felt the stigma of being an adopted "bastard," a fact which gave literal dimension to Baldwin's claim that as the descendants of slaves he was himself a "bastard" of Western modernity built from capitalism and slavery.

David Baldwin and Emma Berdis Jones had many children to whom Baldwin would be the eldest, and often caregiver. As Baldwin put it, his mother was "given to the exasperating and mysterious habit of having babies. As they were born, I took them over with one hand and held a book with the other."[4] Baldwin's siblings included a brother George, born in January 1928; Barbara, born in 1929; Wilmer, born in 1930; David, his closest lifelong sibling, born in 1931; Gloria, born in 1933; Ruth, born in 1935; Elizabeth, born in 1937; and Paula Maria, born in 1943, ironically on the day his stepfather David Baldwin died, a coincidence that became the springboard for one of Baldwin's most famous essays, "Notes of a Native Son."

The combination of multiple children, Depression-era conditions in Harlem—where unemployment in the 1930s reached 50 percent—his father's low-wage job, and the oppressive ceiling of racism in America enabled Baldwin to see his family life and upbringing as allegories for the systemic, historic oppression and struggles of African-Americans. About David Baldwin, himself a migrant from the slave port city of New Orleans, Baldwin later said, "My father left the South to save his life. They were hanging niggers from trees in uniforms in 1919 and my father left the South therefore. Millions of us left the South therefore. And came to Chicago where we perish like rats, in New York where you perish like rats."[5] Baldwin refers here to what has been dubbed by historians the "Red Summer" of 1919 when African-American soldiers and workers were beaten and killed on the streets of cities like East St. Louis or on the "killing floor" of Chicago slaughter houses by white workers after filling their jobs during World War I. It was these events which inspired the Caribbean poet Claude McKay to urge African-Americans to die "fighting back" in his famous Harlem Renaissance Shakespearian sonnet, "If We Must Die."[6]

Baldwin's schoolteacher, Orilla Miller, also remembers visiting the Baldwin family railroad apartment where Emma was forced to cook, clean, and perform all the labor by hand for her husband and nine children without help, a cruelty deepened by her job as a domestic worker in white people's homes at a time when that work was one of the only jobs available to black women. Baldwin's acute sensitivity to his mother's devotion to her children, as well as her own personal suffering, was rewarded by deep loyalty to her throughout his life, and constant efforts to improve her material conditions when he began to earn money as a writer. Ironically, she survived him by twelve years, living in the relative comfort and stability of a New York apartment he purchased for her and his siblings while alive.

But it was the particular hardships—and his harsh reactions to them—of his stepfather's life that provided Baldwin with the most powerful and lasting early lessons about race, poverty, and masculinity, lessons which would shape many elements of his life, including his own sexuality. Baldwin knew intuitively, and came to know it experientially from the example of his family, that racism and capitalism combined to try and crush the life from what W.E.B. Du Bois called defiantly the "souls of Black folk."[7] David Baldwin developed an authoritarian personality within the home that was meant to exercise power in the only sphere of his life he could control, yet poverty and immiseration constantly outran his efforts to hold back the tide of suffering, racism, and self-abnegation. For the young James Baldwin, his father's entrapment and rage were tragic microcosms of the life of black people and black families. As he later told the poet Nikki Giovanni, "You know when you're called a nigger you look at your father because you think your father can rule the world—every kid thinks that—and then you discover that your father cannot do anything about it. So you begin to despise your father and you realize, Oh, that's what a nigger is.' But it's not your father's fault and it's not your fault."[8] Baldwin also said of his father, "it seemed to me that the most terrible thing that happened, and he was a very proud man, was that he couldn't feed his children … He had no power. He was always at the mercy of some other man, some other man who was always white."[9]

Baldwin here demonstrates a recurrent insight in his writing on U.S. and Western racism and capitalism, reversing the "causation" of personal suffering from victim to system, from subaltern to oppressor, from exploited to exploiter. Baldwin often singled out the word "nigger" as the invention of a exploitative system that needed to scapegoat black suf-fcring as a means of avoiding guilt, responsibility, and blame for social inequality. As he later put it in a 1963 documen-tary film *Take This Hammer*, "We have invented the nigger. I didn't invent him. White people invented him ... he's unnec-essary to me, so he must be necessary to you. I'm going to give you your problem back: You're the nigger, baby, it isn't me."[10] In other instances, Baldwin specifically blamed ruling elites—from southern plantation owners to factory bosses to government officials—for creating racist terms and ideas in order to keep blacks and whites divided from each other. The idea of the "nigger," then, Baldwin understood to be a long-standing American idea to make one group feel superior to another, to maintain divide and rule for the powerful. From his stepfather, too, who eventually descended into mental illness, Baldwin developed the resilient insight that "you can only be destroyed by believing that you really are what the white world calls a NIGGER."[11]

A critical dimension of Baldwin's life as a child and in his intellectual, artistic, and spiritual development was his stepfa-ther's work as a Pentecostal storefront preacher, and the latter's zealous, fundamentalist religious devotion. Under David Baldwin's stern directive influence, young James attended Abyssinian Baptist Church on 138th Street in Harlem, and later joined the Mount Calvary of the Pentecostal Faith Church on Harlem's Lenox Avenue. As a result of these experi-ences, Baldwin underwent a religious conversion and became a young minister at Fireside Pentecostal Assembly in Harlem. From the age of 14 to 17, he preached there regularly.

For Baldwin, the black church and religiosity represented both the excitement and ecstasy of worship, music, poetry, and communion. The Bible and scripture, as we will see, were also dominant influences on his mature oratory and literary styles. Most importantly, the black church and religion came to represent for Baldwin what Marx called the "sigh of the oppressed" in a heartless world. As Baldwin wrote in his 1948 essay, "The Harlem Ghetto":

> There are probably more churches in Harlem than in any other ghetto in this city and they are going full blast every night and some of them are filled with praying people every day. This, supposedly, exemplifies the Negro's essential simplicity and good-will; but it is actually a fairly emotional business … religion operates here as a complete and exquisite fantasy revenge: white people own the earth and commit all manner of abomination and injustice on it; the bad will be punished and the good rewarded, for God is not sleeping, the judgement is not far off.[12]

The most vivid account of Baldwin's youthful time as a minister and religious convert is actually fictional: his thinly veiled autobiographical novel *Go Tell It On the Mountain*, published in 1953, and the book that set him fully on the path of his literary career. The novel's title refers to the Negro spiritual of the same name gathered and published by the first African-American collector of the genre, John Wesley Work, Jr. The spirituals—sacred and secular songs sung first by slaves as what W.E.B. Du Bois called "sorrow songs" of work and woe—became canonized and popularized through groups like the Fisk University Jubilee Singers who toured the world singing them in concert in the late nineteenth century. The lyrics of "Go Tell It On the Mountain" assume the voices of angels announcing the birth of Jesus Christ: "Down in a lowly manger | The humble Christ was born | And God sent us salvation | That blessed Christmas morn." In Baldwin's novel, the young protagonist, John Grimes, appears fated from the first page of the book to fulfill his historical destiny as a preacher meant to carry forth the word of God:

> Everyone had always said that John would be a preacher when he grew up, just like his father. It had been said so often that John, without ever thinking about it, had come to believe it himself. Not until the morning of his fourteenth birthday did he really begin to think about it, and by then it was already too late.[13]

Baldwin cleverly embeds tension and irony in this opening paragraph that foreshadows the multiple personal and emotional struggles of his protagonist. John's decision to become a preacher is not his own but something "everyone" said would happen. The passage suggests community and paternal pressure as a guiding hand on an unconscious child. Ironically, John's own ability to think and choose for himself arrives "too late" after he embarks on his short-lived preaching career. The paragraph tells us of an enormous conflict between father and son, community and individual, fate and free will.

Indeed, the writing of *Go Tell It On the Mountain* was the first and most important literary aspiration of young James Baldwin's career, a personal obsession and ambition that began when he was all of 17 years old, and coincided with the year he left the church for good, and moved from Harlem to Greenwich Village in New York. The book then is about a break with the church as much as an immersion in it, and about the trauma of both as impetus for Baldwin's literary career. These creative conflicts and tensions are foretold in Baldwin's numerous drafts and notes on the book.

The novel's original title was *Crying Holy*, a phrase Baldwin used in reference to black church music (gospel mainly) in his later essay "Letter from a Region of My Mind." The passage refers to the "visceral" power of the church and its gospel and spiritual traditions: "There is no music like that music, no drama like the drama of the saints rejoicing, the sinners moaning, the tambourines racing, and all those voices coming together and crying holy unto the Lord."[14] The draft title is one of the first indicators of the enormous impress of black music on Baldwin's life, a story well documented by the likes of scholars like Ed Pavlić, who note that for Baldwin African-American music—jazz, blues, spirituals, gospel—were guiding lights and metaphors for black creativity, improvisation, joy, suffering. In many cases, they were also direct literary templates for his own work, as in the important novella "Sonny's Blues," to be discussed later.

But early notes and drafts of the book also foreground the fictional representation of young James Baldwin's real emotional and spiritual battles with his stepfather, the Pentecostal preacher who "fated" him to preach. "At seventeen," he wrote in one draft note for the book, "Johnnie Rogers [later changed to John Grimes] realizes that he has always hated his father. His father is Deacon Rogers. The head-deacon of a fanatically strict church … He forces his children to lead incredibly secluded and narrow lives to their detriment."[15] Baldwin's childhood sympathies for his real-life mother, Emma Berdis, are also embedded in the drafts: "The mother is a meek, frightened woman completely under her husband's domination." She "sympathizes with her children but is unable to help them. Her love for her husband (though she is not much more to him than a convenient piece of furniture, by whom he feeds his ego, begets children, and satisfies his bodily craving) her fear of the wrath of God, her captivity to convention, make her a pallid and unimportant person in the household."[16]

The original plot line for the book also underscores the tenacity and fatalism of Baldwin's real-life psychological struggle with his father. About the young protagonist Johnnie, he writes, "His frustrated, bored and repressed life makes him increasingly neurotic and bitter. His hatred for his father must always be concealed. He is always being told that he is lost, that he must get saved."[17] Significantly, Baldwin also wrote his own roiling sexuality, longings, and confusions into the story of paternal repression. "None of the children have been given anything resembling adequate sexual instruction, so that at fourteen, Johnnie's body is still a good deal of a mystery to him. A homosexual lures him into a hallway and attempts a perversion of sexual intercourse with him. Johnnie flees in terror. Now he feels irredeemably lost and unclear."[18] Johnnie then lurches towards heterosexual conformity, attempting sex with Sylvia, a young woman whose Christian faith combined with his own "morbid, neurotic, emotionally repressed state and feeling of guilt" results in a "stormy conversion to religion."[19]

Here sexual crisis, anxiety, repression, and identity ambiguity are the impetus for faith, not the love of God. The hallway episode Baldwin later recounted in autobiographical form in his essay "Freaks and the Idea of American Manhood." Baldwin later said of himself, "I didn't have any human value. And that was why I joined the church."[20] Baldwin's oft-stated reflections on the gender and sexual fluidity of his own youthful urgings—embodied in the epigraph to this chapter about his self-imaging as both male and female—was, in the earliest incarnations of what became Go Tell It On the Mountain, among the most vital of themes. Indeed, the Oedipal conflict, inflected by Johnnie's queer desire, is the center of the draft notes for Crying Holy. When the paternal Deacon slaps him for desiring sex, "For the first time Johnnie thinks of killing his father"—and does, putting cyanide in his communion cup. In a melodramatic plot twist, Johnnie's brother, Roy, is blamed for the killing, and dies in the electric chair. Johnnie meanwhile stays silent, a "dead drunk in a harlot's room."[21]

Almost all of these plot imaginings would be revised out of the final text of *Go Tell It On the Mountain*, which we will discuss in more detail in Chapter 2. However, the early draft notes for the book are important for indicating the prominence of queer sexuality in young Baldwin's life and writing. Another draft chapter, for example, set on Charles Street in Greenwich Village, includes scenes of male cruising, interracial sex, and titles—"The Prisoner" containing intimations of some of Baldwin's later, more explicit writings on homosexuality, like "The Male Prison," his 1961 essay on the gay French author André Gide. The early draft notes also indicate how David Baldwin's masculinity and authority were clear challenges to the identity formation of a sexually indeterminate young Baldwin, and how the weight of sin in Christianity outweighed salvation in his mind. Finally, the book's themes of brotherly love—and betrayal—and feminist compassion for African-American women in oppressed circumstances, would redound in later Baldwin books and plays, like *Blues for Mister Charlie*, *Just Above My Head*, and *Tell Me How Long the Train's Been Gone*—as would one final theme—taking responsibility for the death of someone, a centerpiece of the 1956 novel *Giovanni's Room*.

* * *

Baldwin once described his formal education as a reprieve and escape from the oppressive religiosity and conformity of his home life. "School," he wrote, "was a kind of refuge from home. From my father." "I read my way through two libraries by the time I was thirteen," he once said,[22] and "I read myself out of Harlem."[23] Books, and school learning, provided Baldwin with a secular alternative to his dogged scriptural training. Among the earliest important influences on Baldwin was Harriet Beecher Stowe's *Uncle Tom's Cabin*— the first serious book Baldwin read—and the work of Henry James and Charles Dickens, who helped commit Baldwin to a mode of literary realism. His public school education was also buttressed by important contemporary events. He was born in the midst of the Harlem Renaissance, a flowering of literary, visual, and cultural production by black artists, many of whom like Baldwin's family had arrived in New York City from the South. The Harlem Renaissance was also an international affair: one of its inspirations was the contemporary "Irish Renaissance" in the arts that produced the likes of James Joyce and W.B. Yeats; another, Caribbean migration to the U.S., which produced important Harlem-based writers like the Jamaican Claude McKay, cited earlier.

Eventually, Baldwin would be directly touched by architects of the Renaissance: his junior high-school French teacher Countee Cullen was a breakthrough poet of the Renaissance, and its poetic star, Langston Hughes, was one of the first African-American writers to call Baldwin to a career in letters. Thus even though Baldwin was too young to experience it as an artist, and later diminished the Renaissance as something that "was not destined to last very long," we can perceive his Harlem Renaissance "roots" as another element shaping his life as an intellectual and writer.

A second major influence on his education was the impress of leftist political thought on a young, impressionable, searching mind. Baldwin was five when the stock market crashed and millions of Americans were thrown out of work. His family's already dire poverty deepened. As he later recalls of that period, "I learned something every poor kid does. All you have to figure out is how you are going to outwit those forces which are determined to destroy you."[24] He also wrote of this period, "I knew that people were suffering and dying all around me and it wasn't their fault."[25] Many people with a similar consciousness turned to the left, joining the Communist Party and other socialist organizations active in New York City. Baldwin himself was eleven when the "Popular Front" period was decreed by the Communist International in Moscow, and the fight against fascism in the Western world was conjoined to an emphasis on fighting racism: "Black and White Unite and Fight" became a widely used slogan in left circles. Indeed, Harlem from the early 1920s to the period of World War II was a literal hotbed of leftist activity and thought that by the 1930s created an accessible culture for a curious, sharp-minded boy like Baldwin seeking to develop an analysis of racism and economic inequality. After all, by Baldwin's own account, it was his first encounter with the police as a ten year old that began to educate him in the sociology of his own life. "[T]hey both beat me up," he recalls, "They knocked me down, and left me lying flat on my back in that empty parking lot. I never forgot. I still remember lights of that cop car going by and then I understood something. That's when hatred begins."[26] We might then see Baldwin's youthful education and political training as a self-conscious struggle to blast the Harlem ghetto "out of existence" as he once put it. That would mean both learning to expose through his writing the ghetto's inequalities to a wider world, and by doing so end them, and to actually leave that place behind.

Baldwin's formal public education began at Public School 124 (P.S. 124) in Harlem. The school was significant for having the first black principal in the city's history, Gertrude Ayers. As Baldwin recalls, the black teachers there were "laconic about politics but single-minded about the future of Black students."[27] Even during his time as an elementary school student, Baldwin attempted to assist his family financially by shining shoes and selling shopping bags with his brother George to supplement his parents' meager incomes as factory worker and paid domestic.[28] A flashpoint in Baldwin's early political education occurred while he was an elementary school student: in 1935, when he was ten, Lino Rivera, a Puerto Rican youth of 16, was arrested and accused of shoplifting at the S.H. Kress department store on 135th Street, not far from his home (Harlem was, as Baldwin recalled it, not an "all-black" community during his youth; East Harlem earned the name "Spanish Harlem" after the turn of the century for the massive Puerto Rican migration there after the U.S. annexed, occupied, and colonized the island in 1898). Rivera's arrest triggered rumors that he had been beaten to death in the store's basement, possibly by police. The rumors sparked a massive uprising in Harlem, with the police and locally owned businesses viewed as symbols of Harlem oppression and disenfranchisement the targets. Baldwin would later refer to the 1935 (and later 1943) Harlem riots as inspirations for his important essay "The Harlem Ghetto." In it, Baldwin described black urban rebellions as what Martin Luther King, Jr. once called the "language of the unheard."

A more direct link between Baldwin's formal and political education also occurred in 1935 when Orilla Miller (also known to Baldwin as Bill) arrived as a teacher at P.S. 124. Miller was a white woman from the American Midwest. Her father was a populist and Farmer's Cooperative organizer. After attending Antioch College, Orilla came to New York City to attend Teachers College. She soon joined the Communist Party of the United States and gained employment in the education division of the Federal Theater Project (FTP). The FTP was a creation of Franklin Roosevelt's New Deal Works Progress Administration, one of many federally funded cultural programs designed to employ artists during the

Depression. It was well known for housing leftist sympathiz-
ers and doing innovative, politically progressive productions.
Sometime in 1935 or 1936, Miller asked to be transferred to
Harlem to teach. She was assigned to Baldwin's P.S. 124, where
her task was to put on plays with the students.

Miller recognized Baldwin's uniqueness immediately. "I
realized that he was just a remarkable child," she recalled later
in an interview with Lynn Scott.[29] Baldwin's intellectual pre-
cociousness was for Miller matched only by the direness of
his family's economic circumstances. For Baldwin, the two
came together in his reading of Charles Dickens's novels, the
subject that first brought he and Miller together in discussion.
"We would have these long conversations up in the attic," she
later said.[30] In particular, it was Dickens's *A Tale of Two Cities*
that conjoined them. Baldwin recalls reading it "over and over
and over again."[31] In the novel, he later wrote, "it had been
Madame Defarge [an organizer of the French Revolution]
who most struck me. I recognized that unrelenting hatred, for
it was all up and down my streets, and in my father's face and
voice."[32] In 1936, when Baldwin was twelve, Miller took him
to see the 1935 Metro-Goldwyn-Mayer film adaptation of the
novel at the Lincoln Theater on 135th Street in Harlem. To
do so, Miller requested the permission of Baldwin's parents.
Baldwin later recalled that his father hated the idea of a white
woman taking his child from the home, but that his mother
quietly supported the idea. In 1936, Miller also took Baldwin
to see his first play, Orson Welles's FTP production of William
Shakespeare's *Macbeth* set in Haiti with an all-black cast at
Harlem's Lafayette Theater. The so-called "Voodoo Macbeth"
was a landmark in anti-racist American theater, and a touchstone for what scholar Michael Denning calls the "Cultural
Front" ambitions of the American Popular Front Left to
create a workers' culture.[33] The play also indexed the rise of

anti-imperialist sentiment on the U.S. left motivated by events like Mussolini's invasion of Ethiopia in 1935 (a hugely important moment of solidarity for African-Americans in the U.S.).

The influence of Miller's life and instruction on Baldwin was significant and long-lasting. In *The Devil Finds Work*, his book on cinema, he recalled her introduction of him to movies and theater as life-shaping influences. He frequently referenced cinema in his essays and fiction as a boyhood portal out of the strict and domineering influence of home. "The language of the camera," he once wrote, "is the language of our dreams."[34] Movies also became for Baldwin both cultural texts by which to understand race and politics in America, and an inviting medium for a writer to reach a wider audience. Later, for example, Baldwin would write a screenplay about the death of Malcolm X, to be discussed in Chapter 6. Baldwin also identified his embrace of theater with the secularization of his own life: he was forbidden to attend plays until he broke with the church, he wrote, and came to understand the church itself as a staging ground for his own dramatic life. From an early age he also understood the theater as a space for radical black culture, attending the New York stage adaptation of Richard Wright's blockbuster novel *Native Son*, also directed by Welles, where the left-wing actor Canada Lee made a deep impression: "his physical presence, like the physical presence of Paul Robeson, gave me the right to live."[35] Finally, from his childhood exposure, writing for the theater compelled him: later we will examine in detail his two most successful plays, *The Amen Corner* and *Blues for Mister Charlie*.

Politically, even at twelve, Baldwin understood the import of his relationship to a radical white female mentor who was an open critic of capitalism and an advocate for the socialist side in the Spanish Civil War. In 1936, for example, Orilla's husband, Evan, took Baldwin to a May Day parade organized by the Communist Party. As he later wrote, "I understood, as Bill had intended me to, something of revolution—understood, that is, something of the universal and inevitable human ferment which explodes into what is called a revolution."[36] Baldwin would also later remember himself as a "convinced fellow traveler" of the left in this period—"carrying banners, shouting East Side, West Side, all around the town. We want the landlords to tear the slums down!"[37] Yet it would take years, Baldwin wrote, before he understood how black people—and black proletarians like his father—could fit into any revolutionary scheme, though by the 1960s upheavals, as we shall see, Baldwin would begin to see black revolution as a real possibility.

The second order of influence of Miller was more personal but equally political. As Baldwin later wrote in *The Devil Finds Work*,

It is certainly partly because of her ... that I never really managed to hate white people—though, God knows, I have often wished to murder more than one or two ... .

From Miss Miller, therefore, I began to suspect that white people did not act as they did because they were white, but for some other reason, and I began to try to locate and understand the reason. She, too, anyway, was treated like a nigger, especially by the cops, and she had no love for landlords.[38]

Baldwin here provides a self-conscious, retrospective translation of the influence across his life of the politics of interracial unity. His anti-essentialist understanding of "whiteness" not as biological category but as constructed by society would remain with him for the rest of his life. So too would his confidence that some white people, though not all, could build solidarity across the color line by giving up racism or clinging to a fictitious white identity. As Baldwin later brilliantly put it in the film *The Price of the Ticket*, "As long as you think you're white, there's no hope for you."[39] Finally, Baldwin's astute attention to Miller's sense of economic and political justice—"she had no love for landlords"—comported with an organic anti-capitalist sensibility in his youth that would set him searching across his next decades, the 1940s especially, for socialist, Marxist, and anarchist ideas for reading, study, organizational attachment, and intellectual development. Put another way, the quest to "Try to locate and understand the reason" for racism, and interracial unity, burned at the core of his political education, set ablaze in part by Miller's anti-racist, anti-capitalist example. As he put it in a letter to her nearly 50 years later, "You do know, my friend, how much that example meant to me, later, when my time for choices came. You do not know how much you helped me to get beyond the trap of color."[40]

When Baldwin was twelve, in 1936, he enrolled at Frederick Douglass Jr. High School in Harlem, named after the famed self-emancipated slave and abolitionist. One of his teachers there was Herman W. Porter, a Harvard-educated math teacher who would take him to the 42nd Street New York Public Library to conduct research.[41] According to Baldwin biographer James Campbell, Porter said that Baldwin wrote "better than anyone in the school—from the principal on down."[42] Baldwin used his talents as editor-in-chief of *The Douglass Pilot*, the school's student publication. It was also at Frederick Douglass that Baldwin met Countee Cullen, who encouraged him to write poetry and, Baldwin says, implanted the idea he later adopted for himself to live in France. Cullen also recommended to Baldwin that he attend DeWitt Clinton High School in the Bronx, from which he himself had graduated. DeWitt Clinton had the reputation of being a top school whose graduates included the musician Fats Waller and the actor Burt Lancaster.

The decision to attend DeWitt Clinton in the fall of 1938 turned out to be momentous for Baldwin. Baldwin seized every opportunity at DeWitt Clinton, including the opportunity of friends and mentors, to develop his exceptional writing ability and his emerging desire to be a writer. While his grades outside of English and History were poor or mediocre, Baldwin threw himself into work on *The Magpie*, the school literary magazine. On the magazine staff were three people who were to become long-time friends: Emile Capouya, later the literary editor of the progressive magazine *The Nation*; Sol Stein, Baldwin's first intimate Jewish friend and future editor, whose relationship would provide important reflection on Jewish and black life in the U.S.; and Richard Avedon, later one of the most important photographers of the twentieth century, and a future Baldwin collaborator, as we will discuss. Baldwin wrote both prose and poetry for *The Magpie*. One short poem, "Youth," seemed to carry a theme of artistic aspiration akin to James Joyce's Stephen Daedalus in *Portrait of the Artist as a Young Man*:

Beloved, do not warn me
    Of birds too highly flown;
Your word is not enough for
    Me—
I must have my own."[43]

A Baldwin short story published in *The Magpie*, "Mississippi Legend," was an adjunct to Baldwin's interest in sexual repression and liberation evidenced in his notes for "Cry Holy." The story is a fable about a southern woman, Mattie, who has sex with a young man. Though the community outcasts her, everyone's crops go to ruin except hers. Handwritten Baldwin notes for the story include the names "*New Masses Republic Nation Liberty*," periodicals to which presumably he intended to submit the story, though there is no record of its professional publication. The *New Masses* is an important indicator and foreshadowing of Baldwin's political consciousness; it was the magazine closely associated with the U.S. Communist Party, where some ten years later he would publish a poem, to be discussed in Chapter 2. Finally, Baldwin also published an interview in *The Magpie* with Countee Cullen.

Baldwin also left a distinguishing mark intellectually on his teachers, one of whom would return to his life in an especially political way. The instructor for one of his English courses at DeWitt Clinton was Abel Meeropol. Meeropol had himself graduated from DeWitt Clinton in 1921 and had been teaching English there for more than 15 years by the time Baldwin entered his class. Meeropol was a member of the Communist Party and a staunch anti-racist. In 1939, under the pen name Lewis Allan, Meeropol wrote the lyrics for "Strange Fruit," a searing political ballad protesting the lynching of African-Americans. The song's poignant lyrics and haunting imagery make it to this day the best-known anti-lynching song in U.S. history: "Southern trees bear a strange fruit, Blood on the leaves and blood at the root, Black body swinging in the Southern breeze, Strange fruit hanging from the poplar trees." The song exploded into public consciousness when the great jazz and blues singer Billie Holiday recorded it, making it the signature anti-racist song of the U.S. left during the Popular Front period.

The teenage Baldwin did not know his English teacher was a Communist. But in 1974, well after Baldwin's fame was established, Meeropol wrote him a letter to tell him of their braided lives. In the letter Meeropol remembers Baldwin's striking use of imagery—"the houses in their little white overcoats"—in an assignment to write about a scene of winter. He also tells Baldwin that he is the adoptive father of Michael and Robert Meeropol, the sons of Ethel and Julius Rosenberg. Meeropol adopted the boys after their birth parents, Communists both, were executed by the U.S. for allegedly passing on information to the Soviet Union about U.S. atomic weaponry. The case against the Rosenbergs was the singular U.S. political melodrama of the Cold War and McCarthyite hysteria. In recent years, evidence for and against the cooperation of the Rosenbergs with the Soviets has preserved the story in public memory. In the same letter, Rosenberg tells Baldwin that he is the author of the song "Strange Fruit."

Baldwin's response, like his retrospective letter to Orilla Miller about her leftist politics, reveals much about the arc of his life's understanding of race, racial cooperation, and capacity for solidarity. The letter reads in part:

My dear Mr. Meeropol:

Your letter is completely unanswerable because it drags up out of darkness, and confirms, so much. What it confirms is something I must always somewhere have believed (without knowing that) about the connection between one human life and another—how each of us, whether or not we know it, or can face it, is tied to the other. But the attempt to state such a thing is banal; better, simply, to trust it and recognize it as unanswerable.

I don't remember what you remember. I remember only the black-board, and the bottomless terror in which I lived in those days—but if I wrote the line you remember, then must have trusted you.

It never occurred to me, of course, that one of my
teachers wrote *Strange Fruit*—though that also seems,
in retrospect, unanswerably logical—nor could it have
occurred to me that one of my teachers raised the Rosenberg children. It's a perfectly senseless thing to say but I'll
say it anyway: it makes me very proud.[44]

It is also while a student at DeWitt Clinton that Baldwin dated
the beginnings of his life—or what he called his "career," as an
artist—though typical of his life to come, via roads not taken
or traveled by others heretofore, and inclusive of his deepening adolescent racial and sexual consciousness. In "The
Price of the Ticket," a late-in-life essay, Baldwin recounted
his high-school classmate Emile Capouya telling him "about
this wonderful man he had met, a black—then, Negro, or
Colored—painter and said that I must meet him."[45] Capouya
was referring to Beauford Delaney, who the former had met
one day in Greenwich Village after playing hookey from
school. As it happened, Baldwin was working what he called
a "Dickensian job" in a Canal Street garment district sweat-
shop after school not far from the Village. The money was to
support his family, though his life at home was increasingly
strained, particularly owing to conflict with David Baldwin. I
"was getting on so badly at home that I dreaded going home:
and, so, sometime later, I went to 181 Green Street, where
Beauford lived then, and introduced myself."[46]

The introduction transformed Baldwin's life. Beauford was,
like Baldwin, black, and gay, and the son of a preacher. He was
also an artist. "Beauford," he later wrote, "was the first walking,
living proof, for me, that a black man could be an artist …
. He became, for me, an example of courage and integrity,
humility and passion."[47] Delaney imparted these examples to
Baldwin in several ways. "I learned about light from Beauford

Delaney," he later wrote, "the light contained in every thing, in every surface, in every face."[48] It was because of Delaney that Baldwin began to really *see* the textured reality of street life around him through the "poverty and uncertainty" of first his Harlem, then his Paris neighborhoods. As Baldwin later put it describing the role of the artist, "Society must accept some things as real; but he must always know that visible reality hides a deeper one, and that all our action and achievement rest on things unseen."[49]

For Baldwin, trained in Christian eschatology, Delaney's painterly "light" also carried what he called "the power to illuminate, even to redeem and heal." Beauford's work, he wrote, "leads the inner and outer eye, directly and inexorably, to a new confrontation with reality."[50] Put in aesthetic terms, Baldwin testifies here to a commitment to a transcendent realism that would characterize many of his early novels, and even his non-fiction essays. Baldwin ever rejected modernist abstraction in his work in favor of a textured literary portraiture—as mentioned earlier, Henry James, one of the greatest painters of "the social," was his earliest significant literary influence. The term "confrontation with reality" also indexes Baldwin's commitment to an art that impacts the world, or redirects it. As he put it later, "Ultimately, the artist and the revolutionary function as they function, and pay whatever dues they must pay behind it because they are both possessed by a vision, and they do not so much follow this vision as find themselves driven by it. Otherwise, they could never endure, much less embrace, the lives they are compelled to lead."[51] From Delaney, a black, queer artist, then, Baldwin was learning to demand from his young self a direct encounter with material reality, an encounter that would not just study the world but "redeem," heal, or change it.

A second life-changing effect of his encounter with Delaney was aural. Scholars sometimes refer to black music as having two traditions: Saturday night (jazz and blues) and Sunday morning (spirituals and gospel). Baldwin, who had grown up almost strictly on spirituals and gospels was suddenly introduced to the secular tradition in black music, a moment that would begin to galvanize his emotions and emotional life into the form of art. As he recalls from meeting Delaney that fateful adolescent day:

> I walked into music. I had grown up with music, but now, on Beauford's small black record player, I began to hear what I had never dared or been able to hear ... in his studio and because of his presence, I really began to *hear* Ella Fitzgerald, Ma Rainey, Louis Armstrong, Bessie Smith, Ethel Waters, Paul Robeson, Lena Horne, Fats Waller. He could inform me about Duke Ellington and W.C. Handy, and Josh White, introduce me to Frankie Newton and tell tall tales about Ethel Waters. And these people were not meant to be looked on by me as Celebrities, but as a part of Beauford's life and as part of my inheritance.[52]

Baldwin here introduces "inheritance" as the right and responsibility of the black artist to create transformative cultural expression on behalf of the race. A few years later, Baldwin would go to see the great contralto African-American vocalist Marian Anderson in concert at Carnegie Hall after she was banned by the reactionary racist group Daughters of the American Revolution from singing at a building they owned, Constitution Hall. For Baldwin, the concert linked him back to Delaney's lessons about the black artist: "If Beauford and Miss Anderson were a part of my inheritance, I was a part of their hope."[53] Baldwin also introduces in the passage above the importance of art and music as collaborative and communal, a lesson gleaned from the "call and response" pattern of black church reciprocity between minister and congregation, here refigured as the shared experience of black art with a kindred spirit: it was Beauford's "presence," he writes, that allowed him to hear black music properly.

The discovery of black secular music at age 16 also coincided with Baldwin's actual crisis of faith: by 1941, his senior year of high school, Baldwin's confidence in the church, Christianity, and his father's authority were simultaneously collapsing, abetted in part by David Baldwin's poor health, the continued economic immiseration of his family, and Baldwin's own yearnings for spiritual, sexual, and artistic freedom. As he put these processes in his description of the character Johnny in his notes to "Cry Holy," "It is not long ... before Johnnie's intellectual apparatus begins to question many of the 'facts' presented by the church. His emotional need, however, and again his fear and weakness cause him to saddle his doubts for nearly two and a half years. Then he begins to yield in secret to the natural demands of his youth."[54] At 17, his senior year of high school, Baldwin preached his last sermon. Later, in his essay "Notes of a Native Son," Baldwin would remember his "cooling off" from the church as a declaration of his desire to write, not preach. In *Go Tell It On the Mountain*, his autobiographical novel about his life in the church, Baldwin also makes it clear that one of the "natural demands" of his youth was same-sex desire, an urge that had nowhere productive to go, that he could see, while wrapped in the cloth of the ministry and Pentecostal theology. The price of sin was simply too high to pay in that milieu.

Baldwin's "break" from the church, then, was the first of many radical declarations of independence in his life. Later, he would also attribute it to Orilla Miller's challenge, from the left, to its soothing, reactionary comforts. But at 17, Baldwin needed more than a break from the church. Home life had become unbearably repressive, while Greenwich Village, Beauford Delaney, books, and music seemed to be opening up another world entirely, a life of Baldwin's mind and desires. The question then, a recurring one in Baldwin's itinerant, nomadic life, of where to go, needed to be answered, but there was no question that he would go.

Beyond his break with the church, the traces of Baldwin's early years connect everywhere across his life and career as a writer: in the autobiographical *Go Tell It On the Mountain*; in his seminal essays like "Notes of a Native Son" linking critical events in his past like the death of his father to his development as a thinker and artist; in his twisting attempts to maintain relationships with his mother and many siblings during his peregrinations to Paris, Istanbul, Africa, and other parts of Europe; in his portraits of black families—a common theme in many of his books, and especially of fraternal relations modeled on his own. From the 1970s onwards, as he reached middle age, Baldwin turned more to his Harlem familial past to tell stories in books like *Tell Me How Long the Train's Been Gone* and *Just Above My Head*. In 1976, Baldwin wrote his only children's book, *Little Man, Little Man: A Story of Childhood*, drawing from his own Harlem past. And finally, in his battle to find places in the world to live his life as an out gay man who without question left home at an early age—like so many queer teens of his time—just to live.

Perhaps Baldwin's most direct statement on black childhood in America, including his own, came in 1963. Speaking to a group of school teachers mere months after Martin Luther King's March on Washington, and well into the civil rights movement, Baldwin affirmed that what W.E.B. Du Bois called "double consciousness" was a tragically direct experience for black children. "[A]ny Negro who is born in this country and undergoes the American educational system runs the risk of becoming schizophrenic," he argued.

> On the one hand he is born in the shadow of the stars and stripes and he is assured it represents a nation which has never lost a war. He pledges allegiance to that flag which guarantees "liberty and justice for all." He is part of a country in which anyone can become president, and so forth. But on the other hand he is also assured by his country and his countrymen that he has never contributed anything to civilization—that his past is nothing more than a record of humiliations gladly endured. He is assumed by the republic that he, his father, his mother, and his ancestors were happy, shiftless, watermelon-eating darkies who loved Mr. Charlie and Miss Ann, that the value he has as a black man is proven by one thing only—his devotion to white people. If you think I am exaggerating, examine the myths which proliferate in this country about Negroes.[55]

The resolution of this contradiction for Baldwin was consistent with his message that the only way to improve a ghetto was "out of existence," and that children themselves, who were its victims, also carried the promise of its destruction:

> Now if I were a teacher in this school, or any Negro school, and I was dealing with Negro children, who were in my care only a few hours of every day and would then return to their homes and to the streets, children who have an apprehension of their future which with every hour grows grimmer and darker, I would try to teach them—I would try to make them know—that those streets, those houses, those dangers, those agonies by which they are surrounded, are criminal.

I would try to make each child know that these things are the result of a criminal conspiracy to destroy him. I would teach him that if he intends to get to be a man, he must at once decide that he is stronger than this conspiracy and that he must never make his peace with it. And that one of his weapons for refusing to make his peace with it and for destroying it depends on what he decides he is worth.[56]

Baldwin's call for a revolution in America's education system was also a call for a new conception of black childhood and black life that would destroy the "nigger" forever. Baldwin's own rejection of that idea was in many ways the most critical test of his own young life. It was a trial by fire, from which he emerged stronger and in many ways reborn.

2

Dissidence, Disillusionment, Resistance: 1942–48

He is a lad of sterling character, always eager to work and very responsible in carrying out assignments.

Wilmer T. Stone, letter of reference for James Baldwin,
October 16, 1941[1]

I have been in and out of the Village for three years now— from seventeen to twenty. I think the time is fast approaching when I must get out for good. There is death here. Every- where people are sick or dying or dead.

James Baldwin, letter to Tom Martin, September 2, 1944[2]

The contemporary sexual attitudes constitute a rock against which many of us flounder all our lives long; no one escapes entirely the prevailing psychology of our times.

James Baldwin, review of Stuart Engstrand's
The Sling and The Arrow, 1947[3]

I think that art is positive and that it is directly responsible to life … I can see no virtue in art divorced from life or art which distorts or negates it.

James Baldwin, letter to Tom Martin, September 2, 1944[4]

Baldwin received his high-school diploma in January of 1942 and entered the most exploratory and economically tenuous period of his life. Though he didn't know it when he finished school, he was about to enter his last stage for some time of prolonged stay on American soil. The decision to leave the U.S. culminating this period is readily marked by an eclectic series of encounters with a harsh, savage, wartime world outside of Harlem. Baldwin was proletarianized by work, hardened by encounters with racism, buffeted about sexually by competing urges—his queerness dawning—and slowly, incrementally self-educated in prevailing radical political thought. Baldwin became both worldly and bitter, anxious and angry, and unsure that he wouldn't end his life—or the lives of others—out of the inferno of his rage. He would emerge from this second baptismal encounter with the world committed to exile to Paris primarily as a means of staying alive.

Baldwin initially thought after finishing high school that he would attend City College in New York, a public university in Harlem that was famous for educating working-class, immigrant, and leftist students. But he was broke, lacking the money to pay tuition and expenses, and so resigned himself to work. The U.S. declaration of war against Germany, Japan, and Italy in 1941 had created a temporary space in the workforce for black workers (and women) and Baldwin took advantage. He gained a job laying railroad track at an army depot under construction in Belle Mead, near Princeton, New Jersey. His good friend from high school, Emile Capouya, was employed at the same workplace. The relationship preserved a lifeline for Baldwin to his past and his aspiration to write, and it was during his time as a laborer that he continued to make notes towards *Crying Holy*, the book that would become *Go Tell It On the Mountain*. While working in Belle Mead, Baldwin roomed with a local family in New Jersey, sending part of his salary to his family in Harlem, and visiting New York City on weekends, including his new-found friend Beauford Delaney.

Baldwin's work at the military depot provoked his first encounter with workplace racism, an experience that echoed the discrimination faced by thousands of African-Americans fighting in a segregated wartime army, often facing harassment or threats of lynching, especially in southern U.S. military bases. It was such treatment that spurred the *Pittsburgh Courier*, a prominent African-American newspaper, to launch a "Double Victory" campaign during the war: defeat fascism abroad, defeat racism at home.[5] Baldwin recorded his own local experience this way: "I learned in New Jersey that to be a Negro meant, precisely, that one was never looked at but was simply at the mercy of the reflexes one's skin caused in other people. I acted in New Jersey as I had always acted, that is as though I thought a great deal of myself—I had to act that way—with results that were, simply, unbelievable. I had scarcely arrived before I had earned the enmity, which was extraordinarily ingenious, of all my superiors and nearly all my co-workers."[6]

Because he openly defied attempts to demean him at work, Baldwin became known as a rebel—"It began to seem that the machinery of the organization I worked for was turning over, day and night, with but one aim: to eject me." He was fired.[7] With the help of a friend, he managed to get back on the payroll, only to be fired again. But it was the wide-scale, systemic nature of racism in New Jersey that provoked his deepest responses and left the most lingering emotional and political traumas. "I knew about jim-crow but I had never experienced it. I went to the same self-service restaurant three times and stood with all the Princeton boys before the counter, waiting for a hamburger and coffee; it was always an extraordinarily long time before anything was set before me."[8] On his last night in New Jersey, Baldwin went to the movies with a white friend in Trenton. Afterwards the two went to a restaurant, "American Diner." When they tried to order a hamburger and cup of coffee, they were told "We don't serve Negroes here"[9] and left into the night. Baldwin was in a rage: "I wanted to do something to crush these white faces which were crushing me."[10] He decided to enter a fashionable restaurant where "I knew not even the intercession of the Virgin would cause me to be served."[11] When a waitress appeared, Baldwin wrote later, she repeated the refrain, "We don't serve Negroes here." Baldwin snapped: "There was nothing on the table but an ordinary water mug full of water, and I picked this up and hurled it with all my strength at her. She ducked and it missed her and shattered against the mirror behind the bar."[12] Baldwin's first conscious physical strike back against racism produced an epiphany: "I could not get over two facts, both equally difficult for the imagination to grasp, and one was that I could have been murdered. But the other was that I had been ready to commit murder. I saw nothing very clearly but I did see this: that my life, my *real* life, was in danger, and not from anything other people might do but from the hatred I carried in my own heart."[13]

Baldwin's meditation subtly contextualizes the real and potential violence of an America at war not just against "enemies" abroad but African-Americans at home. The night of his act of rebellion, he noted, was the time of a "brown-out" when the lights in American cities were dimmed to preserve resources for the war. But the effect on Baldwin was the "force of an optical illusion, or a nightmare ... People were moving in every direction but it seemed to me, in that instant, that all of the people I could see, and many more than that, were moving toward me, against me, and that everyone was white."[14] Baldwin's wartime nightmare is a lynching fantasy, and his hurling of a water mug an act of survival. Baldwin would later write a fictional version of this episode into his third novel, *Another*

Country, and refer for the rest of his life to his "hatred" for racism—and his fear of the destruction or self-destruction caused by it—as a prime motivator for leaving America.

The firings from construction work took Baldwin back to Harlem to live briefly with his family, and to a meatpacking job, which he also promptly lost. Meanwhile, Baldwin spent part of 1941 as a student in a writers' workshop on the short story taught by the Communist Mary Elting at the Writers' School of the League of American Writers.[15] The League was an association of poets, novelists, journalists, and literary critics formed by the Communist Party in 1935. It was something of a "front" for the Communist Party. Some members were Communists, others "fellow travelers," in line with the Communist International's "Popular Front" strategy launched the same year to build cross-class alliances. The League had emerged out of discussion within the John Reed Clubs, the literary groups formed by the U.S. Communist Party in 1932, and where writers like Richard Wright began to hone their unpublished work. One of the League's missions (like the mission of the Communist Party during the Popular Front) was to recruit black members and support black culture. In January 1942, Baldwin was one of 20 young writers awarded a scholarship by the League, as reported in the January 19, 1942 *Daily Worker*.[16] It was this experience of the League, in addition to his marching in a May Day parade, that Baldwin was likely referring to when he described himself as a "committed fellow traveler" to the Communist Party during the period of his youth and adolescence. We will return momentarily to a deeper analysis of Baldwin's shifting political leanings in this period.

Baldwin was away from home, including at one temporary 5th Avenue address, when the next titanic personal event in his life occurred: the death of his stepfather, David, on July 29,

1943. David's mental health had begun to deteriorate in the years prior. To Baldwin, his stepfather's rage and decline were symptomatic of the racist economic system that ground him down. He was, he wrote, "certainly the most bitter man I had ever met." Much of his consuming anger had been directed at poverty and white people—"The only white people who came to our house," remembered Baldwin, "were welfare workers and bill collectors."[17] At the same time, his stepfather's death connoted deep, personal lessons about his life history and whither to direct it. His stepfather's "tremendous power" had come from his pride in his blackness, but "it has also been the cause of much humiliation and it had fixed bleak boundaries to his life."[18] "I saw that this had been for my ancestors and now would be for me an awful thing to live with and that the bitterness which had helped to kill my father could also kill me."[19]

Baldwin's penchant for reading history as personal allegory was animated by the fact that the death of his stepfather coincided with his own nineteenth birthday, the birth of his last sibling, Paula, and most importantly, the 1943 Harlem riots. Just a month before David Baldwin's death, on June 20, black residents of the Belle Isle Park section of Detroit rose up in rebellion against acute housing shortages, high unemployment, and police brutality. The rebellion was part of a wave of wartime black uprisings, including in New York, Los Angeles, California, and Mobile, Alabama, fueled by the sharpened contradictions of racism and inequality at home as black soldiers died on the front-lines of war. In Detroit, more than 6,000 federal troops were called in to smash the rebellion. At least 25 African-Americans were killed, hundreds wounded, and whole black areas of Detroit, like Paradise Alley, razed to the ground.

Baldwin's 1948 essay "Notes of a Native Son" conjoins these events as a kind of prophetic injunction, an anticipation of the motif Baldwin would develop to narrate God's warning to the world against racist oppression in *The Fire Next Time*. "It seemed to me that God himself had devised, to mark my father's end, the most sustained and brutally dissonant of codas. And it seemed to me, too, that the violence which rose all about us as my father left the world had been devised as a correction for the pride of his eldest son."[20] The Harlem riot was itself provoked by community response to police violence: a black soldier was shot in the back by a white policeman. Rumors that he was dead ignited long-simmering rage over rampant racism and poverty, having the effect, Baldwin notes, "of a lit match on a tin of gasoline." The rebellion targeted white-owned businesses, symbols of wealth and racial disparity, triggering in Baldwin's analysis of American capitalism a recurring theme: "To smash something is the ghetto's chronic need. Most of the time it is the members of the ghetto who smash each other, and themselves. But as long as the ghetto walls are standing there will always come a moment when these outlets do not work."[21]

The Harlem riots posed for Baldwin for the first time the question of the relationship between personal rage and public political expression. His stepfather's life, and death, became a metonymy for Harlem's—and black people's—struggle to survive the oppressive weight of history. "This was his legacy: nothing is ever escaped."[22] Baldwin thus formulated for the first time a personal dialectic, one shaped by, and consonant with, his evolving understanding of history as contradiction:

It began to seem that one would have to hold in the mind forever two ideas which seemed to be in opposition. The first idea was acceptance, the acceptance, totally without rancor, of life as it is, and men as they are: in this light of his idea, it goes without saying that injustice is a commonplace. But this does not mean that one could be complacent, for the second idea was of equal power: that one must never in one's own life, accept these injustices as commonplace but must fight them with all one's strength.[23]

Baldwin's formulation of a "unity of opposites" carries echoes of Marx's famous exhortation from the *Eighteenth Brumaire*: "men make history, but not under circumstances of their own choosing." How do we know to read Baldwin's 1948 dialectical meditation as under the influence of Marxism and Marxist thought? The biographical record here is important, and yet underexplored. Baldwin biographer James Campbell describes this period of Baldwin's life—the early 1940s—as "years when he himself was flirting with socialist groups and standing on picket lines,"[24] but does not delve deep into these claims. Biographer David Leeming suggests that Baldwin's progressive sympathies were shaped by Jewish classmates in public school who were children of the Amalgamated Clothing Workers Union. Douglas Field comes closest to explicating most fully Baldwin's political thought and evolution in this period of his adolescence. Field focuses on the influence on Baldwin of Eugene Worth. Worth was a young African-American intellectual who became Baldwin's closest friend by the time he was 19 years old. When they met, Worth was a member of the Young People's Socialist League (YPSL), and urged Baldwin to join. By Baldwin's account he did, sometime around 1943.

The YPSL (commonly pronounced "yipsel") was ensconced in a broader milieu of the anti-Stalinist left. The youth group of the Socialist Party of America, whose best-known leader was Norman Thomas, in the late 1930s it had been a battleground between militant Trotskyists and more moderate social democrats—torn apart in 1937–38, when the Trotskyists broke away to form the Socialist Workers Party (SWP), led by James P. Cannon and Max Shachtman. In 1940, a split in the SWP generated a new group led by Shachtman, the Workers Party, around which were gathered a substantial coterie of influential writers and intellectuals who impacted substantially on the YPSL circles to which Baldwin had been drawn. Some went on to influence such journals as *Partisan Review*, *Commentary*, the *New Leader*, and *Dissent*.[25]

Baldwin himself was unclear in his own public utterances about exactly when he joined the YPSL. In his most revealing comments about his political orientation in this period, he wrote that Worth "urged me to join, and I did. I then outdistanced him by becoming a Trotskyite—so that I was in the interesting position (at the age of nineteen) of being an anti-Stalinist when America and Russia were allied."[26] Later, in a letter to Orilla Miller written when he was 31, in 1955, Baldwin wrote of this period, "After my father died, I bounced around in the classic bohemian fashion, messed around in politics—made it all the way from the Stalinists to the Anarchists in what I think must be record time."[27] In a 1984 interview with *Paris Review*, Baldwin described himself as a "young Socialist" in this period.[28] Finally, in a 1984 interview with Richard Goldstein, Baldwin refers to a "brief stint in the Socialist Party"[29] without elaborating on when he joined, the longevity of his membership, or actions he might have been involved with.

Baldwin's circumspectness is best filled out by a rendering of the archival trail he left behind. That trail suggests that Baldwin was a member of the YPSL around 1943, and was also heavily recruited by the Workers Party to join. The Baldwin archive, for example, includes an invitation card to a meeting with the featured speaker, Japanese-American activist Ina Sugihara, on the topic of "The Japanese-American Relocation Program and Its Effects." The talk referred to the horrific internment of Japanese-Americans by the Roosevelt government undertaken immediately after the bombing of Pearl Harbor on December 7, 1941. Sugihara was herself a member of the Socialist Party and its Young People Socialist League, whose name appeared on the invitation. Baldwin's archive also includes a copy of *Challenge!*, which since 1933 had served as the official newspaper of the YPSL of the Socialist Party. *Challenge*'s line on the war conformed to both Baldwin's anti-Stalinism and his opposition to the war. As a May 1944 editorial put the matter, support should go neither to the "world-sucking imperialists of Britain and America, with their totalitarian Soviet ally, or the terrorists of Europe and Eastern Asia."[30]

Baldwin's archive also includes multiple copies of *Labor Action*, the newspaper of the Workers Party, suggesting that in the period of 1944–45—the dateline for the papers—he was a subscriber. More evidence of Baldwin's contact with the Workers Party comes in the uncorroborated reminiscences of labor activist and Workers Party member Stan Weir. Weir recalls meeting Baldwin when he was 18 years old and working at the Calypso, a restaurant and nightclub on MacDougal Street in Greenwich Village. Some time in 1942 or 1943, Baldwin took a job there as a waiter after being referred by Beauford Delaney to the restaurant owner Connie Williams, a Trinidadian. The job came just in time for Baldwin after losing his job at the meatpacking plant, and was part of his shift to spending more time in Greenwich Village as a refuge from his stepfather's Harlem home in the year before his death.

As Douglas Field notes, the Calypso was a "favored hangout for artists, musicians, actors, and political radicals."[31] There, Baldwin met among others the one-time Communist Party member, novelist, and poet Claude McKay; Harlem Renais-

sance intellectual, philosopher, and writer Alaine Locke; and
the Trinidadian Marxist C.L.R. James. Of some importance,
McKay and Locke were both gay, and it was in this period
of Greenwich Village life that Baldwin recorded in both his
fiction and personal reflections the clearest beginnings of his
own queer urgings and desires: "I am a homosexual," he wrote
in his diary, without revealing this to his family.[32] Baldwin
would later write out fictionalized versions of his time at the
Calypso in renderings of black musical and cabaret life in
stories like "Sonny's Blues" and the novel *Just Above My Head*.

Weir, for his part, was 22 and a member of the Merchant
Marines when he recalls meeting Baldwin (the Marines were
the wartime branch of the service to which many leftists
enlisted as they did not tend to engage in combat, primarily
acting as an adjunct to the U.S. Navy and delivering wartime
materiel). The two boarded together after Weir was hired as a
dishwasher at the Calypso. By his account, Weir tried recruit-
ing Baldwin to the Workers Party, but was rebuffed:

He already knew that it was the product of a split with
orthodox Trotskyism and with Trotsky, but he paused
longer than usual before tackling a difficult subject. "None
of your Shachtmanites, if you will, have ever patronized me.
You know that, like you, I do not like this war; you know
I agree with you that after all the destruction and death it
will probably end with more, not fewer dictatorships in this
world. And I agree with you on much more, but what you
are really asking of me is impossible. It took you months to
become fully aware that I develop relationships that include
what is sexual with men. It would have taken you longer if
it were not for the presence of a sophisticated Black woman
like Catherine Shipley, born and raised right here in the
Village. The two of you left here last night after you and I

had finished eating together. I saw it happen. She told you without alarm, just out there before you reached the corner. You had known it, and did not know it, because you had buried it. Yes, homosexual is a hard word to accept. You knew instantly that what she said was true. You did not turn on me, but you buried it still another time."[33]

This anecdote is rich with insight into Baldwin's political and personal dispositions in the early 1940s. His proximity to Trotskyism, and caution about openly identifying with a Trotskyist organization, hints at several political dynamics in his evolving thought. First, it indicates the firmly anti-capitalist direction in his thinking that would continue throughout his life. His anti-capitalism was rooted most firmly in an appreciation of Africans and African-Americans as an exploited class: "After all," he said in 1964 with *Transition*, "we have been functioning ... for 400 years as a source of cheap labor."[34] As late as 1972, nearing 50, Baldwin still envisioned the possibility of socialism in the U.S.[35] Second, where he had perceived himself to be a "committed fellow traveler" during the 1930s and up through his affiliation with the League of American Writers, the Communist Party's shifting line on the Soviet Union— for example the 1939 Stalin–Hitler non-aggression pact, and its retreat on the fight against racism during the war in order to support the Soviet Union—rankled a young Baldwin. This helped convince him that American and Soviet Communism were both variants of Stalinism owing to the Communist Party's more or less total dedication to Moscow's direction. Stalinism, for Baldwin, meant the authority of the party taking primacy over socialist political principles. Thus he was critical of the actor, singer, and songwriter Paul Robeson, a fellow traveler to the party, for failing to understand "the nature of political power in general, or Communist aims in particular."[36]

At the same time, Baldwin was more loyal to dissent from Stalinism than fidelity to Trotskyism or party ideology. There is no evidence that he was deeply read in Trotskyism. Even the work of C.L.R. James, the most famous black Trotskyist, did not seem to exercise influence on his thinking.[37]

Baldwin's hesitation to join the Workers Party may also indicate an uneasiness about the relationship of organized politics to art and art-making, a tendency that we shall see informed his perceptions as a literary critic under the influence of the Trotskyist left. Baldwin was openly critical of Richard Wright's *Native Son*, which was written while a member of the Communist Party, and whose influence Baldwin felt deleterious to his art. Baldwin's suspicion that the Workers Party might not welcome his homosexuality is also critically important. His preservation of what might be called sexual self-determination is a broader indicator of a tendency documented by numerous scholars of failures by U.S. socialist and Communist groups to adequately comprehend and support gays and lesbians, despite having advanced positions on questions of gender equality and social reproduction, and some openly gay comrades. Here, Weir's inability to perceive or recognize Baldwin's sexuality made him something in his own mind like an invisible man.

Finally, Baldwin's general anti-capitalist orientation belies important affiliations with other African-American writers of his generation who were likewise turned first towards and then away from the Communist movement during World War II. Baldwin was drawn to the U.S. left during the broad heyday of its influence on African-Americans—as he later put it to Nikki Giovanni, "in those years the Communist Party was in a sense the only haven for a young American black writer."[38] Indeed, between 1920 and 1950, the commitment to fighting racism made the Communist and socialist left, for many black intellectuals and writers, an indispensable resource and part of their lives. Claude McKay, Langston Hughes, Richard Wright, Ralph Ellison, Margaret Walker, Dorothy West, and Gwendolyn Brooks, for example, were all either Communist Party members or fellow travelers at some point during this period. Many of these writers and intellectuals also underwent disillusionment with the left at this time. As Barbara Foley has shown, Ralph Ellison's sturdy Cold War anti-Communism was presaged by a profound disillusionment with the party's wartime retreat on the fight against racism. Richard Wright and Chester Himes were both turned against the Communist Party by the party's oscillating perspectives and, in Wright's case, a perceived hostility to the individual vision of the black artist—or at least his own. Within this historical pattern, Baldwin *is* relatively unique among mid-century black writers for acknowledging Trotskyist influence on his thought. More often, black writers who had a one-time allegiance to Communism or socialism in this period went significantly to the right—like Ellison—or eventually settled for some version of liberalism or black nationalism. Baldwin established early in his life a propensity for "third-way" politics—neither capitalism nor Soviet Communism—that would sustain itself into the 1960s and 1970s in important ways to be discussed.

Baldwin's political "bouncing around" in the period of the war, as he referred to it, also included some level of engagement with anarchism. Baldwin's archives include multiple issues of the U.S. anarchist publication *Why?*, edited by William Young and published in New York City. The issues, non-continuous, begin in March 1943 and conclude in November 1944. In the same period, Baldwin apparently subscribed to a British anarchist publication, *War Commentary*. Issues in his archive begin July 1943 and conclude April 1944.

Why? and *War Commentary* were independent of each other but shared several political perspectives reflective of Baldwin's political thinking in this period. Baldwin acknowledged inheriting from Orilla Miller a dedication to the anti-fascist struggle in Spain. *Why?* and *War Commentary* were both significantly influenced by the tradition of anarcho-syndicalism in the Spanish Civil War. *Why?* was especially allied with Proudhonism—"Property is theft"—as an alternative to what it called a "totalitarian State under one guise or another."[39] That position would have aligned itself with Baldwin's "neither Washington nor Moscow" analysis of Stalinism and U.S. capitalism during the war. For a British publication, *War Commentary* also paid close attention to racial conditions in the United States. A November 1943 article titled "Negro Mutiny" was a report on 14 African-American soldiers charged with attempting to kill two army police sergeants in the Devon town of Paignton. Baldwin routinely collected newspaper stories from the U.S. press of black troops at war or returned from war who had experienced some form of racism or mistreatment, for example a 1945 *New York Post* story headlined "The Veteran Problem: He'll Be Bitter."[40] Finally, the anti-war politics of both anarchist publications would have aligned with Baldwin's leaning—tendency is too decisive a word—to conscientious objection. Baldwin was never drafted to the military, but in June 1943 did receive from the Selective Service an "Order Referring Registrants to Another Local Board for Preliminary Physical Examination Only," and according to his FBI file did register. Yet the same file that included that order contained a copy of "The Conscientious Objector under the Selective Service and Training Act of 1940," a pamphlet published by the National Service Board for Religious Objectors. The YPSL, which Baldwin did join, also supported those resisting conscription, organizing protests against the National Service Act which often resulted in arrest.

Baldwin left virtually no written traces of his activities related to anarchist politics. The only tangible evidence of something like participation is the uncorroborated claim by anarchist Diva Agostinelli that Baldwin attended a meeting in New York sponsored by *Why?*, where he read an early draft of *Go Tell It On the Mountain*.[41] The dates cited in Agostinelli's claim make this possible. Whether true or not, however, Baldwin's apparent intellectual interest in and reading habits around anarchism substantiate his assertion that the period after his father's death was one of tremendous political experiment and consideration. What is most clear is that Baldwin was seeking a systemic alternative to the world of the United States that he knew, the same world that had nearly driven him to murder in New Jersey; taken his father in tubercular madness; and was continuously threatening to drive him to the deepest levels of poverty and alienation, and undermine his aspirations to be a writer.

* * *

Wilmer Stone's 1941 letter of recommendation for a "sterling lad" setting out into the capitalist world did not, as we have seen, batter down the walls of discrimination Baldwin faced in the employment market. After his temporary stints laying railroad, working in sweatshops and meatpacking, and waiting tables, Baldwin was pleased to gain jobs with one foot in the publishing world. For a brief time, he worked as a messenger for the progressive newspaper *PM*. In September 1944, now 20, he went to work as a galley boy in the composing room of the *Morning Telegraph* newspaper. From there Baldwin wrote one of his most revealing and self-reflective letters. The letter was addressed to his close friend Tom Martin. Martin had been a foreman at the military plant where Baldwin had laid railroad track. He then joined the military and was deployed to Italy. Letters to Baldwin from Martin indicate that the latter had leftist political sympathies and an intense homoerotic attachment to Baldwin, referring to him as the "dark love of my life."[42] Their correspondence is one of a number of letters from the period between Baldwin and men who he met in New York before going off to war. In general, these letters indicate Baldwin's sociality and openness to a variety of friendship types.

The letter to Martin suggests the degree to which Baldwin saw his friend as an intellectual sounding board. Much of it is about Baldwin's self-reflection, as an aspiring writer, on the nature of good art: "I am indifferent to schools of art," he writes, while asserting that "I think that art is positive and that it is directly responsible to life … I can see no virtue in art divorced from life or art which distorts and negates it."[43] Baldwin's letter appears to be a criticism of high modernism—in the same letter Baldwin says Joyce is "no good" after the publication of *Portrait of the Artist*, when he wrote his most abstract novels like *Finnegans Wake*—and that he is "dubious" about T.S. Eliot, famous for his erudite, allusive poetry.[44]

But it is Baldwin's private expressions of anguish—or outsiderness— that reveal him as his own Portrait of the Artist trapped in a bourgeois society from which he feels near total estrangement:

Dear Tom:

This letter is being begun under exceedingly adverse conditions. I am at work and surrounded by the model Americans of our time. Every one here is some degree of "successful"—which is to say they have held down the same job (successfully) for the last fifty years. They are all very proud of it. I am, of course, a misfit. (Have I ever been anything else?)

I have been in and out of the Village now for three years—from seventeen to twenty. I think the time is fast approaching when I must get out for good. There is death here. Everywhere people are sick or dying or dead.

The parties are wasteful, the love affairs futile and acrid.[45]

Baldwin's plaintive lament that he is not cut out for a world of commerce and achievement anticipates the complaints of the beatnik writer generation that followed. So, too, does his portrait of a dying New York and a "lost generation" of friends like himself almost too poor to live, too estranged to thrive. Another letter to his friend Sheldon Biegel from 1944, unfinished, reports that he has just lost his job—possibly the one at the *Telegraph*—has pneumonia, and is broke. "I am in the unique position of not being able to eat," he writes.[46] In December 1944, Baldwin wrote to Jackson MacLow asking for books to read and "the $6 you owe me."[47] For a brief time in 1944, Baldwin was employed as a postal worker. Tax documents indicate he earned $47.25 before losing that job.[48] He also returned for a short time to work for the defense department. A January 1945 letter from the Credit Union of the Office of War Information notifying Baldwin of his termination asks him to come in to repay, with interest, a $10 loan.[49] In February 1945, he received a notice of termination from *PM*. A bank book from this period shows a balance of $25.

Baldwin's references to "futile and acrid" love affairs also bespeaks the tumult of a queer life attempting to find itself and speak its name. Baldwin's decision to live in Greenwich Village in this period put him in closer contact with his friend Beauford Delaney, the Calypso, the queer streets. In a late-in-life essay,

"Freaks and the Ideal of American Manhood," he recounts a variety of sexual experiences, including being taken at 16 under the wing of a man of 38, a Harlem racketeer, who "fell in love with me" and to whom Baldwin showed his poetry.[50] At 19, he would wander into movie houses on 42nd Street, and near the public library, observing gay men longing for each other, and "would find myself in bed with one of these men, a despairing and dreadful conjunction, since their need was as relentless as quicksand and as impersonal, and sexual rumor concerning blacks had preceded me."[51] Meanwhile, homophobia was rampant—Baldwin heard from the streets the words "faggot" and "pussy" hurled his way,[52] and his sexual desire was still a secret to his family, one awkwardly kept by Baldwin. As David Leeming notes, "In New York he was increasingly recognized as a homosexual, and Baldwin still had enough of the preacher's outlook to want to 'shield' his mother from the 'details of my peculiarly lonely life.'"[53] Baldwin did have male lovers in the Village. David Leeming writes that he modeled a relationship between David, the protagonist of his novel *Giovanni's Room*, and Joey, a younger man, on a relationship Baldwin himself had with a young Italian boy in the Village in this period.[54] At the same time, Baldwin was compelled to consider heterosexuality and heteronormativity by a mainstream world that sneered homophobically at the queer: at one point he met and considered marrying a girlfriend, only to break off their engagement, an oscillation that would redound in the plot of *Giovanni's Room*.

All the while, Baldwin tended his craft. From 1942 to 1945, he continued to work on drafts of *Crying Holy*. His confidence in the autobiographical novel may have been stoked by the success of Richard Wright's memoir *Black Boy*, published in 1945—Baldwin saved several reviews of the book. He also wrote and submitted several short stories to periodicals, gaining nibbles but no publications. His publishing frustrations seeped into correspondence. A letter from 1944 complains that, "Books are tailor-made, tailored-to suit the fashions, the media, the prejudice of the public."[55] In the spring of 1944, considering his hand at playwriting, Baldwin took a theater class at the New School.[56] Both attachments would last the rest of his life, as we shall see. Baldwin's interest in the theater was also piqued by the ongoing renaissance in African-American theater around him, including the development of the American Negro Theater in Harlem.

In late 1944, Baldwin earned something like his big break. Richard Wright had ascended to become the leading light of African-American letters on the heels of his bestselling, Book-of-the-Month Club novel *Native Son* (1940). Baldwin was a fan, and admirer. He requested and received a meeting with Wright to share the manuscript of his work-in-progress, *Crying Holy*. Wright liked the work, and recommended it to an editor at his own publisher, Harper and Brothers.

In November 1945, Baldwin received a $500 grant from *Harper's* Eugene F. Saxton Memorial Trust to continue work on the novel. Shortly thereafter, a draft was rejected by both Harper and Doubleday, and Baldwin returned to work on it. He also drafted, and abandoned, another novel, *Ignorant Armies*, whose title was drawn from Matthew Arnold's famous Victorian poem, "Dover Beach."

The Arnoldian allusion is an indicator of Baldwin's breadth of reading in this period, and the early influence of canonical Western authors. They included Balzac, Flaubert, Dostoevsky, and especially the American novelist Henry James. Significant to the remainder of his career, it was Baldwin the critic and public intellectual who broke through to a reading public even before the novelist. On April 12, 1947, Baldwin published a book review of Maxim Gorky's *Best Short Stories* in *The Nation*, a progressive periodical with a largely white liberal and left reading audience. Gorky was, for Baldwin, important for his concern for what he called in the review the "wretchedness of people" in reference to his masterwork, *The Lower Depths.*[57] He was also, however, a cautionary example for the modern novelist. At a moment when a brand of realism, and social realism, dominated the American novel, Baldwin singled out Gorky for an expanded vision that, to his mind, transcended sentimental—meaning pitying or dogmatic—depictions of human life. The "dismal failure of present-day realist novels," wrote Baldwin, was that they "do not ever indicate what Gorky sometimes succeeded in projecting—the unpredictability and the occasional and amazing splendor of the human being."[58] And further: "If literature is not to drop completely to the intellectual and moral level of the daily papers, we must recognize the need for further and honest exploration of those provinces, the human heart and mind, which have operated historically and now, as the no-man's land between us and our salvation."[59]

Baldwin's call for sympathy and complexity in literature points to two directions in his thought that eventually synthesized into a whole. Baldwin's insistence that literature create a fully dimensional humanism was rooted in an appreciation that literature can raise individual suffering to a collective level. As he put it in his essay "The Artist's Struggle for Integrity," "When I was very young ... I assumed that no one had ever been born who was only five feet six inches tall, or been born poor, or been born ugly, or masturbated, or done all those things which were my private property when I was fifteen. No one had ever suffered the way I suffered. Then you discover, and I discovered this through Dostoevsky, that it is common. Everybody did it."[60] Or as Baldwin later put it in an interview with the poet Nikki Giovanni, "suffering is your bridge" to other people's lives.[61] Literature's democratizing function also compelled Baldwin's reading of Shakespeare: "The greatest poet in the English language found his poetry where poetry is found: in the lives of the people. He could have done this only through love—by knowing, which is not the same thing as understanding, that whatever was happening to anyone was happening to him."[62] In all three of these instances, including Gorky, Baldwin implicitly centers his personal suffering as human suffering, and finds in the creation of art a bridge between them. It is what might be called a vernacular theory of universal culture. Following from this, "salvation" in Baldwin's schema, means the capacity of literature to raise political and ethical reflection to a higher level irrespective of the subject, or the writer.

This point is made in deeper, dialectical fashion in a companion review of Gorky's novel *Mother*, Baldwin's second major publication, published in the *New Leader* six months later. The *New Leader* had begun publication in 1924 by the Socialist Party of America. Under the direction of editor Sol Levitas in the 1940s, the journal became liberal and anti-Communist, specifically anti-Stalinist. Among other notable writers to publish there were Max Eastman, Ralph Ellison, George Orwell, Theodore Draper, and Daniel Bell. Baldwin's review of Gorky's novel of the revolutionary socialist underground in Russia subtly articulated a theory of art implicitly opposed to what was called in the 1930s "proletarian culture." In response to Gorky's insistence that "art is the weapon of the working class," Baldwin writes:

The phrase has always brought to my mind the image of a soldier rushing into battle waving a volume of Shakespeare on the point of a bayonet. Art, to be sure, has its roots in the lives of human beings: the weakness, the strength, the absurdity. I doubt that it is limited to our comrades; since we have discovered that art does not belong to what was once the aristocracy, it does not therefore follow that it had become the exclusive property of the common man—which abstraction, by the way, I have yet to meet. Rather, since it is involved with all of us, it belongs to all of us, and this includes our foes, who are as desperate and as vacuous and as blind as we are and who can only be as evil as we are ourselves.[63]

Baldwin's aversion to proletarian literature as a type stems from a skepticism expressed at various stages of his life about the political potential of the United States working class specifically, and of Marxism as a theory to bring revolution. He was ever mindful of long-term practices of discrimination in American labor unions, for example, which caused him retroactive doubt about Marxism's use as a tool for liberation. By the 1970s, for example, in a fit of political despair alien to him when young, Baldwin wrote, "For Marx and Engels, the presence of the black man in America was simply a useful crowbar for the liberation of whites: an idea which has found issue in the history of American labor unions."[64] At the same time, and at a deeper level, Douglas Field has persuasively interpreted Baldwin's theory of art as revealing the long-term absorption and influence of Trotskyism. Field notes that Baldwin's book reviews and essays from this period, including his review of Gorky, exhibit a "keen dislike of ideologically driven art and criticism."[65] The latter view was popularized during the late 1930s in the journal *Partisan Review* by editors Philip Rahv and William Phillips, who published two influential essays by Trotsky: "Art and Politics," and "Manifesto: Towards a Free Revolutionary Art." There, Trotsky distanced himself from the "proletcult," or proletarian culture movement that had been initiated in the Soviet Union in the 1920s, and significantly influenced the development of proletarian literature in the United States. This followed from earlier essays like 1924's "Class and Art," in which Trotsky argued that "One cannot approach art as one can politics, not because artistic creation is a religious rite or something mystical … but because it has its own laws of development."[66] These views also became a fundamental consensus of the so-called "New York intellectuals," who used journals like *Partisan Review* and *New Leader* to popularize the perspective. Significantly, in 1949 Baldwin published his most famous, breakthrough essay, "Everybody's Protest Novel," a criticism of Richard Wright's 1940 novel *Native Son*, in *Partisan Review*.

We will take up the essay in more detail in Chapter 3, but note here that Baldwin both identified with—and was identified by—writers and editors associated with anti-Stalinist culture and cultural criticism. They helped to open a door that Baldwin was eager to walk through. Baldwin, in turn, seemed in his literary criticism of the 1940s to reflect a general orientation argued for in Trotsky's *Literature and Revolution* that capitalism, rather than producing class society and class struggle as the subject of great art—a tenet of proletcult—actually inhibited its full development. Baldwin's subtle joke then, that art does not belong just to "our comrades" or the "common man"—Stalinist "abstractions" in his formulation—offers up something like a Trotskyist universalism: as Trotsky put it in his 1938 "Manifesto: Toward a Free Revolutionary Art," written with André Breton, "The need for emancipation felt by the individual spirit has only to follow its natural course to be led to mingle its stream with this primeval necessity: the need for the emancipation of man."[67]

At the same time, Baldwin's reactive cynicism about art from a left point of view would set the stage for perhaps the

most controversial moment of his career—his criticisms of
Richard Wright. We will examine this in detail in Chapter 3.
Here, it is important to note that Baldwin's writings on politics
and literature during the Cold War, including Communism
and anti-Communism, at times carry a whiff of American
nationalist exuberance, or triumphalism, that is an ideological adjunct of his 1940s anti-Stalinism. As he put it to his
friend Sol Stein in a letter written at the height of the Cold
War, "America is the last stronghold of the Western idea of
liberty. And I certainly think that this idea should dominate
the world," and "it is perfectly clear that if America is not
dominant, Russia will be. I, personally, prefer to see America
dominant."[68] The rise of Black Power and black revolutionary
groups like the Black Panthers, who considered themselves
Marxists, eased Baldwin away from some of this liberal chau-
vinism, and gave him more optimism about the chances
for revolution in America. His trajectory is a reminder that
others from the New York intellectual milieu of this period—
Irving Kristol, Norman Podhoretz, Sidney Hook, to take three
examples—moved much further to the right as the Cold War
deepened, the seeds of their anti-Stalinism morphing into
a much fuller and full-blown anti-Communism later titled
"neoconservatism."

Lastly, it is notable that the majority of writers and editors
associated with the 1940s Trotskyist and anti-Stalinist left
were Jewish. Many had, like Baldwin, been members of the
YPSL. Baldwin's intellectual understanding of racial oppression was shaped by this Jewish milieu. Nathan Abrams has
gone so far as to argue that Baldwin was "the black equivalent
of a New York Jewish intellectual."[69] In "The Harlem Ghetto,"
cited earlier, Baldwin argued that "Jews, like Negroes, must
use every possible weapon in order to be accepted, and must
try to cover their vulnerability by a frenzied adoption of the

customs of the country."[70] In 1948, Baldwin was awarded a Rosenwald Fellowship for a proposed collaboration with photographer Theodore Pelatowaki to document storefront churches in black communities. Rosenwald was a Jewish millionaire and philanthropist. In notes for the project Baldwin offered that the book would examine "the growing estrangement between the church and the Negro people, the conflict between the paradise beyond the sky and the ever-growing hope and determination not to wait that long and not to take much more."[71] Significantly, Baldwin sought to model this emancipatory narrative on the book of Exodus, "the story of the Jewish exile up until the exodus led by Moses out of Egypt."[72] "It becomes apparent that the Negro in this country operates actually on that level as an exile."[73] The project was never finished, but demonstrates the intellectual and theological roots of Baldwin's early apprehension of black-Jewish oppression and resistance. Indeed, Baldwin's understanding of inequality and discrimination, and the potential for interethnic, cross-racial alliance, were shaped in part by his sympathetic relationship to Jewish friends and colleagues; his outrage at fascism and the Holocaust; the creation of the state of Israel—to which Baldwin nearly fled in 1948—and the prevalence of anti-semitism in the U.S. Significantly, Baldwin's life arc also includes a movement from supporting the state of Israel to supporting Palestinian liberation and becoming staunchly anti-Zionist, as well as a contested critique of Jewish "whiteness" in the U.S., a topic we will explore in future chapters.

Baldwin also used his platform as a newly popular book reviewer to introduce into his public writing incipient queer themes and thoughts. In doing so he both preserved and expanded his formula for, and example of, sympathetic art. In 1947, again for *New Leader*, he reviewed Stuart Engstrand's novel *The Sling and the Arrow*. The book is the story of a schizophrenic personality. Significant to Baldwin, the novel attributes the schizophrenia to a childhood trauma: the protagonist, at twelve, is discovered in what Baldwin calls "homosexual play" with a young neighbor. From that point, the character's life is a kind of "expiation and flight, an obsession to prove to his dead father that he was masculine entirely and had been cleansed of his sin." Baldwin continues: "Here is a dilemma known to all of us: Herbert's terrible guilt, the compulsion to be accepted, his helplessness in the face of the war within him. The contemporary sexual attitudes constitute a rock against which many of us flounder all our lives long; no one escapes entirely the prevailing psychology of the times."[74]

Baldwin here mediates the individual and the universal through queer identity: Herbert's "dilemma" of being homosexual is made a larger signifier for the sexual anxieties of coming-of-age generally in a heavily repressive society. The "us" is both Baldwin, all queers, and all those who have sex. As he later put it in an interview with Richard Goldstein, "The so-called straight person is no safer than I am, really. Loving anybody and being loved by anybody is a tremendous danger, a tremendous responsibility ... ."[75] In his essay "The Male Prison," his first full-length exploration of queer identity on the writer André Gide, Baldwin asserted that "the prison in which Gide struggled is not really so unique as it would certainly comfort us to believe, is not very different from the prison inhabited by, say, the heroes of Mickey Spillane"—a "tough-guy" detective writer.[76] This gesture towards relationality and universalism competed often in Baldwin's thought with the particularity of queer sexuality. In his pathbreaking essay "Freaks and the American Ideal of Manhood" (1985), for example, which we will explore in more detail later, Baldwin argued that to be called "queer" or faggot is "being told simply that you have no balls."[77] The essay proposes that the "ideal" of heteronormative masculinity by definition excludes, marginalizes, and makes deviant the "freakish" queer subject. The argument is finite, and specific.

Yet in 1947, Baldwin's articulations of queer subjectivity were more muted—if not partially self-closeted—critiques of what he called "prevailing psychology." His review does criticize Engstrand for presenting a queer pathology in his book, a "study of human helplessness" rather than a "personality."[78] But the record of Baldwin's public writing in this early period must be scanned carefully to discern queer moments breaking through. Alan Wald delivers a rare moment of such insight in his discovery and analysis of Baldwin's first-known poem published in a public journal in 1946, one year before his essay on Engstrand. The poem, titled "Nursery Rhyme," reads as follows:

Until the sunless dawn arise
    Jack, be patient, Jack, be wise,
And dry your eyes.
Until the sunless dawn come up
    Stare at the wormwood in the cup
And drink it up.
Snatch at the tabloid, catch the train,
    Reel through the infinite inane.
Silence the roaring brain.
Rest for the weary, hope for the dead;
    These are the pages you have read;
All your fathers left unsaid
Is yours to grapple, yours to face.
You are appointed a cripple's pace.
These days are watching the world grow sick, The dead lie
    rotting.
        Come, Jack, pick

Your way past the dead, though the dead lie thick.
Jack be nimble, Jack be quick.[79]

"Nursery Rhyme" was published in *New Masses*, the journal associated with the Communist Party. It is Baldwin's only known published work there. Its placement bespeaks to us, once again, his general leftist orientation, and a catholic tolerance for publishing in left journals regardless of their political orientation. *New Masses* and *New Leader*, for example, would have been at odds over Stalinism.

In a perceptive reading, Wald notes that the poem "seems to call for forbearance in the face of capitalist misery until the inevitable moment of revolution"—the long wait for the sunless dawn to "arise." Yet Wald also notes that the phrase "sunless dawn" likely originates in Victorian art critic Walter Pater's *Studies in the History of the Renaissance*. Pater evinced a queer aesthetic in his own work, and may have been introduced to Baldwin by Beauford Delaney. In *Studies*, the phrase "sunless dawn" refers to what Pater called the "cold light" in Botticelli's famous rendering of Venus rising from the sea. In combination with Baldwin's reference to a "sunless dawn"— one without the "red sun" of revolution imminent—Wald reads Baldwin's intertextual reference to suggest that "sexuality may be liberated from its ruling-class chains, but the wisdom of experience reminds one that sources of despair reside in the unpredictable and sometimes overwhelming powers of desire."[80] Indeed, Baldwin's poem is shot through with latency and unfulfillment, not consummation: "Rest for the weary, hope for the dead; | These are the pages you have read" likely refers to Marx's famous assertion in the *Eighteenth Brumaire* that, "The tradition of all dead generations weigh like a nightmare on the brains of the living"[81]—Jack is indeed "weighted down" by the "inane" tabloids and the curses of fathers, perhaps, Wald notes, Baldwin's own. The plea to Jack to be "nimble and quick" among the dead may also serve as Baldwin's self-referential advice to navigating the revolutionary left as a queer man: recall his admonition to Weir about his invisibility to comrades.

These pregnant lines from "Nursery Rhyme"—"These days are watching the world grow sick | The dead lie rotting | Come, Jack, pick | Your way past the dead, though the dead lie thick"—also return us to one of our epigraphs, Baldwin's 1944 letter to Tom Martin, and his lament that "There is death here. Everywhere people are sick or dying or dead." Clearly, Baldwin's characterization of death and illness was a metaphorical commentary on the spiritual, and political, state of the United States as rendered in "Nursery Rhyme." The poem and the letter likewise offer two dialectically related responses to these conditions: revolution and exile.

We should keep these coordinates in mind, as they capture much of the movement of Baldwin's physical and political life henceforth. Baldwin's constant motion from place to place, country to country—"Jack be nimble | Jack be quick" was its own commentary on the difficulty of accommodating himself to what he perceived as oppressive social forces operating across the Western capitalist world: racism, nationalism, xenophobia, homophobia. It was, in other words, a drastic political response to political problems. By the end of 1947, Baldwin was at something of a crisis and crossroads: his career as a writer was beginning to take shape, and was suddenly perhaps possible, while his economic situation was dire, his love and sex life a quandary and a mess, and his relationship to the American state increasingly bitter, cynical, and estranged. The beginnings of the Cold War in 1946, and the announcement of the McCarthy hearings and trials, were for Baldwin an ominous foreshadowing of a generalized repression he felt especially vulnerable to as a queer, black leftist: gays and lesbians were fired by the hundreds by the federal government as Communists were chased out. The Red Scare was also Pink. Too, Baldwin saw immediately that colleagues on the black left—Paul Robeson, W.E.B. Du Bois, Richard Wright, Langston Hughes—were immediately imperiled; Robeson in particular wound up paying enormous costs for his political life by being blacklisted as a performer. It would take time for Baldwin himself to be ensnared—the FBI would open its file on him in 1960, after some initial fame.

In this context, the theme of personal and political mortality in "Nursery Rhyme" should return us to Baldwin's reflections on the traumatic encounters with racism in New Jersey. Baldwin recognized that staying alive itself was a basic challenge in America for a young, queer, black man with revolutionary leanings. "Jack be nimble | Jack be quick" was another way of speaking this fundamental truth. Finally, there was the momentous example of his best friend: in 1946, Eugene Worth, who had recruited Baldwin to the YPSL, leaped from the George Washington Bridge, killing himself. The event would haunt Baldwin's life forever: he would use it as the basis for the dramatic turning point of his 1962 novel *Another Country*. He would also later reflect that while they were never lovers, that Worth loved him, and that Baldwin wished perhaps they had been. In the short term, though, Worth's death was the death of one variant of revolutionary optimism—Worth had, after all, recruited him to the YPSL. "Nursery Rhyme" might be seen, then, as a specific epigraph and epitaph for that life and that dream. Both confronted Baldwin again with the most existential of political crises.

And so he jumped.

3
Political Exile and Survival: 1948–57

I split. I had to split, otherwise I would be dead.[1]

James Baldwin, Dialogue with Nikki Giovanni

I am not—as you know—one of those who object to men being lovers, but I think that it is necessary to face facts, and the facts are that two men cannot be married unless one of them is willing to cease being a man—which destroys— more effectively than anything else could, the whole point of their having been lovers in the first place.[2]

James Baldwin, letter to Mary Painter, 1954

I was very poor when I got to Paris. I slept in the streets and under bridges and I slept with the Africans, the Algerians and the underside of Paris. It was very good for me … In France, the Algerian is the nigger.[3]

James Baldwin, interview with *The Black Scholar*, 1973

This world is white no longer, and it will never be white again.[4]

James Baldwin, "Stranger in the Village," 1953

In April 1948, Baldwin published "The Image of the Negro," a review of five recently published novels, all by white liberal authors, all taking up questions of race in the United States.

Most famous among the titles was Sinclair Lewis's *Kingsblood Royal*. Baldwin was generally savage in his assessment. "These novels have in common a subterranean assumption," he wrote, "unspoken by the emancipated, but living in our culture and apparently shared by the novelists themselves: the assumption that whiteness is a kind of salvation and that blackness is a kind of death."[5] Baldwin also pilloried the books for privileging "protest" over craftsmanship: "Granting the initial debasement of literary standards, the arrival of the protest novel was inevitable. The question forever posed by the existence of the protest novel—a kind of writing becoming nearly as formalized as those delicate vignettes for the women's magazines—is whether or not its power as a corrective social force is sufficient to override its deficiencies as literature."[6]

The review exposed a double crisis in Baldwin's life: driven to the brink by joblessness and racism in the preceding decade—recall his mug-throwing episode in New Jersey—the aspiring novelist was confronted with a slew of books seeming to condone and consecrate the overwhelming and immutable power of racial oppression. The second crisis was related to the first: Baldwin desperately needed a language, a voice of his own, by which to smash back at this jeopardy—his "Harlem Ghetto" essay published just two months prior had been a *crier de couer* for the destruction of the world that had created him. But these books under review were dull commercial artifacts that readers of the journal *Commentary*—the venue for this review—and his wider circle of "New York intellectuals" would have agreed were failures to the cause of art. "Protest literature" was Baldwin's lacerating coinage for literature that seemed to straitjacket at once the black writer—and the black subject—in an iron cage.

And so Baldwin escaped. In November 1948, he boarded a plane for Paris. The decision was in many ways the most momentous he ever took. He arrived in Paris temporarily free of his most existential dread—that America might destroy him: "I knew that if I went on ... I would go under, if I stayed I would certainly kill somebody."[7] Thus, Baldwin referred to the subsequent days in Paris as "the best and the most important years of my life."[8] The decision concretized first and foremost his commitment to write. It also removed him from the suffo-cating species of American racist pressures he felt constantly encroaching, and the slowly unfolding debacle of the Cold War and McCarthyite period which he later described as a "national convulsion."[9] The move also provided him with the emotional time and physical space to consider and define his sexuality away from his family, especially his mother. In these ways, Baldwin was more an involuntary political exile from America than a willful expatriate. "No one really wishes to leave his homeland," he later wrote.[10]

At the same time, the move placed Baldwin self-consciously in an important historical stream: of American and African-American intellectuals who saw in Paris and Europe a site from which to measure the historical and geographical arc of their lives. As Baldwin put it in "A Question of Identity," an essay he wrote immediately upon his arrival, "From the vantage point of Europe he [the American] discovers his own country. And this is a discovery which not only brings to an end the alienation of the American from himself, but which also makes clear to him, for the first time, the extent of his involvement in the life of Europe."[11]

Yet precisely because of his peculiar status as an *African-American* abroad, Paris would explode in Baldwin's consciousness a deep, global realization of what he called—to return to our beginning—the condition of being a "bastard of the West." For:

> when I followed the line of my past I did not find myself in Europe but in Africa. And this meant that in some subtle way, in a really profound way I brought to Shakespeare, Bach, Rembrandt, to the stones of Paris, to the cathedral at Chartres, and the Empire State building, a special attitude. These were not really my creations, they did not contain my history; I might search in them in vain forever for any reflection of myself. I was an interloper; this was not my heritage.[12]

Baldwin would feel both newly imagined and newly alienated on Europe's shores. Settling down in the heart of imperial Europe offered him a "double consciousness," for example of colonialism, that was a sequel to his comprehension of racism in America. In "Stranger in the Village," also written in this period in Paris, he described himself as "strangely grafted" to Western history by colonialism and the slave trade: "Europe's black possessions remained—and do remain—in Europe's colonies, at which remove they represented no threat whatever to European identity. If they posed any problem at all for the European conscience, it was a problem which remained comfortingly abstract: in effect, the black man, *as a man*, did not exist for Europe."[13] Especially when confronted with the French colonization of Algeria, whose war for independence broke out six years into his residency in Paris, Baldwin began to perceive himself as a worldly citizen politically responsible for the plight of what Frantz Fanon called, in his powerful book of the same name, the "wretched of the earth." Baldwin's early years in Paris were thus a struggle to accommodate himself as a man of the "West," pushed and pulled by militant currents against that idea in the form of the rising anti-colonial movement in Africa and Asia. This contradiction would culminate in 1956, when Baldwin attended a Conference of Negro-African Writers and Artists organized by the anti-colonial Negritude movement as a reporter on the event. There and after, Baldwin would begin the slow process of tearing himself away from Western moorings, though not without an internal ideological struggle over the meaning of doing so.

And yet this emergence of a new and public James Baldwin was complicated by two other dominant notes in Baldwin's private life: chronic struggles with poverty, and intimate relationships that both expressed and rebelled against Baldwin's desire for stillness, security, queer desire, and most of all love. Baldwin's staggered, abiding affections for two men in this period, Lucien Happersberger, Swiss and white, and Arnold, African-American, combined with illness, pressure to write, and fatigue at his constant mobility, drove Baldwin first to contemplation of suicide, then to an attempt. His letters from this period are shot through with intimations of his mortality and destruction. "I seem, in the main, to be quite a conglomeration of poses, most of them disastrous. And I'm beginning to think that I'm perhaps a somewhat dangerous person, and have been wrong, hopelessly wrong, about almost everything all of my life."[14] Even literary fame brought Baldwin dim analogies to personal disaster: "In a few months I'll have survived being thirty-two, which is when Hart Crane died, and I know why."[15] Yet through it all Baldwin wrote, and published, and did not perish, and became in the eyes of the world a major writer and intellectual, and with those adopted new-found burdens of responsibility. This period, 1948 to 1957, then, might be considered the most pivotal and contradictory in Baldwin's life. Its numerous conflicts and themes would find articulation in his groundbreaking and breakout books from this period: *Go Tell It On the Mountain*, *Notes of a Native Son*, and *Giovanni's Room*.

* * *

Baldwin arrived in Paris by plane on November 11, 1948. He had approximately $40 to his name, the tail end of the Rosenwald Fellowship he had earned for the uncompleted photo book on black churches.[16] He was greeted at the airport by a friend from Greenwich Village and checked himself into the Hotel de Rome. His first significant social meeting was with the African-American writer Richard Wright. Wright had moved to Paris in 1947, fearful that he would be called to testify before the House Un-American Activities Committee because of his membership in the Communist Party. Wright had joined the party in 1932, and left some time in the early 1940s. Baldwin also met, through Wright, Themistocles Hoetis (aka George Solomos) and Asa Beneviste, both aspiring writers. Together, they told Baldwin of plans to publish a new literary magazine, called *Zero*.

Baldwin, however, needed less expensive accommodation first, so checked into the cheaper Hotel de Verneuil. There he would broaden his social circle, meeting the Norwegian journalist Gidske Anderson, and the English socialist Mary Keen, then employed as a translator at the World Federation of Trade Unions. He also met in short time the writers Truman Capote and Saul Bellow, evidence of the rising literary reputation he carried from the U.S. While at Hotel de Verneuil, Baldwin also dove down to his writing. He continued to work on drafts of *Crying Holy* and started another novel, never finished, about Greenwich Village. He continued to read, especially the work of Henry James. James's decision to leave the U.S. for Europe when he was 32—and to write about Americans in Paris, as in his classic novel *The American*—hovered around Baldwin's literary imagination of exile.

In Baldwin's own account, his next major decision was to produce a "declaration of independence" from America and its political and literary influences over his life.[17] That declaration was the essay "Everybody's Protest Novel." The essay was published in the first issue of *Zero* magazine in the spring of 1949 (republished in June that year by the New York intellectual journal *Partisan Review*). The essay begins as a criticism of Harriet Beecher Stowe's bestselling nineteenth-century novel *Uncle Tom's Cabin*. Stowe's novel was famous for being both a melodramatic condemnation of slavery meant to move readers against it, and an atavistic portrait of black people, the slave "Uncle Tom" becoming forever a symbol of the stereotypically subservient African-American.

For Baldwin, Stowe's novel was "self-righteous" and full of "virtuous sentimentality" covering a "mask of cruelty" directed against the complexity of black humanity.[18] As such, it reminded Baldwin of the sentimental "protest" novels by white liberals he had reviewed in America just before leaving, what he called later the "'be kind to niggers' and 'be kind to Jew' books," which in his mind confirmed ideas about white supremacy and non-white inferiority.[19] The controversial part of Baldwin's essay entered near the end, when he introduced for comparison with *Uncle Tom's Cabin* Richard Wright's own bestselling novel *Native Son*. Wright's protagonist is 18-year-old Bigger Thomas, an angry, destitute ghetto dweller on Chicago's South Side at the height of the American Depression. Thomas is physically and financially trapped by circumstances of racism and capitalism. Dire material conditions force him into the accidental murder of a young white woman, then a second, intentional murder of his black lover. Falsely accused of raping the white woman, he is condemned to death. The novel, written when Wright was in the Communist Party, clearly blames capitalism for Bigger's tragedy: society, his Communist lawyer argues in the book, is the criminal, not Bigger.

For Baldwin, Bigger was himself a narrow, reductive stereotype of black life. "All of Bigger's life is controlled, defined by his hatred and his fear." Thus:

Below the surface of this novel there lies, it seems to me, a continuation, a complement of that monstrous legend it was written to destroy. Bigger is Uncle Tom's descendant, flesh of his flesh, so exactly opposite a portrait that the contemporary Negro novelist and the dead New England woman are locked together in a deadly, timeless battle; the one uttering merciless exhortations, the other shouting curses … . For Bigger's tragedy is not that he is cold or black or hungry, not even that he is American, black; but that he has accepted a theology that denies him life, that he admits the possibility of his being sub-human and feels constrained, therefore, to battle for his humanity according to those brutal criteria bequeathed him at his birth.[20]

Baldwin's criticism should remind us of his call for "complexity" of character and sympathy in Gorky, and his suspicion of ideologically driven art. Baldwin thought Wright had stacked the social deck so strongly against Bigger Thomas that he had no choice, or chance, or agency, to become fully human. For Baldwin, this was tantamount to saying that black people could not become fully human: "The failure of the protest novel lies in its rejection of life, the human being, the denial of his beauty, dread, power, in its insistence that it is his categorization alone which is real and which cannot be transcended."[21]

Baldwin's essay struck several powerful chords in the public arena and the world of letters. Wright was the reigning giant of African-American literature. Baldwin appeared to be taking him down. In 1949, the "protest novel," or social realism, was still a popular genre. Baldwin's essay seemed to call for its death. More importantly, who was James Baldwin—himself an unpublished novelist, all of 25, with just a few book reviews under his belt—to dictate the terms of literary production for novelists black or white? To answer this question, literary historians have tended to read "Everybody's Protest Novel" not just as Baldwin's self-declared "declaration of independence" but his Oedipal death blow against a literary father. Later, Baldwin would acknowledge truth to both claims, saying of Wright, "unconsciously I think I turned him into my father, not the father that I knew."[22] We will revisit those moments subsequently. Important for this stage of Baldwin's life and work is comprehending how Baldwin's criticisms of American literature about race was an explicit attempt to clear ground for both new subjects, and new approaches, namely his own: simultaneous with writing and publishing "Everybody's Protest Novel," Baldwin was nearing completion of his autobiographical novel *Go Tell It On the Mountain*—to be the first in-depth treatment of the complex and repressive aspects of the black church—and beginning to conceive his novel of queer love and life, *Giovanni's Room*, which he would call, not coincidentally, "another declaration of independence."[23] Put another way, if Baldwin was taking down literary "fathers," he was also in the process of imagining, creating, and queering new types of "native sons"—the title of his book of essays of 1955 that would include that phrase as an homage to and break from the influence of Richard Wright.

The affective scope of Baldwin's essay on protest literature was enhanced by its republication in *Partisan Review*, which by

1949 had become perhaps the preeminent U.S. literary journal of the anti-Stalinist left. Yet notoriety did not rescue Baldwin from dismal quotidian agony in Paris. He spent the summer after publication of the essay clerking for an American lawyer. Broke, he borrowed money from an American friend. David Leeming reports that, desperate for money, Baldwin agreed to take a job singing in an Arab nightclub, though it is not clear that he ever performed there.[24] He was by several accounts also frequently ill. In the fall of 1949, he took a trip with Themistocles Hoetis and Gidske Anderson to the south of France but was hospitalized twice for an inflamed gland. On returning to Paris, in December, another misfortune generated one of Baldwin's most penetrating essays about France in the 1950s.

On December 19, 1949, Baldwin was arrested and charged by the police with being a "receiver of stolen goods." Specifically, he was accused of stealing a bed sheet from a hotel on the Rue du Bac. As he later wrote in the essay "Equal in Paris," the accusation resulted when Baldwin borrowed the bed sheet from an American friend who had stolen the same sheet and moved from one hotel to Baldwin's own. But the French police suspected Baldwin, and locked him up. The experience launched Baldwin into a complex meditation on identity. In New York, he noted, the police would have immediately identified him as a troublesome black man, and treated him accordingly. Yet for the Paris police, "I was not a despised black man. They would simply have laughed at me if I had behaved like one. For them, I was an American."[25] This insight is important for looking two ways at once in Baldwin's life. In the essay "A Question of Identity" cited earlier, "The American in Europe is everywhere confronted with the question of his identity, and this may be taken as the key to all the contradictions one encounters when attempting to discuss him."[26] Yet his arrest gave Baldwin a new foil for contradiction: in jail, he is struck by the vast preponderance of North African inmates, a recognition that triggers a memory of seeing Arab peanut vendors harassed on the streets. He also notes that where he perceives his arrest as "a lower point than any I could ever in my life have imagined—lower, far, than anything I had seen in that Harlem which I had so hated and so loved"—for the North Africans incarceration was "simply another unlucky happening in a very dirty world ... the truth was that they were far more realistic about the world than I, and more nearly right about it."[27]

Baldwin here recognizes the privileged distinction of American nationality in a Western imperial country as a counterpart to colonial abjection. It is 1950, and Algeria and North Africa are under French domination, its own "exiles" second-tier citizens in France as announced by their prominence in Parisian jails. This is what Baldwin means by their arrest being just "another unlucky happening in a dirty world," and that they are more "right" and "truthful" about its political meaning. A gleaning of his own embededness in the "dirty world" of French colonial racism comes near the end of the essay, in the courtroom, after his acquittal, which is accompanied by laughter from French judicial administrators:

It could only remind me of the laughter I had often heard at home, laughter which I had sometimes deliberately elicited. This laughter is the laughter of those who consider themselves to be at a safe remove from all the wretched, for whom the pain of living is not real. I had heard it so often in my native land that I had resolved to find a place where I would never hear it any more. In some deep, black, stony, and liberating way, my life in my own eyes, began during that first year in Paris, when it was borne on me that this laughter is universal and can never be stilled.[28]

This moment of conscious, universalizing solidarity would stay with Baldwin for some time: it was fully five years before he wrote about it, and he would return to it retrospectively to confess to the impactful presence of North Africans, Arabs, and Algerians in Paris during his time there. In his 1972 book *No Name in the Street*, Baldwin wrote this passage which could also serve as a postscript to his prison encounter with North Africans: "The Arabs were together in Paris, but the American blacks were alone … I will not say that I envied them, for I didn't, and the directness of their hunger, or hungers, intimidated me; but I respected them, and as I began to discern what their history had made of them, I began to suspect, somewhat painfully, what my history had made of me."[29] He would also revisit the period around 1952, as a run-up to the Algerian War, when "Algerians were being murdered in the streets, and corralled into prisons, and being dropped into the Seine, like flies."[30] Baldwin would even note that "Everyone in Paris, in those years, who was not, resoundingly, from the north of Europe was suspected of being Algerian … Turks, Greeks, Spaniards, Jews, Italians, American blacks."[31]

In March 1950, Baldwin published the short story "The Death of the Prophet—A Story," in *Commentary*, a journal of the anti-Stalinist left, further cementing his reputation for alignment with New York intellectuals. The biographical note published with the story described him as "the most promising young Negro writer since Richard Wright,"[32] an irony that would take on new meaning again soon. A letter from his *Commentary* editor, Robert Warshaw, shows Baldwin broke again, pleading for a loan, unrequited.[33] Meanwhile, he continued drafting notes and an outline for *Go Tell It On the Mountain*, temporarily titled *I, John*, in reference to the protagonist John Grimes.

But the most significant element of Baldwin's personal life to change and deepen in 1950 was his relationship to the young Swiss painter, Lucien Happersberger. Baldwin had met Happersberger not long after his arrival in Paris. By 1950, they were lovers. Happersberger was bisexual, and married to Suzy Happersberger. Baldwin would become godfather to their children. Baldwin saw Lucien as a painterly muse, an intimate confidante, and a stabilizing force in his life. David Leeming contends that from the start of their relationship Baldwin wanted a mate, Happersberger a friend. In the winter of 1951, they went together to live in the small Swiss village of Loèche-les-Bains for three months, residing in the Happersberger family cottage. Poverty and illness alternated there with nights of heavy drinking and comradeship. Meanwhile Baldwin wrote, completing the manuscript of *Go Tell It On the Mountain*. His time in Switzerland also produced the ideas for one of his earliest seminal essays, cited earlier, "Stranger in the Village," published in the mainstream liberal periodical *Harper's Magazine* in October 1953. It became the final essay in Baldwin's 1955 essay collection *Notes of a Native Son*.

As with "Equal in Paris," Baldwin uses counterpoint to narrate identity crisis as political allegory. Because no one knows his name in the Swiss village, "I remain as much a stranger today as I was the first day I arrived, and the children shout *Neger! Neger!* [the black! the black!] as I walk along the streets."[34] Baldwin's exoticism is underscored in the all-white village—"I was simply a living wonder"—and the distance he feels from Europe, and European history and culture, is underwritten by a growing consciousness of his personal imbrication in colonial history: "Out of their hymns and dances come Beethoven and Bach. Go back a few centuries and they are in their full glory—but I am in Africa, watching the conquerors arrive."[35]

Baldwin's historical memories of oppression and exploitation in the essay—slavery and colonialism—also beget a dialectic of resistance: "The black man insists, by whatever means he finds at his disposal, that the white man cease to regard him as an exotic rarity and recognize him as a human being."[36] The African-American stands poised to play a special role in this resistance, having been used as a foil for the nation's settler-colonial origins, "when Americans were scarcely Americans at all but discontented Europeans,"[37] and used slavery and racism to build a "new world" from the old one Baldwin now inhabits. The essay's transatlantic perspective culminates in a prophetic warning that history is about to reverse itself:

> The time has come to realize that the interracial drama acted out on the American continent has not only created a new black man, it has created a new white man, too. No road whatever will lead Americans back to the simplicity of this European village where white men still have the luxury of looking on me as a stranger. I am not, really, a stranger any longer for any American alive … It is precisely this black-white experience which may prove of indispensable value to us in the world we face today. This world is white no longer, and it will never be white again.[38]

Who or what is the "agent" of this seeming call to social revolution? Answers lie elsewhere in Baldwin's essays from the period, like "Journey to Atlanta," also included in his first essay collection, and its assertion that "Since Negroes have been in this country [the U.S.] their one major, devastating gain was their Emancipation, an emancipation no one regards any more as having been dictated by humanitarian impulses";[39] or in his celebration of the 1943 Harlem riots in "The Harlem

Ghetto"; or within France itself. Years after writing "Stranger in the Village," Baldwin would recall that his arrival in Paris in 1948 coincided with nascent rumblings in the North African colonies, and a devolving French empire in South East Asia: "The Arabs," Baldwin wrote, "were not a part of Indo-China, but they were part of an empire visibly and swiftly crumbling, and part of a history which was achieving, in the most literal and frightening sense, its *denouement*."[40] Baldwin's essay then looks both backward to the long arc of subaltern rebellion against slavery, and forward to emergent anti-colonial struggles that would dominate the 1950s and 1960s. Continuity and rupture are all in his proclamation that the world "will never be white again."

Completing the manuscript of *Go Tell It On the Mountain* in Switzerland was also a momentous achievement for Baldwin: he had begun it more than ten years earlier, moving through multiple drafts and iterations. Notes for the book written while in Paris suggest a number of competing influences on Baldwin's thinking about the final draft, including James Joyce's *Portrait of the Artist as a Young Man*; in an "Outline" for the novel in 1950, he describes John Grimes in terms parallel to Stephen Daedalus, the protagonist of Joyce's novel, claiming he must move from a "blasted" heritage and personality to become the "uncreated conscious of his race."[41] Other notes from the period confirm Baldwin's desire to move past the model of Richard Wright or the "protest novel": "I am not concerned, either, with the stock situations of American Negro fiction. Rapists and rapees, shot-gun toting sheriffs and murderous black boys exist, but can, I think, be left quite safely for the moment to the popular press and to the liberal movement."[42] Finally Baldwin sought to anchor the book in black historical oppression. The novel, he wrote, would create a "more complex social organism ... than those faced by the slaves."[43]

The finished text of *Go Tell It On the Mountain* contains four themes that bear attention as markers of Baldwin's early career and thought. The first is the historical ties of southern black migrants to the North back to the South, and their chronic disappointments at the "promised land" of northern opportunity. This theme is put succinctly in the experience of the character Esther, the mistress of John Grimes's father, Gabriel, who dies giving birth to his first son, Royal. "There was not, after all, a great difference between the world of the North and that of the South which she had fled; there was only this difference: the North promised more" writes Baldwin. "And this similarity: what it promised it did not give, and what it gave, at length and grudgingly with one hand, it took back with the other." For Elizabeth, the birth mother of the hero, the same is true: "The world in which she now found herself was not unlike the world from which she has had, so long ago, been rescued."[44]

The second is the oppressed, gendered lives of black women. Early critics of Baldwin's work like Trudier Harris tended to see black women as stereotypically rendered. Harris argued that black women were narrowly confined to traditional roles like mother, sister, or wife. She noted that women in his novels like *Go Tell It On the Mountain* "come closer to being stereotypes than perhaps any others in Baldwin's work."[45] Harris is correct that women in the novel occupy traditional roles, and are connected to the church. But Baldwin also writes explicitly about gendered constraints on their lives. Gabriel's sister, Florence, is initially forced to stay behind in the South to care for her mother after her brother leaves for the North. Baldwin writes of her: "'Yes,' said Florence, moving to the window, "the menfolk, they did, all right. And it's us women who walk around, like the Bible says, and mourn. The menfolk, they did, and it's over for them, but we women, we have to keep on living and try to forget what they done to us.'"[46] As noted earlier, Baldwin also dramatized the absolute patriarchal authority of John's father, Gabriel, over his wife Elizabeth. The novel clearly directs sympathy to Elizabeth. This theme of women's lives restricted by men would return through many of Baldwin's later books.

The third theme is queer sexuality. John Grimes is filled with yearning for Elisha, a fellow altar-boy in his father's church, and member like him of the choir. Several passages in the book index the conflation in John's mind between queer desire and John's coming-of-age. This one is most vivid:

John stared at Elisha all during the lesson, admiring the timbre of Elisha's voice, much deeper and manlier than his own, admiring the leanness, and grace, and strength, and darkness of Elisha in his Sunday suit wondering if he would ever be as holy as Elisha was holy. But he did not follow the lesson, and when, sometimes, Elisha paused to ask John a question, John was ashamed and confused, feeling the palms of his hands become wet and his heart pound like a hammer.[47]

The novel ends with John symbolically choosing Elisha over both his father and a life in the church. This homoerotic epiphany signals John's break from both: "Then he turned away, down the long avenue, home. John stood still, watching him walk away. The sun had come full awake. It was waking the streets, and the house, and crying at the windows. It fell over Elisha like a golden robe, and struck John's forehead, where Elisha had kissed him, like a seal ineffaceable forever."[48]

The fourth, related to the prior, is music and language. The foreground to the consummation of John's love for Elisha is a moment of religious ecstasy where John speaks in tongues on the "threshing floor" of the church. Bodily, linguistic, and musical ecstasy all merge. Ed Pavlić notes a key scene near the end of the novel when John emerges with Elisha from the church after immersing himself in music. "Where joy was, there strength followed; where strength was, sorrow came—forever? Forever and forever, said the arm of Elisha, heavy on his shoulder."[49] As Pavlić notes, it is no coincidence that Elisha is the church piano player, and joy comes directly from bodily contact with him.[50] This, too, is an aspect of *Crying Holy* for Baldwin: the possibility, including the pleasure and anguish, of love between men.

Go Tell It On the Mountain was published by Knopf in May 1953. Reviews were generally positive. Langston Hughes sent Baldwin a congratulatory letter, but offered a slightly patronizing assessment of the book, calling it a "low-down story in a velvet bag."[51] The backhanded compliment started a low-level skirmish between the writers of each one's assessment of the other. Baldwin would later say that Hughes had not gotten enough out of his talents. To some extent, the feud was another indication of Baldwin's upstart challenge to the African-American literary status quo, including his public criticism of Richard Wright, which had deepened in November of 1951, when Baldwin published a second essay criticizing Wright's writing. That essay, "Many Thousands Gone," was published in *Partisan Review*. In it, Baldwin widened his criticism of African-American protest writing in ways that might have offended Hughes, too. Baldwin notes that *Native Son* reflected a shift in African-American writing:

The Negro, who had been during the magnificent twenties a passionate and delightful primitive, now became, as one of the things we were most self-conscious about, our most oppressed minority. In the thirties, swallowing Marx whole, we discovered the Worker and realized—I should think with some relief—that the aims of the Worker and the aims of the Negro were one. This theorem ... seems now to leave rather too much out of account; it became, nonetheless, one of the slogans of the "class struggle" and the gospel of the New Negro.[52]

Baldwin's uncharitable characterization of the Harlem Renaissance (also known as the New Negro movement) in which Hughes took part, and the proletarian literary movement that followed it, was again an attempt to clear literary and critical ground for his own work. *Go Tell It On the Mountain* had neither the sentimental racialism of some Harlem Renaissance writing, or the anti-capitalist militancy of Wright's early fiction. Baldwin's "Many Thousands Gone," however, was the last straw for Wright, who in a famous contretemps, more important to critics than to Baldwin, accused the latter of "betrayal," and their relationship permanently soured. To this reader, Baldwin aimed specifically in "Many Thousands Gone" to make further space in the literary arena for treatment of two largely autobiographical themes: religion and queer sexuality. These were to be the topics of his next two major works: the play *The Amen Corner*, and the novel *Giovanni's Room*.

* * *

The commercial and critical success of *Go Tell It On the Mountain* pushed Baldwin's private and public life in several directions at once, creating numerous emotional and artistic tremors. Much of this is conveyed in Baldwin's correspondence with Mary Painter, an economist at the American embassy in Paris who Baldwin first met in 1951 and with whom he developed a lifelong friendship. Though she was neither an artist nor literary intellectual, Baldwin adopted Painter as a confidante in his letters. Because she had means, he also relied on her at times for financial support. Their relationship is indicative of the catholic social world Baldwin created during this period: ranging from Painter, an architect of the Marshall Plan, to a swirl of writers and entertainers who became social contacts, including the novelist Chester Himes, the singer Bobby Short, and a new acquaintance, a young Maya Angelou.

Baldwin's letters to Painter show him groping for means to secure a Knopf book advance "because I can't afford to starve anymore,"[53] and rampaging uncertainty about how to hold together stable romantic relationships with Lucien and Arnold. Baldwin first wrote to Painter about this from Switzerland, asking for a $100 loan. In January 1954, another letter complained, "I haven't got any cash."[54] The struggle was real. Baldwin traveled all the way from Paris to New York in June 1952—borrowing money from Marlon Brando—to secure a $250 advance from Knopf when it showed interest in publishing *Go Tell It On the Mountain*. In June 1954, Baldwin achieved a significant financial reprieve, winning a Guggenheim Fellowship. That was followed in short order by a fellowship to write at the MacDowell Colony in Petersboro, New Hampshire, and in 1955, at Yaddo, a writers' colony in Saratoga Springs, New York. These fellowships literally kept Baldwin from starving.

It is also in this period that Baldwin wrote the letter to Painter cited at the head of this chapter, that "two men cannot be married unless one of them is willing to cease being a man."[55] For Baldwin, this problem was made tangible by Lucien's actual marriage to Suzy—the embodiment of his traditional "manhood"—and by Arnold's self-doubts about his own sexuality. Arnold, Baldwin wrote to Mary Painter, can't make his mind up about anything.[56] Between 1953 and 1956, Baldwin lived alternately with Arnold (and sometimes other gay male friends, like Beauford Delaney) in a range of places: Paris, Clamart, just outside of the city, Ibiza, and Corsica. Baldwin's letters to Painter present him as madly in love with Arnold, and despondent about the possibility of permanence with him. In October 1955, in the midst of a break-up with him, Baldwin wrote to Painter to say, "Arnold is leaving in a few hours; and, yet, I'll be glad that it's over; and I won't hang myself and I won't rush into that sea which is roaring outside. But I scarcely know how I'll drag myself through these hours."[57] And yet not long later, in early 1956, Baldwin nearly crashed and burned after another fight. He took sleeping pills and phoned Mary Painter, who rushed over and forced him to vomit.[58] David Leeming reports that on another occasion, after another break-up with Arnold, Baldwin did walk into the sea, thinking of Virginia Woolf's suicide.[59]

Baldwin's difficult queer relationships are wrapped within contradictions endemic to his heteronormative times. As he put it to Painter in a letter, women can offer men "safety" but "love between men predicates not only the inevitable suffering but the very real possibility of becoming absolutely bankrupt."[60] Baldwin's conflation of his material and emotional states of privation is significant: he lived on the margins even of his own celebrity in order to preserve a queer life. This is a subtext to one of Baldwin's most important declarations about why he left the U.S. in 1948 just as his literary fortunes were beginning to improve. As he told Arthur Crossman, "I could see that I could become a member of the club but the price was too high for me. It meant that I would imperceptibly become estranged from the world that produced me. I would become an American success. That's a very dangerous thing if you're black. It simply wasn't for me."[61] In addition to "race," the world that produced Baldwin was a world of gay male love. That world was more within reach, and more anonymous, in Europe, but no guarantee of permanence or security, especially given his own tenuous finances. Thus neither relationship, with Lucien nor Arnold, was stable or "fixable" in this period, Baldwin deciding that what Lucien needed was "his freedom" to practice art and live a family life, while Arnold came to represent the impossibility of a fixed relationship itself, a "dream of what my life could have been."[62]

Despite the private chaos, Baldwin's writing career in this period exploded: the publication of *Go Tell It On the Mountain* was followed by a request by his friend and former high-school classmate Sol Stein, an editor at Beacon Press, to put together a book of essays and reviews. That book, the aforementioned *Notes of a Native Son*, was published by Beacon in 1955. A dossier of his intellectual work from a major press legitimated Baldwin's arrival as a public intellectual. In the same period, Baldwin completed at Mac-Dowell the manuscript for the play *The Amen Corner*. Later, Baldwin would recall, "Writing *The Amen Corner* I remember as a desperate and even rather irresponsible act—it was certainly considered irresponsible by my agent at the time."[63] The play was Baldwin's attempt to break into theater, and black theater, at a ripe moment. He had already taken a class at the Actors Studio where he had met Marlon Brando and soon the famous filmmaker Elia Kazan. As noted earlier, Baldwin had been enamored of theater's potential for black drama by both Orson Welles's *Macbeth* and Paul Green's adaptation of Richard Wright's *Native Son*. A major moment, then, was the decision by the poet Owen Dodson's Howard Players in 1955 to perform the play at Howard University, an important historically black university in Washington, DC.

Baldwin said he wrote *The Amen Corner* for two reasons: to revisit afresh after four years abroad a story about the church and black family somewhat like his own—his native Harlem is the setting of the play. Second, to destroy expectations by the market that he simply write "diminished versions of *Go Tell It On the Mountain*" forever. The play itself, *Amen Corner*, features as its primary drama the relationship between the Harlem Church pastor, Margaret Alexander, her teenage son, David, and her husband, Luke. The play is about, in Baldwin's words, Margaret's dilemma of "how to treat her husband and her son as men and at the same time to protect them from the bloody consequences of trying to be a man in this society."[64] As such it is a rewriting of *Go Tell It On the Mountain*, the maternal caregiver here central, while staying with that book's theme of how black masculinity—fathers and sons especially—navigate a racist, economically savage world. The play ends with Margaret learning that through love she "gains herself" while preserving the men in her family. Love, here for Baldwin, is less religious love than the selfless dedication, especially of women, to preserving black life. Fittingly, Baldwin's mother, family, and Lucien all came to see the closing performance of the play after a four-day run. Reviews were positive. Baldwin was ecstatic. "[T]he theater, honey," he wrote to Mary Painter in May 1955, "is going to be hearing from me."[65]

The success of *The Amen Corner* was buttressed by news that Dial Press and Michael Joseph publishers in London had accepted for publication the manuscript of *Giovanni's Room*. The novel had vexed Baldwin for nearly ten years. The story was inspired primarily by Baldwin's life. The novel's protagonist, David, is a (white) American living in exile in Paris. Like Baldwin, he has had sexual encounters with men (one of

David's earliest experiences in the novel is inspired by Baldwin's sexual meet-up with a young Italian boy in Greenwich Village), but flirts with heterosexual relationships: Baldwin's with Suzie, whom he nearly married, and David with Hella, a white American woman with him in Paris. Early in the book, David meets Giovanni, a poor street criminal, described by Baldwin as a "gangster."[66] Critic David Leeming notes that Giovanni, an Italian, bears some resemblance in real life to Lucien Happersberger, Baldwin's Swiss lover, like Giovanni a lover of food and wine. David and Giovanni begin an intense, physical, sexual relationship which David keeps secret from Hella. David is clearly ambivalent in his queer desire, Giovanni is not. In time, David rejects him, driving Giovanni to thievery, murder, arrest, and his own execution. Hella returns to America, in Baldwin's words, "vindictive against all men."[67] For Baldwin, David has destroyed both of them by his "guilt and his ambivalence."[68] In a famous essay published much later on his own queerness, Baldwin said that the novel is "about what happens to you if you're afraid to love anybody. Which is much more interesting than the question of homosexuality."[69]

Since its publication, *Giovanni's Room* has been recovered as a landmark in queer writing in the U.S., and an avatar of contemporary gay literature. Queer black studies scholars Roderick Ferguson and Robert Reid-Pharr have pointed out that Baldwin uses homosexuality in the novel to consider the marginalization of racialized subjects (Baldwin himself said that he made David white because the complexity of writing about race and homosexuality openly was more than he was ready to take on).[70] Matt Brim, in a recent study, has focused on David's whiteness as a signifier of privileged difference, something Baldwin alerts the reader to in this description of David in the first paragraph of the book:

I stand at the window of this great house in the south of France as night falls, the night which is leading me to the most terrible morning of my life. I have a drink in my hand, there is a bottle at my elbow. I watch my reflection in the darkening gleam of the window pane. My reflection is tall, perhaps rather like an arrow, my blond hair gleams. My face is like a face you have seen many times. My ancestors conquered a continent, pushing across death-laden plains, until they came to an ocean which faced away from Europe into a darker past.[71]

Baldwin's invocation here of American "manifest destiny"— westward expansion via Indian genocide—implicates David from the first in the demise of Giovanni. David Leeming uses this example in part to argue that "David is representative of the failure of white America, and Giovanni is just as clearly the embodiment of what Baldwin sees as the outlook of the black man."[72] Beyond the racial theme, Baldwin uses mirror imagery and claustrophobic rooms throughout the novel to suggest how both David and Giovanni are trapped in a heteronormative social matrix that destroys their love. This was the theme, in part, of a critically important essay Baldwin had written and published in 1954 while drafting *Giovanni's Room*, a review of the gay French novelist André Gide. Titled "The Male Prison," the essay argued that "when men can no longer love women they also cease to love or trust each other, which makes their isolation complete. Nothing is more dangerous than isolation, for men will commit any crimes whatever rather than endure it."[73] This theme redounds in themes of violence, mutilation, castration (Giovanni dies by guillotine), and murder in the novel. David describes a queer pedestrian on the street as "like a mummy or zombie ... or something walking after it had been put to death,"[74] and of himself: "The body in the mirror forces me to turn and face it. And I look at my body, which is under sentence of death."[75] Yet buried within this social death is a dialectical dream of the queer body as emancipation. David also thinks:

I long to crack that mirror and be free. I look at my sex, my troubling sex, and wonder how it can be redeemed, how I can save it from the knife. The journey to the grave is already begun, the journey to corruption is always, already, half over. Yet, the key to my salvation, which cannot save my body, is hidden in my flesh.[76]

For all of its dark trauma and tragedy, Baldwin, and the world, considered publication of *Giovanni's Room* a triumph. It received very good reviews and was nominated for the National Book Award. The book went into a second printing in six weeks. All of these results surprised Baldwin. He had been wracked with worry during the writing process that publishers would censor the novel—"Don't know what on earth they expect me to censor out—there are only about three or four dirty words and only two bedroom scenes: both these heterosexual and far less explicit than is the current fashion."[77] Its success also overcame what he expected to be a savage critical reaction: "It will, I'm afraid, be condemned as one of the most unpleasant confections ever produced by an American. I can't help that … I think of my grim fable of helpless isolation, sexual terror, guilt, death, and acceptance as being most affirmative."[78]

Indeed, *Giovanni's Room* was a pivotal moment in Baldwin's life and the history of gay and lesbian writing. In it he wrote publically for the first time of gay life as his life. He uncloseted themes from *Go Tell It On the Mountain*—John Grimes's queer longings. He combined an open account of gay life with a ringing critique of American racial history, settler-colonialism, and white supremacy: Giovanni adjudges that David's American sense of time is "like a parade chez vous—a triumphant parade, like armies with banners entering a town."[79] Baldwin also wrote sympathetically of women restricted and unloved by men in a sexist society, a theme also explored in *Go Tell It On the Mountain*. Hella's response to David's complaint that he feels "trapped" by her is, "Ah! ... men may be at the mercy of women—I think men like that idea, it strokes the misogynist in them. But if a particular man is ever at the mercy of a particular woman—why, he's somehow stopped being a man."[80]

Beyond this personal achievement, *Giovanni's Room* both anticipated and predicted insights from what would become queer theory and gay and lesbian literary studies. Baldwin's preoccupation with David's American "innocence" and sexual ambivalence, and the incarcerated nature of his relationship to Giovanni, foreshadows Eve Sedgwick's famous rendering of the "epistemology of the closet"" "the thematics—of knowledge and ignorance themselves, of innocence and initiations, of secrecy and disclosure, become not contingently, but integrally infused with one particular object of cognition: no longer sexuality as a whole ... but even more specifically, now, the homosexual topic."[81] Baldwin's focus on the body as a performative site of identity in *Giovanni's Room*, combined with his insights about the "male prison" of sexuality, also foretell Judith Butler's argument that gender is a "stylized repetition of acts" through the "stylization of the body"[82]—a theme Baldwin would explore in even greater depth in *Another Country*. And Baldwin's confession of his own ambivalent sexual history through the novel would allow him, and force him, over time, to reckon publically with queer sexuality as a centerpiece of contemporary life. By the time the AIDS crisis reached America in the 1980s, Baldwin would be forced to become, reluctantly, a spokesperson for its devastation. Reckoning with that historical trauma began with the much more private crisis of conceiving, writing, and publishing *Giovanni's Room.*

*   *   *

Baldwin's essay collection, *Notes of a Native Son*, was published in late 1955 by Beacon Press. Baldwin's preface to the book, titled "Autobiographical Notes," reveals a momentary attempt by the author, perhaps nurtured by new-found fame, to position himself as something like a centrist cultural critic whose intellectual independence was a virtue in times of Cold War. Baldwin sounds both like an aesthetic formalist on one hand—"This is the only real concern of the artist, to recreate out of the disorder of life that order which is art"[83] and on the other like a patriotic dissident passable as Cold War liberal:

> I don't like people who like me because I'm a Negro; neither do I like people who find in the same accident grounds for contempt. I love America more than any other country in the world, and exactly for this reason, I insist on the right to criticize her perpetually … . I want to be an honest man and a good writer.[84]

Baldwin presents here like an American version of George Orwell—"My Country Right or Wrong"—himself a contributor to *New Leader*, and a patriotic dissident in his own right. Orwell was responding in his case to the horrors of Stalinism and Fascism on one side, and the reactionary excesses of Torydom and ruling elites. Baldwin's calculus was similarly national in character. In May of 1955, almost coterminous with the publication of *Notes of a Native Son*, Baldwin wrote to Mary Painter that he was about to be invited to join the American Committee for Cultural Freedom (ACCF). The ACCF was an affiliate of the anti-Communist Congress for Cultural Freedom (CCF). Both were funded by the CIA (though Baldwin likely did not know that at the time) as revealed in 1967 by *Ramparts* magazine and the *New York Times*.[85] The purpose of the ACCF and CCF was to encourage U.S. intellectuals to be critical of the Soviet Union. Among its members was Baldwin's friend, Sol Stein, who had encouraged him to put together the manuscript of *Notes of a Native Son*, and helped it get published.

Baldwin's patriotic dissidence would have aligned with Stein's worldview, one Baldwin's 1955 letter at least temporarily endorsed. "I agree, in the main, with their position," he wrote of the ACCF. They are "quite lucid about the extremists of both left and right":

I have no Stalinist leanings, I agree that there is such a thing as a Communist menace though I have some reservations about such language. I agree that it must be fought, that, in such a battle, it is of the utmost importance that one keep a cool head, a rigorously open mind, that one not lose the battle beforehand by allowing hysteria to make us over in the image of the enemy. But such terms do not come easily to me, and I do not even like groups—I do not like the subtle self-righteousness always present in such groups, even when they are right.[86]

This anxious dialectic of attachment and displacement from liberal political citizenship in the West would rear its head in an important piece of writing undertaken by Baldwin in 1956. Baldwin traveled to the Sorbonne in September to cover the First Conference of Negro-African Writers and Artists sponsored by *Présence Africaine*, a journal of the Negritude Movement. Negritude was a Pan-African cultural and political movement first launched in the 1930s by African and Caribbean intellectuals in Paris. The Martiniquan poet, Marxist, and statesmen Aimé Césaire coined the phrase "Negritude" in his poem "Cahier d'un retour au pays natal." Other participants in Negritude included the Senegalese poet Léopold Senghor. In Paris, they together launched the journal dedicated to art which would advance African and Caribbean self-determination and anti-colonial movements. Negritude, influenced by the surrealism of André Breton, also sought to develop an experimental, modernist black aesthetic. When he moved to Paris, Richard Wright became involved with *Presence Africaine*, which by the 1940s had become the leading intellectual journal of the movement.

The Writers and Artists Conference was held Wednesday, September 19 in the Sorbonne's Amphitheater Descartes in Paris. Among the attendees were Alioune Diop, editor of *Présence Africaine*; Senghor; Césaire; the novelist and poet Jacques Alexis, from Haiti; the novelist George Lamming, from Barbados; and the American novelist Richard Wright. The Martiniquan physician and revolutionary Frantz Fanon attended, and spoke, as well. The conference was conceived by organizers as a kind of sequel to the 1955 Bandung Conference in Indonesia. There, leaders of 29 African and Asian decolonizing countries attended, and formed for the first time a historical bloc designated by Jawaharlal Nehru of India as the "Third World." Paramount at Bandung was political independence, especially from the U.S. and Soviet superpowers. This message carried over in speeches at Paris by Diop. Other keynote themes in Paris were the fact of anti-colonial intellectual life as a dissident by-product of Europe and colonization. As reported by Baldwin, Césaire's speech lauded that he "had penetrated into the heart of the great wildernesss and stolen the sacred fire. And this, which was the promise of their freedom, was also the assurance of his power."[87] Here, the conference touched on a deeper vein mined in C.L.R. James's classic book *The Black Jacobins*, published in 1936: that the Haitian revolution was the extension and application of the enlightenment and revolution by the colonies, a theme also touched upon by Richard Wright in his remarks. Finally, for Senghor and Césaire especially, the conference was meant to articulate the uniqueness of Negritude culture as a unifying aspect of the African diaspora. Senghor proposed in his remarks, for example, that, as Baldwin reported it, "the heritage of the American Negro was an African heritage."[88]

Baldwin's published account of the conference, "Princes and Powers," appeared in January 1957, in *Encounter*, a journal associated with the ACCF, and which also received funding from the CIA (Baldwin was unlikely to have known this in 1957). His report is tinged with ideas consonant with his Cold War patriotic dissidence. "Hanging in the air, as real as the heat from which we suffered, were the great specters of America and Russia, of the battle going on between them for the domination of the world. The resolution of this battle might very well depend on the earth's non-European population, a population vastly outnumbering Europe's, and which had suffered such injustices at European hands."[89] Where speakers argued for Negritude unity as a path to independence and victory, Baldwin was cautious and reactive. For example, in reporting W.E.B. Du Bois's message to the conference that he would not attend because "the U.S. government will not give me a passport" (stripped because of his public advocacy for the elimination of atomic weapons by the U.S.),[90] Baldwin called the message "ill considered" as it undermined the effectiveness of the five-person U.S. delegation, and tilted discussion towards a pro-Soviet point of view and against the U.S. as a colonizing force. Baldwin's implicit defense of the U.S. was undergirded by a deeper political attachment to a version of African-American and U.S. exceptionalism:

> For what, at bottom, distinguished the Americans from the Negroes who surrounded us, men from Nigeria, Senegal, Barbados, Martinique—so many names for so many disciplines—was the banal and abruptly quite overwhelming fact that we had been born in a society, which, in a way quite inconceivable for Africans, and no longer real for Europeans, was open, and, in a sense which had nothing to do with justice or injustice, was free. It was a society, in short, in which nothing was fixed and we had therefore been born to a greater number of possibilities, wretched as these possibilities seemed at the instant of our birth. Moreover, the land of our Forefathers' exile had been made, by that travail, our home.[91]

Baldwin proposes that the experience of Western modernity—as opposed to colonialism or feudalism—gives the African-American what Du Bois called "second sight" onto the world. "The American Negro," he writes, "is possibly the only man of color who can speak of the West with real authority, whose experience, painful as it is, also proves the vitality of the transgressed Western ideals."[92] This difference also disavows for Baldwin the Negritude idea of a common African diasporic culture. Baldwin rejects Senghor's argument at the conference that Richard Wright's autobiography, *Black Boy*, is an African text because growing up in the American South "Wright had not been in a position, as Europeans had, to remain in contact with his hypothetical African heritage."[93] "Moreover, *Black Boy* had been written in the English language which Americans had inherited from England, that is, if you like, from Greece and Rome; its form, psychology, moral attitude, preoccupations, in short, its cultural validity, were all due to forces which had nothing to do with Africa."[94]

Considered together, there are several keynotes to Baldwin's early life and career in this report from Paris and Baldwin's "Autobiographical Notes." Baldwin underscores his anti-Stalinist political orientation of the 1940s by sharply rejecting the Soviet Union as a model for African-American and African liberation (interestingly Baldwin did not comment in any detail on Stalin's death in 1953, two years prior, indicating if nothing else that nothing had changed for him in his assessment of Soviet Communism). The pull in Baldwin towards a "free" but flawed American democracy thus emerges in Cold War relief as a kind of lesser of two evils. Baldwin's patriotic dissidence seems a negation of Cold War pressures as much as an affirmation of the validity of an America that had nearly destroyed him before he left it in 1948. Baldwin's soft nationalism is also in some ways a logical extension of Baldwin's as yet underdeveloped internationalism: his suspicion of Negritude solidarity bespeaks a lingering psychological devotion to some idea of himself as a bastard, yet still a child, of the West. The "Third World" that presented itself to Baldwin full frontal in Paris was not yet recognizable. Finally, Baldwin's skepticism about Negritude predicts another contradictory current of his thought: an initial political rejection of black nationalism. Because of its confidence in African diasporic unity, the Negritude movement had great impact on some of the architects of U.S. black nationalism in the 1960s, especially poets and writers in the Black Arts Movement. By the early 1960s, just a few years after the Paris conference, many young black radicals would be en route to Africa inspired by the anti-colonial movement in an attempt to bring it "home" to the U.S. Baldwin's later "truce" with this current of black nationalist politics was hard won.

Indeed, it would take history intervening to move Baldwin past this momentary conjuncture. Specifically, it would take wars of liberation coming full force into his purview, calling him to witness them. The first was the U.S. civil rights movement, the second the Battle of Algiers. Both would begin a transformation of Baldwin into a more confident and auspicious voice for liberation, including his own.

4
Paying His Dues: 1957–63

I went back in '57 because I got terribly tired. It was during the Algerian war ... I got tired and I began to be ashamed, sitting in cafes in Paris and explaining Little Rock and Tennessee ... . It was impossible to sit there and listen to Frenchmen talk about my Algerian friends in the terms that had always been used to describe us, you know, "You rape our women. You carry knives."[1]

James Baldwin, interview with Ida Lewis, 1970

I have a feeling that the Southern police system is very tightly knit and long before I get to Birmingham, I may spit on a side-walk and vanish.[2]

James Baldwin, letter to Mary Painter, 1960

Baldwin spoke before a mass rally of the Washington D.C. chapter of the Congress of Racial Equality for the "Original Freedom Riders" on 6–11–61 and stated in substance that the white race had better realize the emerging strength of the Negro and that he would not care to be in the shoes of the white man when the African nations become stronger.[3]

Memorandum from Baldwin's FBI File, 1963

I began to see that the West—the entire West—is changing, is breaking up; and that its power over me, and over Africans, was gone. And would never come again. So then it seemed that exile was another way of being in limbo.[4]

James Baldwin, interview with Studs Terkel, 1961

The years 1957–62 were a political crossroads for Baldwin. During them, his former life as an African-American dissident was reborn in the guise of cosmopolitan political internationalist. Baldwin was shaken from the torpor of Cold War liberalism by the racist violence of the American South in its response to the civil rights movement, and the structural racism and colonialism of French society as its war against Algeria intensified. These events spurred the development of a non-Western orientation on the "West"—one of his favorite writing subjects from Paris—as he visited for the first time Istanbul, several countries in Africa, and Israel. Both a comparative and an anti-colonial perspective were born in Baldwin via these events. Of note, Baldwin began a ten-year relationship with Turkey, where some of his greatest books were written in whole or in part, and where he nurtured a developing interest in Islam. Indeed, Islam became a nodal point for Baldwin's political transformation: between 1958 and 1962, Baldwin calibrated the rise of the Nation of Islam in the U.S. and the upturn of anti-colonial resistance in North Africa and Europe as part of a remaking of the politics of the black world.

Thus Baldwin's life was frenetic with activist writing, travel, organizing, and speaking in this period. At the same time, his writing career continued to expand in reach and genres. He became an in-demand journalist and rapporteur for intellectual and popular journals and magazines; ventured deeper into theatrical writing and, for the first time, television, both as a writer and commentator; and published two commercially successful books: an essay collection, *Nobody Knows My Name*, the sequel in many ways to *Notes of a Native Son*, and his third novel, *Another Country*. The title of the latter is a unique index to Baldwin's analytical mood in this period. As he toured the American South in 1957, his nerves frayed by the thought that he might be killed as a black interloper in the civil war of the civil rights movement, he wrote, "I've never in my life been on a sadder journey or through a sadder country";[5] while a short time later, writing from Paris to Mary Painter, he would opine, "I am in another country, briefly, but this country is in the difficult world: things are not going well here."[6] What was going poorly in both outposts of the Western world were white supremacy and Western domination, its dying gasps expressed as brutality and repression of non-white citizens. Exile from America and France to Turkey, or Africa, or Israel in this period became a way of thinking in realpolitik terms about the meaning of nations, nationalisms, colonies, colonization, independence, and, eventually, revolution. Movement and mobility provided Baldwin with relief from feeling too much exposure and vulnerability to a single state. Exile would also continue to provide him with emotional space within the queer community even as he struggled to find anything like permanence in a love relationship. Baldwin would emerge from this period transformed: on fire with ideas for the next stage of his political and literary life, and a formal enemy of the U.S. state. These were the consequences and costs of what he called "paying his dues."[7]

* * *

Baldwin arrived by boat in New York from Paris in June 1957. In his 1972 book *No Name in the Street*, he misremembers and misreports his reason for coming. He recalls leaving the 1956 Congress of Negro-African Writers meeting he was covering for *Encounter* and seeing news photographs of Dorothy Counts, a 17-year-old African-American girl, being taunted by white supremacists as she tried to integrate Henry Harding High School in Charlotte, North Carolina (after four days of vicious abuse her parents withdrew her from the school). Yet as Ed Pavlić notes, the Counts event actually took place in 1957. Baldwin's misremembering of fact is however a truthful *emotional* memory of seeing the civil rights movement unfold from Paris and wanting to join it.[8] As he recalled it, the picture of Counts "made me furious, it filled me with both hatred and pity, and it made me ashamed. Some one of us should have been there with her!"[9]

Baldwin returned to America, as these words indicate, to be a witness to history, and to walk in struggle. Thus, in September, after he procured an assignment from *Partisan Review* and the mainstream liberal magazine *Harper's*, to go south to report on the civil rights movement, his first stop was Charlotte. Baldwin's intent was to interview children attempting to integrate schools to try and measure the impact—or failure—of the 1954 Brown vs. Board of Education decision mandating school integration in the U.S. From Charlotte he went to Little Rock, where he met Daisy Bates, a National Association for the Advancement of Colored People organizer and publisher of *The Arkansas State Press*. In 1957, the *State Press* was a leading advocate for the "Little Rock Nine," nine African-American students who attempted to integrate Little Rock Central High School. The case became a national flashpoint of the civil rights movement when racist Arkansas Governor Orval Faubus called out the National Guard to prevent their entry into the school. U.S. President Dwight Eisenhower responded by federalizing the National Guard to ensure enforcement of integration. Later, Baldwin would write bitterly, "It was rather as though small Jewish boys and girls, in Hitler's Germany, insisted on getting a German education in other to overthrow the Third Reich."[10]

From Little Rock, Baldwin traveled to the large capital city of Atlanta, Georgia, to meet Martin Luther King, Jr. for the first time. King had by then established himself as a national leader of the civil rights movement on the strength of his work in helping to organize the 1955 Montgomery Bus Boycott, formally launched by activist Rosa Parks's refusal to give up her bus seat. King had sent Bates a telegram supporting both her and the Little Rock Nine. After his visit, Baldwin would declare King a "great man" in a letter to Mary Painter.[11] Nearly four years later, Baldwin would write a profile of King and his work for *Harper's Magazine*. This first Atlanta visit with King prompted Baldwin to focus on divisions and differences between wealthy African-Americans in Atlanta and its poor black majority, and the precarious position of its black middle class: "On any night … a policeman may beat up one Negro too many, or some Negro or some white man may simply go berserk. This is all it takes to drive so delicately balanced a city mad. And the island on which these Negroes have built their handsome houses will disappear."[12] Baldwin also saw Atlanta, because of its large black population, as an important site in "This war between the Southern cities and states."[13] "When a race riot occurs in Atlanta, it will not spread merely to Birmingham, for example … The trouble will spread to every metropolitan center which has a significant Negro population."[14] Baldwin here draws on his memory of simultaneous black rebellions against racism and capitalism (Detroit and New York in 1943) to effectively predict the uprisings that would seize America's black urban centers in the 1960s.

Baldwin made other stops on his visit: a first was Birmingham, Alabama, where he met one of Martin Luther King, Jr.'s closest aides, the Reverend Fred Shuttlesworth. Shuttlesworth was one of the four founders of the Southern Christian Leadership Conference, which attempted to unify black clergy in the civil rights movement. Shuttlesworth had been beaten by Klansmen that year when he and his children tried to integrate an all-white school. Baldwin also traveled to Montgomery,

Alabama, where he met Coretta Scott King, wife of Martin Luther King, Jr., for the first time. These visits became the basis of several essays published in *Partisan Review* and *Harper's*, and later, in Baldwin's July 1961 essay collection *Nobody Knows My Name*. The essays, "A Fly in Buttermilk," "Faulkner and Desegregation," and "Nobody Knows My Name: A Letter From the South," were relentless in criticizing southern segregation as a system which "has allowed white people, with scarcely any pangs of conscience whatever, to create, in every generation, only the Negro they wished to see."[15] Baldwin blasted what was then called "go slow" thinking on civil rights advocated by "middle of the road" southerners like William Faulkner, who drew Baldwin's ire by declaring in an interview that if it came to a contest between the state of Mississippi and federal government he would fight for Mississippi, "even if it meant going out into the streets and shooting Negroes."[16] On balance, Baldwin's essays about his trip foretell disaster for the South—and the U.S.—if repression, segregation, and white supremacy are not cast out by the strength of the civil rights movement, else "we may yet become one of the most distinguished and monumental failures in the history of nations."[17]

Privately, Baldwin's letters about his southern trip reveal an almost lethal psychological vulnerability regarding besieged black southerners facing down white politicians, banks, juries, police, and media. An October 18, 1957, letter postmarked from the A.G. Gaston Motel in Birmingham—one of the few black-owned hotels in the South, and hence a refuge for Baldwin— describes him as "Having reactions symptomatic of hysteria barely controlled: always on the edge of tears; can't sleep."[18] Birmingham, he writes, is a "city which is busy preparing its doom."[19] An October 1957 letter written after his journey was complete described it as a "grueling trip." He was, he admitted, "Badly frightened in Montgomery, for the first

time, but certainly not the last."[20] "White people," he wrote
to Painter about the success of the bus boycott movement,
"are not taking their defeat in the matter of the busses with
anything remotely approaching grace, and, further, the effect
of Rev. King on the morale and tactics of the Negroes is having
an unsettling effect on their minds."[21]

If Baldwin left Paris to come to America "tired" of the war in
Algeria, he returned to Europe to write his dispatches on the
South with a version of racial post-traumatic stress disorder. In
December, from Lausanne, he wrote to Painter, "I don't think
I have ever suffered before as I have these last few months."[22]
Thinking back on the U.S., he wrote, "I don't believe that love
exists in America, only hideous shadows and parodies of it."[23]
And in a bit of dark but revealing self-parody, he wrote: "Well,
some years from now some bright, untroubled cipher, who
is even now throwing practice rocks, will begin his dissertation on Baldwin thus: 'Around the age of thirty five, Baldwin
underwent an artistic and racial crisis and began to hate
everyone, and took the first great strides towards becoming
that monster whose name is now anathema.'"[24]

A key to understanding Baldwin's sharpened mood lay in
his new-found recognition that the social balance of forces in
Europe and North America were shifting. As he noted above
in his 1961 interview with Studs Terkel, "I began to see that the
West—the entire West—is changing, is breaking up; and that
its power over me, and over Africans, was gone. And would
never come again." Upon returning to Paris in the spring of
1958, Baldwin set himself to two long, unpublished pieces of
writing on the Algerian War and revolution which illuminate
this theme. The pieces provide connecting tissue between the
"civil wars" in his old and new homes.

The first piece, an undated essay titled "Paris, '58," was
written in September of that year, as evidenced by Baldwin's

reference to the Notting Hill Riots in England from August 30 to September 5 in which black neighborhoods in London exploded with rage after racist Teddy boys, inspired by fascist Oswald Mosley's Union Movement to "Keep Britain White," attacked West Indian residents. Baldwin uses the allusion to compare race riots in London and Paris, where, after a week of activity by the *Front de libération nationale* "the French police have invited all North Africans to be off the streets by nine-thirty at night."[25] Baldwin then begins a dissertation on parallels between black struggle in the U.S. and Algerian colonization and resistance. "I remembered," writes Baldwin, "that American Negroes had not been hated as long as they were slaves; they began to be hated when they were slaves no longer. And the French did not hate Algerians ten years ago. They scarcely knew that Algerians existed. But they are beginning to hate them now."[26] "All Arabs," he writes, "have always looked alike to the French and, these days, all of them look like terrorists."[27]

Of special note to Baldwin was the broad criminalization in France triggered by the independence struggle which swept up people like himself: "There are vast numbers of people in Paris, who do not understand French, who do not go to bed at nine-thirty, and whom the Algerians are able to recognize as Greeks, Spaniards, Turks, Persians, Indians, Jews, or American Negroes. This, the French police seem quite unable to do. Already, two friends of mine, both American, one Negro, have been molested with drawn revolvers, who, luckily, had time to look at their papers."[28] Baldwin also provides a materialist analysis of oppression of African-Americans in the U.S. and Algerians in France: "The Mississippi economy demands until today a certain percentage of labor so cheap as to be scarcely indistinguishable from slave labor which ... was also a French necessity. $ explains the presence of so many Algerians to the mainland ... They [the French] have ignored, ill-treated, over-worked, under-paid and mocked them."[29]

Baldwin concludes his summation by hypothesizing a radical synergy of 1958 protests as an index to a possible new political horizon:

> It was all very well to have dark Frenchmen and English-men in the colonies; but it was never expected that these people would actually use their passports, certainly never in such numbers, to cause trouble on the mainland, change the structure of the government, and endanger the peace of the capital ... the North African question, so swollen with blood and human passions, and complicated by the question of religion, is still the mighty question on which the future of France depends ...
>
> It is the history of Europe which makes white a proud color. And it is because Americans were Europeans once, have never gotten over it, nor learned how to deal with it, that Little Rock, as much as Formosa or Algeria, menaces the future of everyone now living.[30]

The second unpublished Baldwin text on Algiers is "Les Evade's," an incomplete, handwritten treatment for a novel likely written in late 1958. In his notes for the novel, under setting, Baldwin writes, "Paris, the Spring/early summer of '58, during the time of the revolt of the generals in Algeria, & just before the de Gaulle election."[31] Baldwin refers here to an attempted putsch in Algeria by colonial administrators seeking a harder line against the Algerian insurrection. The events resulted in the return of Charles de Gaulle to the pres-idency after a twelve-year absence. Baldwin's story describes the character Boona, an Algerian student forced to leave school in Lausanne after his family in Algeria lose their property to the Fellagha and a French raid, and his brother is killed in France attempting revenge. Boona is befriended by Ralph, an African-American journalist for the U.S. national newscast CBS. He is attempting to interview ordinary citizens about the Algerian rebellion. Frenchmen he interviews describe Algerians as "lazy, they carry knives" and as "savages."[32] Much as in Baldwin's description of police dragnets above, the tables turn when Boona himself is stopped by a policeman and asked to show his papers while Algerians are rapidly rounded up and arrested. The story ends with Ralph and Boona discussing whether they have the proper papers to get past the police.

Baldwin's assemblage of Little Rock, Paris, and Algiers onto a map of global struggles for freedom points in several different directions at once. Clearly his visit to the South, combined with witnessing French state repression of Algerians, triggered a new understanding of black urban rebellion, police racism, and state terror as an international phenomenon. Baldwin is also mapping these sites of anti-colonial and anti-racist resistance onto the Cold War (hence the comparison to Formosa, the name for Taiwan, a reference to the so-called "Second Taiwan Strait Crisis" of August 1958, when the People's Republic of China lightly bombed the island claimed by the Republic of China). Baldwin also sees French identity threatened by a challenge from below to the social order. In a sentence echoing what he had written of Americans in essays like "Stranger in the Village," Baldwin wrote of the French citizen, "He has been a Frenchman and a Christian so long that it has never occurred to him that his identity does not rest on eternal foundations."[33] Concomitantly, events of 1957 and 1958 sharpened Baldwin's analysis of state and colonial power: "the Algerians were not fighting the French for justice ... but for the power to determine their own destinies."[34] Finally, "Les Evade's" concluding references to passport papers foreshadowed Baldwin's unfinished novel started later in life and inspired by his real-life Muslim gardener. Titled *No Papers for Muhammad*, the novel was motivated by Baldwin's apprehension of restrictive immigration policies towards non-French subjects, for example Turks. The theme of the book highlights Baldwin's interest in national citizenship, exile, and "limbo" as he described it above, themes and ideas he felt described his own life as an African-American in Europe. We will see these themes reconstituted in *The Welcome Table*, the last major work Baldwin attempted before his death.

* * *

Meanwhile, Baldwin's personal and literary life remained dotted by queer themes: he remained in and out of a love relationship with Arnold, breaking up, reconciling, confessing in frustration at one point that there was a little bit of "blackmail" in their relationship. Baldwin was also determined to transfer the success of *Giovanni's Room* to the theater. He spent part of 1958 at the MacDowell Colony working on a stage adaptation. In May 1958, the famous Actors Studio in New York staged a workshop production. Engin Cezzar, a young Turkish actor and protégé of the famous stage and film director Elia Kazan, was cast as Giovanni. This was a life-changing event for Baldwin. He would befriend Cezzar, and three years later travel to Turkey to begin his long period of partial life there. The Kazan influence was also permanent: Baldwin hoped he would help produce a film version of *Giovanni's Room* starring his friend Marlon Brando. It never happened. According to David Leeming, Kazan also encouraged Baldwin to inject civil rights themes into his creative writing which would give impetus to his composition of the play *Blues for Mister Charlie*, to be discussed in Chapter 5.[35] Baldwin was also motivated to develop theatrical work in this period by seeing the opening of Jean Genet's play *Les Nègres* (*The Blacks*) in Paris in October 1959. The play was a surreal satire on racial and sexual stereotypes using black actors in "whiteface." Genet was to Baldwin's mind a formidable queer outlaw, having been expelled from the French Foreign Legion for "lewd acts." Their relationship would last until the 1970s, when both would become supporters of the Black Panther Party in the U.S. Finally, Baldwin made the acquaintance—and friendship—of playwright Lorraine Hansberry. The brilliant, left-wing, lesbian writer would inspire Baldwin with the groundbreaking success of her 1959 play *A Raisin in the Sun*, the first play by an African-American writer to be cast on Broadway in New York.

The year 1959 was similarly pockmarked by personal anguish for Baldwin about sexuality, and his writing. Both revolved around the composition of his novel *Another Country*. Though he was awarded a two-year, $12,000 Ford Foundation grant to work on the book, Baldwin struggled to write it, in part because the book was a painful retelling of the suicide of Eugene Worth. To honor him, Baldwin created the character of Rufus in *Another Country*, also modeled in part on the character of Sonny from Baldwin's 1957 short story "Sonny's Blues," published in *Partisan Review*. "Sonny's Blues" was its own difficult psychological drama about one brother's narration of the life of another, a jazz musician and addict—both characteristics of Rufus in the novel. Baldwin also intended to give Rufus—and a range of characters in the book—non-conventional sexualities: bisexual, homosexual, straight, non-binary. It is possible that that intention was motivated by what David Leeming perceives as a mild sexual crisis of Baldwin's own in 1959: letters written towards the end of the year, he notes, reveal that Baldwin had relationships with several women that summer, and "considered the picture of himself married, with children, living a thoroughly ordered and domestic life."[36] Real life was precisely the opposite. His love life was unsettled, the writing difficult. "Writing a novel is just fucking hard work, from the time you begin the damn thing until it finally falls from your arthritic fingers," he complained in a letter to Painter.[37] In another letter to Painter, in August 1959, Baldwin sounded exhausted, comparing himself grandiosely to Shakespeare's aging, besieged monarch King Lear: "Lear has authority because he knows mortality. And so do I."[38]

As was often the case, public events pulled Baldwin out of his writer's isolation and into history. On February 1, 1960, four freshman students from North Carolina A & T, an all-black college, sat in at the segregated Woolworth's counter in Greensboro, North Carolina, and demanded service. The four were Ezell Blair Jr., Franklin McCain, Joseph McNeil, and David Richmond. They were surrounded by a threatening mob of racists. The non-violent sit-in drew national attention. It immediately inspired the development of the group Student Nonviolent Coordinating Committee, or SNCC, and new chapters of CORE, the Congress of Racial Equality, a civil rights group that had formed in 1942 and had led prior sit-ins. In the same month, CORE activists in Tallahassee, Florida, sat in at two dime stores, Woolworth's and McCrory's. The students sought to discuss their grievances with managers of the stores but were refused. In March 1960, members of a CORE chapter in Tallahassee helped organize a march of nearly 1,000 black students across the campus at Florida Agricultural and Mechanical University, another all-black college. They were met by members of the White Citizens' Council, a white supremacist group, with bats and knives. In a pattern typical of southern politics of the time, none of the racists were arrested. The students were dispersed by tear gas and 35 were arrested.[39]

Baldwin flew to Tallahassee to interview student protesters on assignment for *Mademoiselle* magazine. He arrived in May. His report on their protests carried two themes. One, that the student protesters represented a radical new generation of black people who, unlike his generation, felt no servility and were impatient for change. As Baldwin put it,

> These students were born at the very moment at which Europe's domination of Africa was ending. I remember, for example, the invasion of Ethiopia and Haile Selassie's vain appeal to the League of Nations, but they remember the Bandung Conference and the establishment of the Republic of Ghana ... Americans keep wondering what has "got into" the students. What has "got into" them is their history in this country. They are not the first Negroes to face mobs: they are merely the first Negroes to frighten the mob more than the mob frightens them.[40]

The second theme is that their protest carried the potential to expand—or collapse—real freedom for Americans of all races:

> It seems to me that they are the only people in this country now who really believe in freedom. Insofar as they can make it real for themselves, they will make it real for all of us. The question with which they present the nation is whether or not we really want to be free. It is because these students remain so closely related to their past that they are able to face with such authority a population ignorant of its history and enslaved by a myth. And by this population I do not mean merely the unhappy people who make up the southern mobs. I have in mind nearly all Americans.[41]

From Tallahassee, Baldwin wrote a letter to Martin Luther King, Jr. in Atlanta. Baldwin had been asked by *Harper's*

Magazine to write a profile of King. In the letter, Baldwin asked if it would be possible to spend a day or two with King to gather information for the profile. He wrote, "The effect of your work, and I might almost indeed, say your presence, has spread far beyond the confines of Montgomery, as you must know. It can be felt, for example, right here in Talla-hassee. And I am one of the millions, to be found all over the world but more especially here, in this sorely troubled country, who thank God for you."[42] Baldwin's finished article, "The Dangerous Road Before Martin Luther King," builds from a flattering, intimate portrait of King the person—"For one thing, to state it baldly, I liked him"[43]—to his larger place in black historical struggles: "He is the first Negro leader in my experience, or the first in many generations, of whom this can be said; most of his predecessors were in the extraor-dinary position of saying to white men, *Hurry*, while saying to black men, *Wait.*"[44] While praising the "rewards" of King's campaign for integration in the South—what King himself called "community"—Baldwin saves his greatest political enthusiasm for the *movement* behind King, like the students in CORE and SNCC:

These young people have never believed in the American image of the Negro and have never bargained with the Republic, and now they never will. There is no longer any basis on which to bargain: for the myth of white suprem-acy is exploding all over the world, from the Congo to New Orleans ... And one of the things that this means, to put it far too simply and bluntly, is that the white man on whom the American Negro has modeled himself for so long is vanishing. Because this white man was, himself, very largely a mythical creature: white men have never been here, what they imagined themselves to be. The liberation of Americans from the racial anguish which has crippled us for so long can only mean, truly, the creation of a new people in this still-new world.[45]

It was also on this second southern sojourn that Baldwin wrote of his fear of being swallowed up by the police—"I may spit on a sidewalk and vanish"—a reference not only to the ongoing attacks with water cannons and dogs on protesters, but the "disappeared" like Emmett Till, the 14-year-old African-American boy from Chicago who was brutally lynched while visiting Mississippi in 1955, his Klan killers protected by the very police Baldwin encountered virtually every day on his southern tour.

Meanwhile, around him, the contours of the civil rights movement were changing. In May of 1960, Ella Baker, a veteran of 1930s political activism, helped students at Shaw University organize the first chapter of SNCC. SNCC was a direct action organization dedicated to grassroots organizing independent of other more moderate sections of the civil rights movement like King's Southern Christian Leadership Conference. The year 1960 was also a monumental one in the African decolonization struggle: no fewer than 17 African countries, including the Congo and Nigeria, earned their independence. Ghana's independence in 1957 (formerly the Gold Coast) attracted a steady stream of African-Americans welcomed by Kwame Nkrumah's leadership, including W.E.B. Du Bois, who moved there permanently in 1961. Generally, the African example was rapidly internationalizing black struggle in the U.S., while providing a threshold for measuring freedom. For Baldwin, there was a wicked irony in African liberation occurring while the U.S. continued its policies of racism, segregation, and violence against black protesters. As he put it in 1961 in a *New York Times* essay, "The way things are going here, all of Africa will be free before we can get a cup of coffee"⁴⁶—a reference to ongoing lunch-counter protests across the South.

Another important moment in the internationalization of the black freedom struggle in the U.S. was Cuban independence in 1959. Fidel Castro was seen by figures like Du Bois as a liberator. In September 1960, Castro stayed at Harlem's historic Hotel Theresa on a visit to speak to the United Nations General Assembly. Among the notables to visit with Castro in Harlem during his stay was Malcolm X. In April 1960, Baldwin was an original signatory to the newly created Fair Play for Cuba Committee (FPCC), a New York-based activist group offering support to Cuba's revolution. Jean Paul-Sartre, Norman Mailer, Truman Capote, and Allen Ginsberg were also supporters. An advertisement for the FPCC in the *New York Times* on April 6, 1960 caught the attention of the FBI, and put Baldwin permanently on its radar as it attempted to monitor, and repress, anything like pro-Soviet, pro-Communist, or "un-American" political activity.

This emerging confluence of Cold War repression, anti-colonial struggle, southern obstinacy in the face of the civil rights movement, and increasing black militancy challenged further Baldwin's abiding aspiration for something like an integrationist response to changing world events. This might best be captured through metaphor. On his 1960 trip south to interview King, Baldwin took time to speak at a black church. "I tried to talk about what it meant to be the maid in this great, strange house called America," he wrote to Mary Painter, "and how the people who had played this role might be enabled to save the house."⁴⁷ The metaphor of the American nation as a "house" worth saving would be revised by Baldwin himself in short time. In his 1963 book *The Fire Next Time*, Baldwin would ask, "Do I really want to be integrated into a burning house?"[48] in reference to the seeming intractability of race problems in the U.S. The difference in these expressions captures Baldwin's political movement across the 1960s. What were its roots and causes?

One was the challenge presented to Martin Luther King's version of civil rights integrationism by the Nation of Islam movement in the United States. Malcolm X's seminal 1965 autobiography captured brilliantly the Nation of Islam's appeal. Malcolm was converted from drug dealer and street hustler by the Nation of Islam's emphasis on black racial unity, political and personal discipline (disavowing drugs, drinking, and smoking), and its powerful counter-history of America as a white supremacist country and of Christianity as a religion of the slave master under slavery. The Nation of Islam's appeal to black economic cooperation and self-development also resonated with poor and working-class African-Americans who felt completely disenfranchised by capitalism.

On April 23, 1961, Baldwin appeared on the television program "The Open Mind" along with Malcolm X, C. Eric Lincoln, and George S. Schuyler. Four years before his book was published, Malcolm had already emerged as the most prominent and militant voice of the Nation of Islam, growing its base among working-class and poor African-Americans especially in New York, Detroit, and Chicago. Earlier that year, black scholar C. Eric Lincoln published the first study of the Nation of Islam, titled *The Black Muslims in America*. The book was in some ways a scholarly rejoinder to "The Hate that Hate Produced," an inflammatory television documentary about the Nation of Islam broadcast on American television in July of 1959. The broadcast provided most viewers with their first televised images of Malcolm X. It included an interview between Malcolm and Louis Lomax describing white Americans as "evil," and Malcolm's speech to a black Christian audience asking, "How did so few white people come to control so many black people?"[49] While pretending to be dispassionate, the program's title, and shallow rendering of Malcolm X's thought, demonized the organization. It presented the Nation of Islam's program for black self-organizing without whites as reactionary. It also failed to comprehend the Nation of Islam's appeal as a critique of Christianity's oppressive role in U.S. history buttressing slavery, racist ideology, and segregation.

These latter themes would become staples of Baldwin's thinking later in the 1960s as he absorbed, and applied, lessons from the rising Black Power movement. Yet on "The Open Mind" broadcast, Baldwin argued strongly against the Nation of Islam's self-organizing as itself reactionary. "The separation of races is what Mississippi wants and what Georgia wants. Now that isn't what I want."[50] He argued that a separatist approach to U.S. racism would simply seek to replace one racial hierarchy with another: "When one takes the road to power, it seems to me that the white world proves this, one ends up where the white world is."[51] Baldwin's argument was buttressed by a recurring theme in his writing from the 1950s, namely that "integration" in the U.S. had been a constant fact in part because of the racial mixing forced by slavery, socially and biologically. Many people in the U.S., he argued, are "neither white nor black."[52] At the same time, while rejecting the Nation of Islam program, Baldwin underscored a need for a radical transformation of U.S. society. The country must get "radical" and "overhaul the entire social fabric" he said.[53] "I can't imagine anything this country can offer me that I any longer want."[54]

Baldwin's sympathy for a project of radical social transformation led him on a political course across 1961 characterized by increasing public political activism, and a new affiliation with what might be called black internationalist currents. In January 1961, Baldwin spoke at a rent strike rally on 117th Street in Harlem to a crowd of 800 people;[55] in February 1961, he agreed to become a sponsor for SANE (National Committee for a Sane Nuclear Policy).[56] In April 1961, according to his FBI file, he helped sponsor a rally to abolish the House Un-American Activities Committee likely organized by the New York Council to Abolish the House Un-American Activities Committee; that group was succeeded by the Emergency Civil Liberties Committee, whose meetings Baldwin also attended.[57] In June 1961, at a CORE rally Baldwin praised African decolonization as a threat to white global supremacy. Also in June of 1961, Baldwin spoke at a forum hosted by the Liberation Committee for Africa. The Liberation Committee had been created in June 1960 and was chaired by Daniel Watts. Based in New York, it was Pan-Africanist in perspective, nationalist politically. In 1963 it would form a journal, *Liberator*. Baldwin's talk at the Liberation Committee forum set the fight against white supremacy in the U.S. in an internationalist context. As he had in "The Open Mind," Baldwin referenced U.S. attacks on the Cuban Revolution as analogous to its repression of the black freedom struggle. He invoked British, French, and Portuguese colonialism as cautionary examples of racial oppression for African-Americans: "No matter what they say now about highways and hospitals and penicillin, whatever was done in those colonies was not done for the natives."[58] Baldwin railed against corporate capitalism as responsible for a materialist culture whose commercial seductions produced a form of political false consciousness: "The only hope this country has is to turn overnight into a revolutionary country, and I say 'revolutionary' in the most serious sense of that word: to undermine the standards by which the middle-class American lives."[59] Baldwin was unspecific about what form revolution would take—"I don't know how it will come about, but I know that no matter how it comes, it will be bloody; it will be hard."[60] And he insisted that what kept open the possibility of radical transformation was the long history of *interraciality* in the United States:

> We in this country now—and it really is one minute to twelve—can really turn the tide because we have an advantage that Europe does not have, and we have an advantage that Africa does not have, if we could face it. Black and white people have lived together here for generations, and now for centuries. Now, on whether or not we face these facts everything depends.[61]

Baldwin's vague assertions of revolutionary potential are an index to past influences and shifts in his thought concordant with his times. They recall the influence of the interracial socialist left as undying embers of imagined solidarity (indeed, in 1962 he signed a clemency petition for Junius Scales, a Communist convicted under the Smith Act meant to criminalize Communist and socialist political organizing). They also reference the idea that the challenge to white supremacy of the civil rights movement created new vistas for interracial struggle. To return to his essay on King cited earlier, ending white supremacy could create a "new people" in Baldwin's version of a New Jerusalem. White people themselves could be emancipated from racism by black struggle.

The U.S. state did not fail to notice Baldwin's rising public presence and radicalization. Baldwin's CORE speech of 1961, as well as his appearance at the Liberation Committee for Africa, were duly noted by the FBI, as was Baldwin's public support for Carl Braden, an anti-racist activist who refused to testify before the House Un-American Activities Committee in 1958 and was sentenced to a year in prison. He was released after nine months early in 1962 after Martin Luther King, Jr. pushed for clemency in his case, with Baldwin's support. Baldwin also made himself an FBI target by signing a letter to the editor in the *New York Herald Tribune*, on June 17, 1961, opposing capital punishment and attacking directly FBI Director J. Edgar Hoover as someone who "uses his enormous power and prestige to corroborate the blindest and basest instincts of the retaliatory mob."[62]

Baldwin's appearance with Malcolm X on "The Open Mind" inspired Norman Podhoretz, editor for the journal *Commentary*, to ask Baldwin to write on the topic of the Nation of Islam. The idea took hold, and Baldwin arranged to meet with Malcolm and Elijah Muhammad, the titular leader of the Nation of Islam, with the idea of turning the meeting into an article. That article, "Letter from a Region in My Mind," would appear in the *New Yorker* magazine in November of 1962, and become, retitled, the first section of Baldwin's 1963 book *The Fire Next Time*. We will turn to discussion of the book later in this chapter, and in Chapter 5. Meanwhile, further invitations to write, and travel, poured in: in July of 1961, *New Yorker* magazine editor William Shawn wrote to Baldwin asking him to write a series of articles for the magazine on the Congo, Ghana, Nigeria, Kenya, and the Republic of Guinea. Nearly simultaneously, Baldwin was invited by the government of Israel to visit that country. These invitations set Baldwin's life and political thought in brand new directions. He decided to accept the invitations and to write a book on Africa with his travels to Israel set as a "prologue."[63] Biographer David Leeming writes that Baldwin intended to include Israel as another "homeland" which had helped give Baldwin his identity.[64] These plans were scrambled mainly by Baldwin's reaction to visiting Israel.

Baldwin left London for Tel Aviv on September 26, 1961. The visit conjured up a memory for Baldwin of a temporary impulse he'd had in 1948 to move to Israel rather than Paris as his expatriate home. Years later, in his 1972 book *No Name in the Street*, he would write, "Four hundred years in the West had certainly turned me into a Westerner—there was no way around that. But four hundred years in the West had also failed to bleach me—And if I had fled, to Israel, a state created for the purpose of protecting Western interests, I would have been in yet a tighter bind: on which side of Jerusalem would I have decided to live?"[65] Baldwin's initial awareness of the apartheid, imperial nature of the post-1948 state of Israel is an important indication of his Trotskyist sympathies in the 1940s: Trotskyists distinguished themselves from supporters of Stalin by not giving uncritical support for the new state of Israel which resulted from formal partition. They argued that a single, democratic state controlled by Arab and Jewish workers was the best outcome for the former British mandate. Thus it is not entirely surprising that Baldwin's trip to Israel in 1961 produced new contradictions.[66] From Israel, Baldwin wrote to Mary Painter on October 7, "A rather gloomy note, am within a stone's—or hand grenade's—throw from the Gaza strip. One is never very far from a border here, all the borders are hostile."[67] And then: "you can't walk five minutes without finding yourself at a border ... and of course the entire Arab situation, outside the country, and above all, within ... the fact that Israel is a homeland for so many Jews ... causes me to feel my own homelessness more keenly than ever."[68]

Baldwin's unease at the segregation of Israel was both a revisiting of past traumas of U.S. racism and a foreshadowing of political shifts to come in his rejection of Zionism. Coming precisely on the heels of his new-found commitment to anti-colonial politics, the visit to Israel produced an epiphany

about the larger contours of Western imperialism. Referring specifically to the Balfour Declaration of 1917 in which
Britain promised Jewish Zionists a state, he would recall the
visit in this way in *No Name in the Street*:

> When I was in Israel I thought I liked Israel. I liked the
> people. But to me it was obvious why the Western world
> created the state of Israel, which is not really a Jewish state.
> The West needed a handle in the Middle East. And they
> created the state as a European pawn ... When I was in
> Israel, it was as though I was in the middle of *The Fire Next
> Time*. I didn't dare go from Israel to Africa, so I went to
> Turkey, just across the road.[69]

We will return to further discussion of Baldwin, Israel,
and Palestine in Chapters 6 and 7. Here, we note the role
his Israel visit played in literally turning Baldwin further
away from a Western, Eurocentric perspective, and towards
an anti-imperialist internationalism. This current in this
thought would be deepened by his first visit and subsequent
stays in Turkey. Baldwin chose Turkey at the invitation of
actor Engin Cezzar, who had played Giovanni in the Actors
Studio workshop production in New York. In her superb
book on Baldwin's long relationship with Turkey, Magdalena
Zaborowska notes that Baldwin arrived "with little money,
depressed by a trip to Israel, and with a severe case of writer's
block that made him desperate to finish *Another Country*."[70]
Baldwin was taken in, housed, and fed by Cezzar and an
extended family of friends. The positive effect was immediate.
Baldwin rewrote and finished the book there, and developed a
permanent sense that Istanbul was a place to get writing done:
over the next ten years he would develop *The Fire Next Time*,
his play *Blues for Mister Charlie*, several novels, and his 1972

book *No Name in the Street* while residing in Istanbul. On his first visit Baldwin also met David Leeming, then a teacher at Robert College in Istanbul. Leeming would become Baldwin's secretary and close family friend, and eventually his biographer.

Of more consequence, Baldwin found something like a temporary third home in Istanbul, after New York and Paris. He made numerous friends among left intellectuals in Istanbul, including the poet and critic Cevat Capan, actress Sirin Devrim, and feminist journalist Zeynep Oral.[71] Zaborowska asserts that Baldwin discovered in Turkey "the intertwining of the erotic and race in a transatlantic context, and his embrace of what we would today call a 'queer' identity, was sharpened and enabled by his Turkish exile precisely because he was free there from the American notions of race and sex."[72] In Baldwin's words, Turkey appealed to him because it was "both in Europe and in Asia … neither Christian nor Muslim."[73] "[I]t is a relief to deal with people who, whatever they are pretending, are not pretending to be Christians."[74] This latter declaration, in context, is important, as Baldwin's long "break" with Christianity and the challenge of the Nation of Islam to it was to be an important theme in *The Fire Next Time*, the manuscript of which Baldwin carried with him into Turkey. Finally, as Zaborowska notes, Baldwin developed in Turkey what were his most explicitly queer novels, including *Tell Me How Long the Train's Been Gone*, to be discussed in Chapter 5. She argues persuasively that Baldwin developed an "erotics" of exile in his work nurtured by the culture and geography of Turkey.

Baldwin signaled the most consequent event of his first visit to Turkey by marking the date of its completion and location—December 10, 1961, Istanbul—on the final page of the manuscript of *Another Country*. He dedicated the book to Mary Painter. As noted earlier, the book had been very difficult for Baldwin to complete. In part, this was due to the explosion of celebrity, publicity, and public demand on his time evidenced by the commissioned magazine assignments. In part, this was owing to Baldwin's decision to dedicate himself to writing about the southern civil rights movement, interrupting his writing of the novel to do so. Further still, Baldwin had a peripatetic tendency to work on multiple projects at once: he completed, and published, *Notes of a Native Son* and *Giovanni's Room* in the time he worked on *Another Country*; he adapted the latter to the stage; he also wrote a television screenplay of "Equal in Paris," his story about spending time in a Parisian jail.

But primarily the book was difficult to finish because of its scope and subject matter. *Another Country* was meant by Baldwin to cover the terrain of his life as lived to date: Harlem, Paris, the American South, Greenwich Village; poverty, work, exile; art, music, writing, sexuality. Where his first two novels had only two or three protagonists, *Another Country* had at least four main characters, and several crisscrossing storylines. Baldwin also had trouble controlling a writing style and voice for the book that was radically new. Where his first two novels had been tightly structured, concisely written exterior social novels, *Another Country* seemed influenced by numerous competing sources: the experimental poetry of the 1950s, expressionist prose fiction by the likes of Henry Miller and Norman Mailer, multiple musical genres—jazz and blues most prominently—and a graphic dedication to recording physical details of sex, music, and alcohol. Indeed, Baldwin himself complained in October 1961, in a letter to Mary Painter, "it seems to me that my style is becoming more erratic, unmanageable, and clumsily loaded than ever—what I wouldn't give to be able to write a straight, straightforward, declarative sentence, free of qualifications, flourishes, and asides!—like Tolstoi, Dostoyevsky, or, even Dickens."[75]

  Baldwin's own clue as to what kind of book he intended—and how readers might approach it—came in its epigraph from one of his oldest influences, Henry James: "They strike one, above all, as giving no account of themselves in any terms already consecrated by human use; to this inarticulate state they probably form, collectively, the most unprecedented of monuments; abysmal the mystery of what they think, what they feel, what they want, what they suppose themselves to be saying."[76] Baldwin suggests here that the characters in his book are a "generation" whose lives and desires do not yet have a vocabulary even to themselves. The passage also points self-referentially to the problem of a writer finding a language to tell the stories of their lives. Seen from a psychoanalytic perspective, Baldwin suggests that "taboo" structures the novel: that which is knowable yet unsayable because it violates social norms. Primarily, in *Another Country*, this taboo is the domain of sex and race: most characters in the book express queer, bisexual, and heterosexual impulses, without ever articulating a "position" on these questions. Similarly, racialized characters seem trapped in their skins, seeking ways out. Sex across races, and interracial relationships, becomes one of those ways.

  Baldwin establishes these taboos as subtexts of the novel's setting, New York City in the post-war period. These two passages describing public social locations—the first a bar, the second a subway train—hint at clashing sexual and racial desires confronting both repression and suppression:

  Some of the men were buying drinks for some of the women—who wandered incessantly from the juke box to the bar—and they faced each other over smiles which werc pitched, with an eerie precision, between longing and contempt. Black-and-white couples were together here— closer together now than they would be later, when they got home. These several histories were camouflaged in the jargon which, wave upon wave, rolled through the bar; were locked in a silence like the silence of glaciers. Only the juke box spoke, grinding out each evening, all evening long, syncopated, synthetic laments for love.[77]

At Fifty-ninth Street many came on board and many rushed across the platform to the waiting local. Many white people and many black people, chained together in time and in space, and by history, and all of them in a hurry. In a hurry to get away from each other, he thought, but we ain't never going to make it. We been fucked for fair.

Then the doors slammed, a loud sound, and it made him jump. The train, as though protesting its heavier burden, as though protesting the proximity of white buttock to black knee, groaned, lurched, the wheels seemed to scrape the track, making a tearing sound. Then it began to move uptown, where the masses would divide and the load become lighter.[78]

Baldwin's novel narrates a social history of routinized racial and sexual intimacy producing, simultaneously, "longing and contempt." Both expressions are "camouflaged in the jargon" of social normativity and commercial culture—the "synthetic laments" of love in popular music. In the second passage, the train itself is a symbol of a modernity—a locomotive of history—which has forged new social relationships heavy with estrangement and alienation. In both passages black and white bodies are the register—or vehicle—for the fundamental contradictions of life under a capitalist system shot through with racism, sexism, heteronormativity, and a dialectical urge within the masses to destroy or leap over both.

Into this matrix Baldwin casts a network of desiring bodies: they are Vivaldo, a poor Italian-American writer; Rufus, a young African-American jazz musician; Ida, Rufus's sister, an aspiring singer; Cass, a bourgeois white woman married to a writer; and Eric, a gay southern American living in exile in Paris as the novel begins. Baldwin signals a dominant theme of the novel by titling Book One "Easy Rider," in reference to W.C. Handy's twelve-bar blues song, one first recorded by American blues singer Ma Rainey in 1924. The song's "easy rider" can refer to an unfaithful lover—usually a male—or, in dirty blues, to a sexually active woman. Book One is thus justly freighted with double meanings and ambiguities about both sexual identity and sexual contact: Vivaldo and Rufus sleep with both white women and black women, sometimes the same woman, and think to sleep with each other. Rufus sleeps with white women in part to punish them for their stereotypical desire for a hypersexual black male. Vivaldo recalls beating a man when he was a boy after he and a group of friends rape him orally. Ida laments that black women are born in America with reputations for being sexually loose (Jezebels), a stereotype rooted in the slave system's rationalization of raping black women. Vivaldo feels "more alive in Harlem" sexually. Vivaldo sleeps with Ida and thinks of her body in racially stereotypic terms as a "jungle" and "savage." Cass, nominally straight, sleeps with Eric, nominally gay. Rufus is haunted by a memory of sleeping with and loving Eric.

These inchoate expressions of social taboo are painful and destructive for most of the characters. They are symbolized dramatically by Rufus's suicide after a meditation on destruction itself. While riding the same train described earlier Rufus thinks:

Suppose these beams fell down? He saw the train in the tunnel, rushing under water, the motorman gone mad, gone blind … and the people screaming at windows and doors and turning on each other with all the accumulated fury of their blasphemed lives, everything gone out of them but murder, breaking limb from limb, and splashing in blood … It could happen; and he would have loved to see it happen, even if he perished, too.[79]

A few pages later, Rufus jumps from the George Washington Bridge, invoking memories of Eric, Leona (the white woman he abusively slept with), and Ida (his sister).

As noted earlier, Rufus's suicide was modeled for Baldwin by Eugene Worth, his dear friend and socialist mentor who died in the same manner. As also noted earlier, it is possible that Worth was romantically attracted to Baldwin. In any event, Worth's suicide brought an end momentarily for Baldwin to his aspiration for the possibility of something like a political transformation of the world. In *Another Country*, Rufus's suicide is the epicenter of a shared historical trauma binding the main characters of the book together. As in other Baldwin narratives, a black male is sacrificed (or killed) as a symbol of a racist social order which can no more bear the idea of black equality than it can alternatives to "straight" sexuality. Rufus dies on this social cross as described by Baldwin in his essay "Freaks and the American Ideal of Manhood":

The American ideal, then, of sexuality, appears to be rooted in the American ideal of masculinity. This ideal has created cowboys and Indians, good guys and bad guys, punks and stud, tough guys and softies, butch and faggot, black and white. It is an ideal so paralytically infantile that it is virtually forbidden—as an unpatriotic act—that the American boy evolve into the complexity of manhood.[80]

At the same time, Rufus is a young Baldwin, as recalled in the same essay, perceived by society as a walking black cock, sleeping with both men and women (including white women) as an expression of anxiety about settling into a queer identity: "At bottom, what I had learned was that the male desire for a male roams everywhere, avid, desperate, unimaginably lonely, culminating often in drugs, piety, madness or death."[81] Rufus's tragedy is compounded by the way this complex of contradictions destroys his own capacity to love. Baldwin here picks up a theme from *Giovanni's Room*—the destruction wrought when love is impossible. All of the characters in *Another Country* remain contained within this alienation, like riders on a fatal train.

Baldwin would later, in the same essay ("Freaks and the American Ideal of Manhood"), open out an analysis of gender and sexuality that can also be used as a key to *Another Country*:

Freaks are called freaks and are treated as they are treated—in the main, abominably—because they are human beings who cause to echo, deep within us, our most profound terrors and desires.

Most of us, however, do not appear to be freaks—though we are rarely what we appear to be. We are, for the most part, visibly male or female, our social roles defined by our sexual equipment.

But we are all androgynous, not only because we are all born of a woman impregnated by the seed of a man but because each of us, helplessly and forever, contains the other—male in female, female in male, white in black and black in white. We are a part of each other. Many of my countrymen appear to find this fact exceedingly inconvenient and even unfair, and so, very often, do I. But none of us can do anything about it.[82]

Baldwin encodes this theme into a late scene in the novel, when all of the major characters attend a film screening featuring Eric, the gay exile for whom nearly all of the characters have an expressed or latent sexual desire. The scene is tipped by Vivaldo's recognition that as he watches Eric on screen, he "for the first time caught a glimpse of who Eric really was." I quote the passage at length to underscore the weight Baldwin gives to the moment:

The camera moved very little during this scene and Eric was always kept in range. The light in which he was trapped did not alter, and his face, therefore, was exposed as it never was in life. And the director had surely placed Eric where he had because this face operated, in effect, as a footnote to the twentieth-century torment. Under the merciless light, the lined, tense, coarse-grained forehead also suggested the patient skull; an effect which was underlined by the promontory of the eyebrows and the secret place of the eyes. The nose was flaring and slightly pug, more bone, nevertheless, than flesh. And the full, slightly parted lips were lonely and defenseless, barely protected by the stubborn chin. It was face of a man, a tormented man. Yet, in precisely the way that great music depends, ultimately, on great silence, this masculinity was defined, and made powerful, by something which was not masculine. But it was not feminine, either, and something in Vivaldo resisted the word androgynous. It was a quality to which great numbers of people would respond without knowing to what it was they were responding. There was great force in the face, and great gentleness.

But, as most women are not gentle, nor most men strong, it was a face which suggested, resonantly, in the depths, the truth about our natures.[83]

Eric embodies an elastic, ambiguous version of Baldwin's notion of the "male in female, female in male." By choosing a cinematic representation of Eric to represent his "true" nature, Baldwin underscores the fictive, constructed nature of gender identity, what Judith Butler calls its "performativity," as noted in our discussion of *Giovanni's Room*. As Baldwin notes above, "We are, for the most part, *visibly male or female, our social roles* defined by our sexual equipment"—social roles Butler calls gender "scripts."[84] The audience reaction here is also important. Vivaldo's denial of the word "androgynous" to describe Eric marks the latter as a "freak" who elicits in Vivaldo the "most profound terrors and desires." At the same time, the omniscient narrator's recognition of Eric's androgyny marks out that "great numbers of people would respond without knowing to what it was they were responding," returning us to the novel's initial theme of taboo: "Abysmal the mystery of what they think, what they feel, what they want, what they suppose themselves to be saying." Finally, the passage links to Baldwin's essay on "Freaks" by describing Eric's androgyny as a universal human condition, what Baldwin calls "a footnote to the twentieth-century torment." As Baldwin put it in a 1965 interview, in words that might serve as a gloss on *Another Country* and this voyeuristic cinematic moment with Eric, "those terms, homosexual, bisexual, heterosexual are 20th-century terms which, for me, really have very little meaning. I've never, myself, in watching myself and watching other people, been able to discern exactly where the barriers were."[85]

Another Country received mixed reviews, but quickly became Baldwin's bestselling novel to date. Because of its representation of both queer and straight sex, the book was also flagged for possible obscenity by the FBI, which gathered a copy, and whose special agent noted its affinities to Henry Miller's *Tropic* books, which had already been banned by the state for sexual content. As scholar William Maxwell notes in his edited edition of Baldwin's FBI file, *Another Country* made it all the way to the hands of J. Edgar Hoover, and would begin a longer confrontation between him and Baldwin which we will take up in Chapter 5.[86] Almost simultaneous with the book's publication and stepped-up public celebrity, Baldwin undertook a new whirlwind of activity: in May of 1962 he wrote to Mary Painter of a trip to London to interview Paul Robeson for *Esquire*, meeting Elia Kazan regarding a possible screen treatment of *Another Country*, and preparing for an off-Broadway production of *The Amen Corner* in the fall of 1962. In July of 1962, one month after the publication of *Another Country*, Baldwin traveled to Africa for the first time with his sister Gloria. He visited Senegal, Ghana, and Sierra Leone. In Conakry, Guinea, he met Ahmed Sékou Touré, the President of the country since 1958 who had helped establish colonial independence from France.

While he had first planned to use the Africa trip as the basis for magazine articles, Baldwin instead returned, as David Leeming puts it, "with his eyes once again on the [civil rights] movement and its most public battlefield, the Deep South."[87] There were two immediate reasons for this. In the fall of 1962, James Meredith, a civil rights activist, had braved racist mobs (and a full-scale riot) to integrate the University of Mississippi, a flagship university in the Deep South. Baldwin had a running feud over segregation with Mississippi writer William Faulkner, noted earlier, who coincidentally died the same year. Baldwin was eager to follow up on his earlier reporting about the South and saw the Meredith case as a good prompt. The second reason, closely related, was that in late 1962 Baldwin finished his essay "Down at the Cross" while in Istanbul. The essay was Baldwin's attempt, fundamentally, to reckon with the totality of the shifting dynamics of the civil rights movement, and specifically to make sense of the role of Malcolm X and the Nation of Islam in the broader political landscape of the United States. Much of the article was based on the interviews with Malcolm X and Elijah Muhammad he had conducted before going to Africa.

The results of that reckoning and the book it would produce would change everything for Baldwin, and to a large extent change the ways Americans thought about the civil rights movement in the United States. It was to be what poet Gwendolyn Brooks might have called his own furious flowering.

5
Baldwin and Black Power, 1963–68

Now we are now engaged in a psychological struggle in this country, and that is whether or not black people will have the right to use the words they want to use without white people giving their sanction to it. And that we maintain, whether they like it or not, we gonna use the word "Black Power" and let them address themselves to that; but that we are not goin' to wait for white people to sanction Black Power. We are tired of waiting; every time black people move in this country, they're forced to defend their position before they move. It's time that the people who are supposed to be defending their position do that. That's white people. They ought to start defending themselves as to why they have oppressed and exploited us.

Stokely Carmichael speech on Black Power, October 29, 1966[1]

Black Power means the recognition that neither the American government nor the American people have any desire, or any ability, to liberate Negroes or … themselves. Well, the job must be attempted, we must save ourselves if we can; and if we can save ourselves we can also save the country; it is now absolutely and literally true that the American Negro is America's only hope.

James Baldwin, interview with Cep Dergisi, 1967[2]

It is not a question of whether they are going to give me any freedom. I am going to take my freedom.

James Baldwin, "What Price Freedom?" 1964[3]

What is the meaning of black self-determination? That question lies at the root of the global Black Power movement of the 1960s. Baldwin was both one of its participants and one of its architects. Beginning at the end of 1962, and immediately into the new year of 1963, Baldwin dedicated his organizing, speaking, and writing to developing a concept of the independent African-American freedom struggle that would undermine racist and economic oppression for a black minority while lifting the majority from under its burden as exploiter and oppressor. Baldwin's conception of Black Power mediated between the separatist nationalism of the Nation of Islam, which he fundamentally rejected, and the mass grassroots political organizing of African-American activists in the South—like the Congress of Racial Equality (CORE), and the Student Nonviolent Coordinating Committee (SNCC)—with whom he allied himself. Baldwin first constellated his thinking on Black Power in his epochal 1963 book *The Fire Next Time*, arguing that black Americans "are very well placed indeed to precipitate chaos and ring down the curtain on the American Dream."[4] By 1966, when Stokely Carmichael coined the term "Black Power," the idea had already assumed dimensions Baldwin had helped to give it.

Baldwin's pathways to a commitment to Black Power were multiple: a recognition that direct action organizing in the South and in the North would most likely win political demands; a profound dedication to black youth organizers, including children, who he saw as the generational hope of the movement; a visceral reaction to white supremacist violence, most notably the murders by Ku Klux Klan (KKK) member Byron de la Beckwith of his close friend Medgar Evers, Malcolm X's calamitous killing in 1965, and James Earl Ray's assassination of Martin Luther King, Jr. in 1968; as well as direct confrontation with the repressive apparatus of the U.S. state. In 1963, recognizing himself as an open target of the FBI because of his public speaking and writing, Baldwin threatened to write a book exposing its oppressive surveillance and harassment tactics, sensing early on the role it would play in helping to destroy individual lives and movements through tactics like COINTELPRO, the vast federal counter-intelligence program which resulted in the murder of Black Panther Party leaders Fred Hampton and Mark Clark.

Baldwin's embrace of Black Power was also directed by international events: the escalating U.S. war against Vietnam and Israel's Six-Day War against Arab countries were decisive in aligning Baldwin with the SNCC and Black Panther parties, each of which viewed these as exemplars of U.S. imperialism and Western racism. The public turn by the SNCC and the Black Panthers against Israeli colonialism and Zionism after 1967 also plunged Baldwin into public rejection of and debate over anti-semitism in the U.S., its contours and consequences, and its relationship to both capitalism and the black freedom struggle. Finally, Baldwin's rising celebrity and status as a queer black radical put him in the crosshairs of both a homophobic U.S. state and masculinist elements in the Black Power movement. "Isn't Baldwin a well-known pervert?" would be a question asked directly by J. Edgar Hoover, and implied by attention in the bourgeois press to his life and work. Baldwin survived and countered these attacks using Turkey and France as refuges, and channeling political responses into new public writing and speaking on gender and queer sexuality, including his revelatory, queer-affirming 1968 novel *Tell Me How Long the Train's Been Gone*.

* * *

Baldwin hurled himself headlong into a future of political notoriety on the first day of 1963, the most momentous single political year of his life. He traveled to Jackson, Mississippi, in order to meet James Meredith, the student who had earlier in the fall integrated the University of Mississippi, and the National Association for the Advancement of Colored People (NAACP) field organizer Medgar Evers, whom he accompanied on a trip to investigate a reported lynching. The trip south was smack dab in the middle of a speaking tour for CORE. In October 1962, Baldwin had spoken on behalf of CORE to students and faculty at Cornell, MIT, Harvard, and Brandeis; in January, he spoke at Dillard University in New Orleans and in North Carolina; in May, he spoke on the West Coast in nine cities over ten days, including Los Angeles and Oakland. The tour was a fundraiser for CORE. As Davis Houck notes, by early 1963 Baldwin was earning up to $500 per speaking engagement; every dollar taken in on the tour he donated to CORE. According to CORE internal documents, Baldwin's speeches earned CORE more than $20,000, and helped to push its membership to over 65,000.[5]

Baldwin conveyed two main themes in his talks to mostly student audiences, including, on the West Coast, high-school students. The first was their need to recognize themselves as agents of change in the world, and to resist the capacity of white supremacy to diminish their self-esteem. "[T]he white culture has operated and is operated deliberately to demoralize all Black people," Baldwin told them. "And demoralization, has, in many cases, been fatal, and in all cases, has been sinister. The effort, therefore, that I must make, to arrive at my identity, is mainly an opposition to the white force of the world."[6]

The second was encouraging young activists to study and learn from U.S. history in order to comprehend the oppression and exploitation of African-Americans:

> [W]e enslaved him because in order to conquer the country, we had to have cheap labor. And the man who is now known as the American Negro who is one of the oldest American citizens and the only one who never wanted to come here, did the dirty work ... I think it is not too strong for me to say, let me put it this way: without his presence, without that strong back, the American economy, the American nation would have had a vast amount of trouble creating its capital. If one did not have the captive toting the barge and lifting the bale as they put it, it would be a very different country, and it would certainly be much poorer.[7]

Baldwin's combined role as mentor, historian, and advocate for struggle on the streets found its literary complement— what might be called Baldwin's movement manifesto—in *The Fire Next Time*, published, fittingly, in the midst of his CORE lecture tour. The occasion for the book was the 100th anniversary of the Emancipation Proclamation intended by President Abraham Lincoln to free the slaves. For Baldwin, "the country is celebrating one hundred years of freedom one hundred years too soon."[8] The book's first section, "My Dungeon Shook," is in the form of a letter from Baldwin to his nephew James. The letter echoes cautionary themes and the avuncular tone from Baldwin's CORE addresses to black youth: "You can only be destroyed by believing that you really are what the white world calls a *nigger*";[9] and, "know from whence you came."[10] From the outset, too, Baldwin invokes the concept of integration to indicate that it is on shaky ground: "Please try to be clear, dear James, through the storm which rages about your youthful head today, about the reality which lies behind the words *acceptance* and *integration*. There is no reason for you to try to become like white people and there is no basis whatever for their impertinent assumption that *they* must accept *you*."[11]

The second, longer essay, "Down at the Cross," explains the challenge posed by the Nation of Islam to the United States' social order in the form of an allegory of Christianity's role in Baldwin's private life and the life of Western imperialism. This two-sided intent is signaled in double epigraphs: one, a reference to a Christian hymn, "Down at the Cross," describing a sinner "cleansed" of sin by the Crucifixion; the second, to Rudyard Kipling's famous call to "Take up the White Man's burden," written to commemorate—and celebrate—the U.S. annexation of the Philippines in 1898, and the beginning of a new racist imperial century in the Western world. Baldwin juxtaposes the epigraphs to suggest that Christianity has been used to "cleanse" and rationalize the sins of the latter.

The first part of "Down at the Cross" locates Baldwin's early loss of religious faith in this matrix. He recounts his days as a childhood preacher in Harlem, fleeing into the church to escape the "wages of sin" abounding in surrounding poverty, violence, drugs, and sex. Yet racism itself also tests Baldwin's faith: "the Negro's experience of the white world cannot possibly create in him any respect for the standards by which the white world claims to live."[12] Over time, Baldwin understands Christianity itself as one of the white world's false standards: "And if His [God's] love was so great, and if He loved all His children, why were we, the blacks, cast down so far?"[13] "I realized that the Bible had been written by white men. I knew that, according to many Christians, I was a descendant of Ham, who had been cursed, and that I was therefore predestined to be a slave."[14] This personal story of negative awakening to Christianity is also an allegory of how Christianity in the West has been used to establish political power and empire in the name of God:

> The Christian church itself—again, as distinguished from some of its Ministers—sanctified and rejoiced in the conquests of the flag, and encouraged, if it did not formulate, the belief that conquest, with the resulting relative well-being of the Western populations, was proof of the favor of God. God had come a long way from the desert—but then so had Allah, though in a very different direction. God, going north, and rising on the wings of power, had become white, and Allah, out of power, and on the dark side of Heaven, had become—for all practical purposes anyway—black.[15]

Baldwin here anticipates his focus and theme: the emergence of the Nation of Islam as a black theological response to Christian domination, wherein an Anglo God is what Malcolm X called the face of the "white devil." He moves to a description of black worshippers listening on the South Side of Chicago to speeches by the Honorable Elijah Muhammad described thusly:

> The white man's rule will be ended forever in ten or fifteen years ... the crowd seemed to swallow this theology with no effort—all crowds do swallow theology this way ... But very little time was spent on theology, for one did not need to prove to a Harlem audience that all white men were devils. They were merely glad to have, at last, divine corroboration of their experience.[16] The South Side proved the justice of the indictment; the state of the world proved the justice of the indictment.[17]

Yet Baldwin also uses his experience of Christianity to reject the Nation of Islam's messages of economic separatism. "In the same way that we, for white people, were the descendants of Ham, and were cursed forever, white people were, for us, the descendants of Cain. And the passion with which we loved the Lord was a measure of how deeply we feared and distrusted, and, in the end, hated almost all strangers, always, and avoided and despised ourselves."[18] Baldwin here rejects separatist ideology as a reinvention of the "Other." The Nation of Islam, he fears, will reproduce racial hierarchy with a new black master. At the same time, Baldwin describes sympathetically the Nation of Islam's call for the self-determination of black people. Describing its plan to demand portions of southern land as "back payment" for slave labor, Baldwin writes:

> All this is not, to my mind, the most imminent of possibilities, but if I were a Muslim, this is the possibility that I would find myself holding in the center of my mind, and driving to war. And if I were a Muslim, I would not hesitate to utilize— or indeed, to exacerbate—the social and spiritual discontent that reigns here, for, at the very worst, I would merely have contributed to the destruction of a house I hated, and it would not matter if I perished, too. One has been perishing so long![19]

Baldwin's complex voicing of this passage is significant. Much as with his writings on the civil rights movement, Baldwin comprehends and presents the most radical demands of the movement as the most socially rational. This tips *The Fire Next Time* towards an embrace of a racial revolution in the U.S.:

> What it comes to is that if we, who can scarcely be considered a white nation, persist in thinking of ourselves as one,

we condemn ourselves, with the truly white nations, to sterility and decay, whereas if we could accept ourselves as we are, we might bring new life to the Western achievements, and transform them. The price of this transformation is the unconditional freedom of the Negro.[20]

Baldwin's repetition of this refrain a moment later—"And I repeat: The price of the liberation of the white people is the liberation of the blacks"—resonates with his early socialist orientation to a world transformed through interracial struggle, an orientation absorbed through the example of people like Orilla Miller. In Marx's famous words, "Labor in the white skin cannot be free where in the Black it is branded."[21] Precisely in this passage, notes E. San Juan Jr., "Baldwin affirms the right of self-determination for all people of color as an organic part of a society-in-the-making, the New Jerusalem he envisioned arising from everyone taking responsibility for what's going on in the world. This was his utopian wager."[22]

Indeed, at the heart of Baldwin's wager is the living history of black freedom struggle as an emancipatory force. Baldwin proposes that the U.S. is on the verge of a racial apocalypse—"A bill is coming in that I fear America is not prepared to pay."[23] African-American struggle to destroy racism and what Du Bois called "the color line" is Baldwin's singular prescription:

Color is not a human or a personal reality; it is a political reality. But this is not a distinction so extremely hard to make that the West has not been able to make it yet. And at the center of this dreadful storm, this vast confusion, stand the black people of this nation, who must now share the fate of a nation that has never accepted them, to which they were brought in chains. Well, if this is so, one has no choice but to do all in one's power to change that fate, and at no matter what risk—eviction, imprisonment, torture, death.[24]

Baldwin's call for the "unconditional freedom of the Negro" was his prophetic caution, or jeremiad, to America, a second coming of God's warning to Noah about the world's imminent destruction: "this time water/the fire next time." The book's lyricism, depth, rage, and appeal to whites to respond to black battles against racism in America made Baldwin an embraceable dissident across a wide political spectrum, from white liberals seeking confirmation that they had a place in the civil rights struggle, to black militants committed to emancipation, as Malcolm X himself would describe it, "by any means necessary." The book sold 100,000 copies in hard cover, gained exceptional reviews, and brought Baldwin a radical new form of celebrity: on May 17, 1963, he was the subject of a cover story in *Time* magazine, the first black author so featured. A week later, *Life* magazine, Henry Luce's strongly pro-American, pro-capitalist publication, featured a photo-story on Baldwin's CORE tour of the South.

Baldwin used his new-found social leverage to enhance black political power. On May 12, he wired U.S. Attorney General Robert F. Kennedy, brother of President John Kennedy, blaming the federal government for failing to protect non-violent black protesters, including children, who had recently been beaten by local police on the streets of Birmingham, Alabama. On May 24, Baldwin organized a group of friends and civil rights activists to meet with Kennedy at his New York City apartment. The group included preeminent black psychologist Dr. Kenneth Clark, Harlem civil rights attorney Clarence Jones, veteran civil rights activist Jerome Smith, playwright Lorraine Hansberry, and actor Harry Belafonte. The meeting was a political farce. Kennedy patronized the group, which responded by berating him and the administration for failing to do anything to advance civil rights. Hansberry, by 1963 a seasoned activist and leftist, was especially incensed, and walked out of the meeting. "I've only met one person Lorraine could not get through to, and that was the late Bobby Kennedy," Baldwin later wrote.[25]

According to scholar William Maxwell, a key fallout of the meeting between Baldwin and Kennedy was ramped-up FBI surveillance of Baldwin and his associates. He was placed on the FBI's "Security Index," indicating that the state considered him a high security risk. In 1963, the FBI wiretapped the phones of Clarence Jones. Jones was heard to say that Baldwin was going to "nail them [the FBI] to the wall" for its dirty tricks.[26] That threat was all the FBI needed to begin a campaign to dig up dirt on Baldwin, including on his sexuality. Maxwell notes that the FBI began "seeding" attack stories on Baldwin in American newspapers to try and damage his reputation.[27] Within a year, Baldwin was publicly promising to write a book, *Blood Counters*, exposing the FBI and its tactics. The FBI also kept note of and attempted to utilize evidence of homophobia within the civil rights movement itself. Tapping the telephone of Stanley Levinson, the FBI heard Levinson claim that both Baldwin and Bayard Rustin—an openly gay adviser to Martin Luther King, Jr.—were "better qualified to lead a homo-sexual movement than a civil rights movement." Rustin, like Baldwin, was gay, and left, and one of Martin Luther King, Jr.'s closest advisers. When Rustin was forced out of the Southern Christian Leadership Conference in 1960 because of threats to "out" his sexuality, Baldwin noted that King lost "much moral credit" in the eyes of young people, clearly understanding Rustin as a victim of homophobia.[28]

This "queer" state profiling of Baldwin was enhanced by heteronormative coverage by the bourgeois press of his new-found literary and political influence. The *Time* magazine cover story described him in hysterical terms as a "nervous, slight, almost fragile figure, filled with frets and fears. He is effeminate in manner, drinks considerably, smokes cigarettes in chains."[29] A profile in *Mademoiselle* magazine published the same month gave Baldwin his own platform to speak back to the straight world of America. "American males," he said, "are the only people I've ever encountered in the world who are willing to go on the needle before they'll go to bed with each other. Because they're afraid of this, they don't know how to go to bed with women either … . I don't know what homosexual means any more, and Americans don't either … If you fall in love with a boy, you fall in love with a boy. The fact that Americans consider it a disease says more about them than it says about homosexuality."[30]

Baldwin's life took a pivotal turn one month later on June 12, when his friend Medgar Evers was assassinated in the driveway of his home in Jackson, Mississippi. Evers was a World War II veteran and NAACP field organizer in Mississippi. He was, like many southern civil rights organizers, an advocate of black self-defense. On June 12, he was emerging from his car when KKK member Byron de la Beckwith shot him dead. Baldwin saw the killing as symptomatic: "he was put to death by the same oligarchy who still intend, with the country's help, to keep the Negro in his place."[31] At the time of Evers's death, Baldwin had been nurturing the idea for a play based on the lynching of Emmett Till, the 14-year-old African-American from Chicago who had been murdered and mutilated by white supremacists in Mississippi in 1955. Evers's death spurred memories for Baldwin of having traveled just months earlier into southern backwoods to investigate another black murder. "When he died," he wrote in 1964, "something entered into me which I cannot describe, but it was then that

I resolved that nothing under heaven would prevent me from getting this play done."[32]

The finished play, *Blues for Mister Charlie*, is Baldwin's homage to the lives of black martyrs like Till and Evers as transformative figures in the civil rights movement's turn from non-violent protest and integration to the beginnings of Black Power. The play is set in a starkly segregated southern town sectioned on stage into "Blacktown" and "Whitetown." The narrative opens with Lyle Britten, a white man, dumping the body of a black man into a pit, uttering the lines, "And may every nigger like this nigger end like this nigger—face down in the weeds!"[33] The body is that of Richard Henry, a young African-American who has returned to his family hometown after moving up north. The plot of the play, quite simply, is who killed Richard. The question is mediated through a political spectrum representative of shifting racial currents in the South: Lyle is a store owner, open racist, and proud southerner with a history of sexually exploiting black women. His wife, Jo, is his loyal second. Opposite Lyle and Jo are Richard and Juanita, the last of which is a young, self-confident African-American student in the midst of joining herself to the civil rights struggle. Over time, it is revealed that she has long loved Richard Henry, and that she is pregnant with his child when he dies. In the proverbial middle are two versions of racial liberalism: Parnell, a white journalist opposed to the worst of southern racism but unaware of his own entitlements; and Meridian Henry, an elder Christian pastor and father of Richard.

The play unfolds as the trial of Lyle Britten. Baldwin uses the play to produce a trial that never was: of the killers of Emmett Till, murdered, according to contemporary lore at the time, because he "wolf-whistled" (made a pass at) a white shopkeeper's wife. This is the false accusation Jo Britten brings against Richard Henry during the trial. Baldwin renders their actual encounter in the play as a taut confrontation between a militant, no-nonsense northern-trained upstart and a paranoid, racist white woman defending her private property. The scene escalates to sexual melodrama when Lyle enters to "protect" his wife from attack, goading Richard into this assertion: "You don't own this town, you white mother-fucker. You don't even own twenty dollars. Don't you raise that hammer. I'll take it and beat your skull to jelly."[34] Baldwin suggests that Richard is a dead man for even considering his own resistance to southern apartheid. As in the Till case, justice remains impossible: the play ends with Lyle going free despite everyone in the play, and the audience, knowing he is Richard's killer.

Blues for Mister Charlie's primary theme is that a new generation of black militancy will be necessary to break the old racist order of the South, and by extension America. Thus the play concludes with Juanita and other black students starting up a march to protest Richard's death and its miscarriage of justice. The play also juxtaposes Richard's gun and his father's Bible as metonyms of the movement, ultimately choosing mass struggle, self-defense, and collective action as a more potent path to black freedom and self-determination than moral uplift, the church, or non-violence. Juanita, meanwhile, prays that she may carry Richard's baby to term so that "everything will not be lost." Here Baldwin foreshadows a novel to come—*If Beale Street Could Talk*—where the prospect of black biological reproduction is meant as a political counterpoint to the disappearance and loss of black life elsewhere, particularly the erasure of black men. This ending both "naturalizes" Juanita's gender and maternity and makes her an emblem of Baldwin's anxiety about black genocide as a by-product of the "long" reign of U.S. racism and violence, from slavery to lynching to Emmett Till. Real life would unfortunately prove exactly as real as Baldwin's fiction: a year after Medgar Evers's killing, two separate trials of his murderer Byron de la Beckwith would result in hung juries (30 years later, in 1994, he would be tried on new evidence and convicted).

Meanwhile, in July 1963, Baldwin ventured further into television work, writing the script for "Take This Hammer," a one-hour documentary film in which Baldwin toured the city of San Francisco interviewing mostly black male youth about racial conditions and joblessness. The film was unique at the time for focusing on racism in a West Coast U.S. city. On August 20, Baldwin gave an important interview in Paris to François Bondy. He told Bondy that American racism against Native Americans and Indians was part of the need for the civil rights struggle, and again acknowledged the reasons for the appeal of the Nation of Islam to African-Americans: "when the Muslim speaker speaks, he is the only person in America speaking about what those cats in Harlem really, really feel ... The only way to stop Malcolm X from speaking in Harlem on Saturday night, is to get rid of Harlem."[35] At the same time, Baldwin was preparing to take part in Martin Luther King, Jr.'s March on Washington. From Paris, he helped organize a solidarity march and wrote a strong letter signed by friends to the U.S. embassy. The letter, dated August 17, said the march "aspires not only to eradicate all racial barriers in American life, but to liberate all Americans from the prison of their biases and fears."[36] Baldwin flew to Washington, DC in order to attend the march on August 28 in person, but did not speak or play a major role. As the March on Washington grew to 250,000 participants, the FBI chased news of obscenity allegations against Baldwin's novel *Another Country*, a constant reminder of the low-level and highly visible repression lodged against what was now the country's most openly queer black novelist.

But where there was still no justice, there was no peace. On September 15, 1963, Klansman in Birmingham, Alabama dynamited the 16th Street Baptist Church during services, killing four young African-American girls in the process: Addie Mae Collins, Carol Denise McNair, Carole Robertson, and Cynthia Wesley. Two other young black men were shot on the streets, one by police. It was the third bombing in Birmingham in a week after courts ordered Alabama schools integrated. The killings drove Baldwin into a state of rage, a compounding of his memories of protesters being beaten in Birmingham earlier that spring, and of the Kennedy administration's refusal to more firmly intervene in the South. On the day after the bombing, he wrote the unpublished "Statement on Birmingham," declaring, "The crimes committed yesterday in Birmingham must be considered as one of the American answers to the March on Washington."[37] "Six kids were murdered in Birmingham on a Sunday and in Sunday school in a Christian nation, and nobody cared," he later wrote, misstating the number.[38] As always, political trauma spurred Baldwin to creative activity. He planned to produce a documentary film called "Birmingham," described in his notes for the project as the city that is "the most rabidly racist in the United States."[39] The project never came to term.

On September 18, three days after the Birmingham bombing, Baldwin held a press conference in New York City where he criticized the Kennedy administration again for lack of action. The New York Times, on September 19, also quoted Baldwin as saying, "I blame J. Edgar Hoover in part for events in Alabama. Negroes have no cause to have faith in the FBI,"[40] a statement that further incensed the bureau, and made it into Baldwin's FBI file. In addition, an FBI wiretap of attorney Clarence Jones reported Baldwin being angry at Martin Luther King, Jr. for not demanding more action from the federal government after the Birmingham bombing, and Jones concurring. As scholar William Maxwell notes, "More often than his Black-Power era reputation would suggest, Baldwin was discovered on the radical side of those lines."[41]

Indeed, Baldwin turned to Daniel Watts's radical black nationalist journal *Liberator* in October 1963 to publish "We Can Change the Country," a manifest declaration of war against—or at least independence from—the U.S. state. Baldwin begins the essay by describing the situation in the U.S. as revolutionary: "we who are on the barricades in this unprecedented revolution are not in the position of someone in the Congo or someone in Cuba. That is, we cannot take over the land."[42] Rather, Baldwin writes, "We have to begin a massive campaign of civil disobedience."[43] That campaign should include breaking laws, and regime change:

> We have already paid a tremendous price for what we've done to Negro people. We have denied, and we are paying for the denial of the energy of twenty million people. No society can afford that. The future is going to be worse than the past if we do not let the people who represent us know that it is our country. A government and a nation are not synonymous. We can change the government and we will.[44]

Baldwin's populist black nationalism and revolutionary chutzpah in the essay were due to several sources cited in the essay: the Cuban Revolution—"I don't see any reason why I should invade Havana. I would much rather invade Miami"[45]— and the example of contemporary proto-Black Power activists like Robert F. Williams. A self-defense advocate and author the same year of the book *Negroes with Guns*, Williams fled the country to Canada, then Cuba, in support of Castro's revolution after being falsely charged by the federal government with kidnapping. Baldwin had supported efforts to defend him. Baldwin's revolutionary mood was also a direct hangover from the Birmingham bombing: "The FBI has not been able to find a single bomber. In Alabama alone, fifty bombings and not one culprit—not yet. The FBI can't find them. Let me tell you why they can't find them. They can't afford to. They stay at the homes of the people who did the bombing."[46]

A final clue to Baldwin's proto-Black Power thought in this pivotal year of 1963 lies in an unpublished interview with Charles Childs, the manuscript of which exists in the Baldwin papers at the Schomburg Library. Childs pressed Baldwin on his Marxism, asking if he didn't consider the "Negro problem" "a problem of the proletariat in America." Baldwin retorted, "There is a Negro problem in this country … If the Marxists were right, the whites and blacks of the Deep South would have united long, long ago."[47] Asked why this had not happened, Baldwin argued, "It's because there are no workers in this country. In this country you don't have workers. You have people who are going to be capitalists … they think they're going to be boss. Again, look at the history of the labor movement in this country. Negroes, they can't help being workers."[48] Pressed further to consider whether socialism is the answer, Baldwin averred that the problem is the "economic system under which we labor."[49] "Socialism," he continued, "refers to a certain, you know, doctrine of distribution which would have to be modified in order to work here. I certainly would not want to live under a Russian regime. On the other hand, there's something wrong with a regime like our own in which so much power is vested in so many people."[50]

If Baldwin's notion of black self-determination was, as E. San Juan argues, a "utopian wager," it was also bounded by recurring skepticism about interracial working-class struggle in the United States, and disillusionment with Stalinism. The shift to Black Power for Baldwin and contemporaries like James and Grace Lee Boggs and Harold Cruse, many of them like Baldwin first educated by socialist, Communist, or Trotskyist politics, was often a negative passage through this question. It was not by any means, as Baldwin knew, a new question: in his 1935 masterwork *Black Reconstruction*, W.E.B. Du Bois contended that the pivotal tragedy in American history was the failure of free slaves and white workers in the South to see their interests in common after emancipation. U.S. labor unions, as Baldwin often noted, especially those in the American Federation of Labor, had long historic records of discrimination against black workers (in June of 1963, Baldwin wrote a letter at the behest of his long-time friend Stan Weir to Harry Bridges of the International Longshore and Warehouse Union (ILWU), supporting his efforts on behalf of black workers in the union; the ILWU was a left-wing union with a militant history, but Baldwin was compelled by Weir's argument that black workers in the union were getting a bad deal). Baldwin's own notion of "false consciousness" expressed in the Childs interview—workers wanting to become bosses—was for Du Bois inflected by what he called the "wages of whiteness," the privileges granted to white workers by the ruling class for aligning their interests with capital over and against their black working-class brothers and sisters. Baldwin would develop his own variation of this argument, as noted earlier, in positing that "as long as you think you're white, there's no hope for you"—referencing the privileges and entitlements of race generated by a system meant to divide and rule.[51]

And yet, Baldwin's indictment of capitalism and the temptations of class struggle and socialism would not die an easy death in his thought, as we shall see. They became, rather, one of the long threads of his evolving, idiosyncratic Black Power philosophy. In late September 1963, Baldwin spoke at the Community Church on East 35th Street in New York City. His speech was reported in *The Worker*, the newspaper of the Communist Party, by James E. Jackson, a long-time member and the paper's editor who had been indicted in 1951 under the Smith Act. Jackson quoted Baldwin as saying, "A vast complex of industrials and wealthy interests make profit out of segregation. Therefore, we must overhaul the system, the economic system ... We must use our economic weight for ourselves and for the liberation of our country from the blood-sucking establishment."[52] While not expressly endorsing socialism, Baldwin also refused to kowtow to Cold War, McCarthyite hysteria: "I do not take oaths before them. I think it is beneath me to say I am not a Communist."[53]

Baldwin ended 1963 with a final flurry of activism. He traveled to Selma, Alabama in support of Freedom Day, organized by the SNCC to register new black voters. Baldwin watched as SNCC lined up hundreds of African-Americans to vote, telling the news media that "The federal government is not doing what it is supposed to be doing."[54] Also in Selma were James Forman, executive director of the SNCC, comedian and civil rights activist Dick Gregory, Howard Zinn, and movement leader and theorist Ella Baker, an SNCC adviser. On November 20, Baldwin and Bayard Rustin spoke at an SNCC leadership training conference at Howard University. Baldwin's transformative year, and the transformative year of 1963, ended fittingly with a nod to freedom struggle: Baldwin joined lawyer Thurgood Marshall, who in 1967 became the first African-American Supreme Court justice, actor Harry Belafonte, and actor Sidney Poitier on a trip to Nairobi to celebrate Kenya's new-found independence. Baldwin was still in symbolic pursuit of that "cup of coffee" that would bridge African and African-American freedom struggles.

* * *

Baldwin continued to toggle between new creative projects, exploding notoriety, and grassroots political activism in 1964. In February, he was elected to the prestigious National Institute of Arts and Letters. On April 23, his play, *Blues for Mr. Charlie*, directed by the left-wing actor Burgess Meredith, once blacklisted during the 1950s, opened at the American National Theater and Academy in Greenwich Village. The play starred Al Freeman, Jr. and Rip Torn, among other cast members. It received solid reviews; its performances were also tracked by the FBI.

Exactly one week after the play opened, six young African-American men were arrested in Harlem. The youth, all between 18 and 20, were charged with killing Margit and Frank Sugar in their used clothing store in Harlem. Mainstream media stories contended that the six were "Blood Brothers," anti-white thugs set out to terrorize and murder. In fact, four of the six had been targeted by the police because of their alleged participation in the so-called "Fruit Stand Riot" on April 17, two weeks earlier. That incident was sparked when a fruit stand operator blew a whistle to bring police to prevent children from taking spilled fruit from his stand. The police beat the children, and several people who attempted to prevent the beating. Two of those attempting to prevent the beating were among the six people arrested.

The case produced racial hysteria about black male youth as criminals, akin to the "Central Park Jogger" case in 1980s New York City, when five black teens were falsely accused of rape and assault.[55] In March 1965, the "Harlem Six," as the youth were known in the press, were convicted of first-degree murder and sentenced to life in prison. While awaiting trial, they were savagely beaten by police. Baldwin, who knew police brutality first hand, took an immediate interest in defending them. In April 1966, he appeared on a "Town Hall" program with the actor Ossie Davis and comedian Dick Gregory to help raise funds for an attempted retrial led by radical attorney William Kunstler. In 1967, the "Baldwin Benefit Committee" as it was dubbed featured Baldwin speaking at a fundraiser at the Village Theater on Second Avenue. In 1968, the convictions of the "Harlem Six" were overturned, in part because confessions had been gained through police torture.

Baldwin's involvement in the case generated one of his most important pieces of reportage, "Report from Occupied Territory," a detailed narration of the story of the Harlem Six intended to demonstrate for readers the police state that was everyday life in black communities. I quote at length:

Now, what I have said about Harlem is true of Chicago, Detroit, Washington, Boston, Philadelphia, Los Angeles and San Francisco—is true of every Northern city with a large Negro population. And the police are simply the hired enemies of this population. They are present to keep the Negro in his place and to protect white business interests, and they have no other function ...

This is why pious calls to "respect the law," always to be heard from prominent citizens each time the ghetto explodes, are so obscene. The law is meant to be my servant and not my master, still less my torturer and my murderer. To respect the law, in the context in which the American Negro finds himself, is simply to surrender his self-respect.[56]

That Baldwin's essay was published in the liberal, and mostly white, *The Nation* magazine made it one of the first by a black writer to widely expose systemic police brutality to people who were not black. Typically, Baldwin was trailblazing in his capacity to create new public spaces for exposing racism in the U.S. The essay was also overtly anti-imperialist. Baldwin compared the violence against black people in Harlem to the U.S. war against Vietnam. Indeed, his metaphor of "occupation" was overtly martial. Black boys going off to fight in Vietnam, he wrote, "are dying there like flies; they are dying in the streets of all our Harlems far more hideously than flies."[57] Baldwin's analysis of American violence abroad "coming home to roost" within its borders seconded a message popularized by none other than Malcolm X in his famous response to John F. Kennedy's assassination on November 22, 1963. Baldwin appeared to be riffing off of Malcolm's trope in a 1964 essay for the collaborative picture-book *Nothing Personal*. The book was a stylish collection of photographs by Baldwin's high-school friend, the award-winning art photographer Richard Avedon. Itself historical commentary and reportage, the book included photographs of civil rights activists in the South like Julian Bond, and American Nazis like George Rockwell. In his framing essay, Baldwin rejected the idea held by many Americans that the violence that killed Kennedy was accidental or incidental. "The America of my experience," he wrote, "has worshipped and nourished violence for as long as I have been on earth. The violence was being perpetrated mainly against black men, though—the strangers; and so it didn't count. But, if a society permits one portion of its citizenry to be menaced or destroyed, then, very soon, no one in that society is safe."[58]

Baldwin was honing his Black Power theme in these essays—the unique oppression of African-Americans as a potential revolutionary force in the United States, and globally. In so doing, he was beginning to align himself more openly with left currents everywhere. In 1964, the same year as the Harlem Six arrest, he published the essay "What Price Freedom?" in the journal *Freedomways*. *Freedomways* had been started in 1961

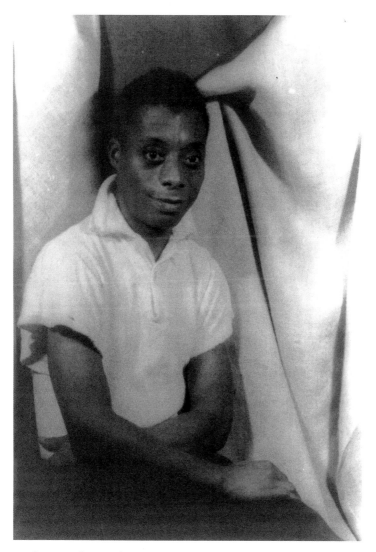

1. Photographer Carl Van Vechten took this portrait of Baldwin in 1955, the year of publication of his essay collection *Notes of a Native Son*. Van Vechten, who was white, was well-known for his portraits of African-American writers and artists of the Harlem Renaissance of the 1920s. (Library of Congress)

2. Baldwin with his friend, actor Marlon Brando, at the 1963 March on Washington. Baldwin did not speak at the March but prior to attending helped organize a petition in support of it in Paris. Brando and Baldwin were good friends; both supported the Black Panther Party later in the 1960s. (U.S. Information Agency; https://commons.wikimedia.org/wiki/Category:James_Baldwin#/media/File:Baldwin_Brando_Civil_Rights_March_1963.jpg)

3. Baldwin lecturing in Amsterdam, 1984. (Sjakkelien Vollebregt, Dutch National Archive)

4. Baldwin in Hyde Park, London, 1968. (Allen Warren; https://commons.wikimedia.org/wiki/Category:James_Baldwin#/media/File:James_Baldwin_37_Allan_Warren_(cropped).jpg)

5. Baldwin on a 1974 speaking tour in Amsterdam, here promoting a Dutch translation of his novel *If Beale Street Could Talk*. In 2018 Director Barry Jenkins (*Moonlight*) adopted the novel for film. (Dutch National Archive)

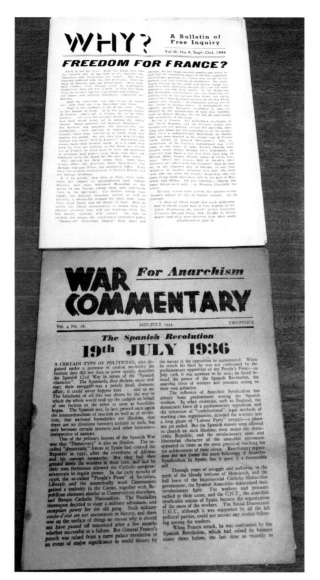

6. Baldwin demonstrated an interest in anarchism in the 1940s. He subscribed to both *Why?*, a U.S.-based anarchist periodical, and *War Commentary*, an anarchist publication produced in the United Kingdom. He likely attended anarchist meetings in New York before leaving the U.S. for Paris in 1948. (Bill V. Mullen)

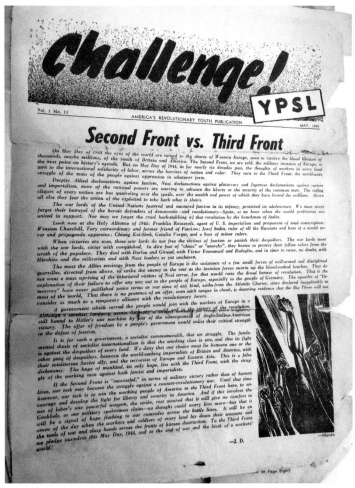

7. Baldwin described himself as a "socialist" and a "Trotskyite" for a brief time during the 1940s. He subscribed at least temporarily to *Challenge!*, the newspaper of the Young People's Socialist League, which he claimed to have joined. This issue from his personal archive is dated 1944. (Bill V. Mullen)

8. Baldwin struggled to make ends meet after graduating high school. In 1944, he worked temporarily for both the U.S. Postal Service, and the Office of War Information. These 1944 government tax forms show him earning a total of $47.25 in the former job and $125.00 in the latter. (Bill V. Mullen)

9. Baldwin's dear friend, mentor and muse Beauford Delaney, a model for Baldwin of what the Black artist could be, painted this portrait of Baldwin around 1957. Meeting Delaney in New York in the early 1940s helped dedicate Baldwin to becoming a writer and artist. (smallcurio from Austin, TX)

FIFTH AVENUE AT FIFTEENTH STREET, NORTH

A.G.GASTON MOTEL
AIR CONDITIONED

TELEPHONE 4-4631

BIRMINGHAM 2, ALABAMA

A. G. GASTON

LOBBY

BEDROOM

MASTER SUITE

COFFEE SHOP

COMPLETELY AIR-CONDITIONED, CENTRALLY GAS HEATED, DELICIOUS MEALS AT COFFEE SHOP, SPACIOUS PARKING COURT, TELEPHONE AND MUSIC IN EACH ROOM, DOWN TOWN LOCATION, PRIVATE BATH AND SHOWER, BEAUTIFUL PATIO AND LOBBY.

A Motel Designed With A Traveler's Comfort In Mind

Dear Mary : —

Having reactions symptomatic of hysteria barely controlled; always on the edge of tears; can't sleep; headaches — have a touch of the flu, or something. Have spent my day walking around the city, talking people, including a white man who works for the Nat'l Conference of Christians and Jews, who, now, is forced - lik to leave Alabama. Can't take any more burning cro the isolation; economic reprisals (credit standing gone. His wife has lost one child due to the strain of being off-beat: he dare not ever leave her alone in their home at night.

So. Negro taxi-drivers - to speak only of th have an even grimmer tale to tell. Have spent evening reading the Southern press and white Cit

10. Baldwin went to the U.S. South in 1957 to report on the Civil Rights movement. In Birmingham, Alabama, he stayed at the A.G. Gaston Motel, one of the few Black-owned hotels in the South, and thus something of a refuge. Baldwin was frayed by the simmering violence underlying Southern racism. In this letter to Mary Painter, Baldwin describes "Having reactions symptomatic of hysteria barely controlled." (Bill V. Mullen)

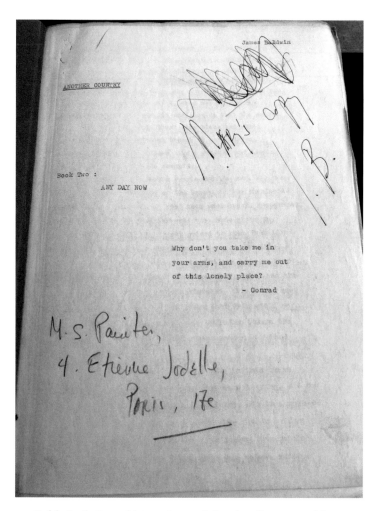

11. Baldwin dedicated his 1961 novel *Another Country* to Mary Painter. This page of the manuscript includes the handwritten inscription, "Mary's Copy." (Bill V. Mullen)

12. Baldwin lived at this address at 81 Horatio Street in Greenwich Village. He wrote parts of his novel *Another Country* here.

James Baldwin (1924-1987)

The great American writer James Baldwin lived in an apartment here from 1958 through 1961. The power and eloquence of Baldwin's varied works impacted ideas about race, class, sexuality, and morality, and played an important role in the civil rights movement. The Village is reflected in the bestselling novel "Another Country," which he worked on while residing here.

Placed by the Greenwich Village Society for Historic Preservation with the generous support of the Two Boots Foundation

13. In 2015, the Greenwich Village Society for Historic Preservation dedicated this plaque to Baldwin's time lived at this Horatio Street address. (Bill V. Mullen)

14. Baldwin in Hyde Park, London. (Allan Warren)

15. In 2014, New York designated 128th Street between Madison Avenue and Fifth Avenue "James Baldwin place." Baldwin lived in the neighborhood at several addresses and attended public school on the block. (Bill V. Mullen)

16. Baldwin attended this public school, P.S. 124, on 128th street in Harlem. It is now called the Harlem Renaissance School. (Bill V. Mullen)

17. The house in St. Paul de Vence in southern France Baldwin purchased in 1971. He spent much of his later years there, and died there in 1987. Scholar Magdalena Zaborowska has explored the role of the house in Baldwin's life in her book *My and My House: James Baldwin's Last Decade in France*. (Daniel Salomons; https://commons.wikimedia.org/wiki/Category:James_Baldwin#/media/File:HouseBaldwinStPaul.jpg)

18. Tombstone of James Baldwin and his mother, Berdis. In Ferncliffe Cemetery and Mausoleum, Westchester County, New York. (Tony Fischer Photography)

by, among others, W.E.B. Du Bois the year he joined the Communist Party; Louis Burnham, also a Communist; and Shirley Graham Du Bois, a member herself. The paper's orientation was to socialism, anti-colonialism, and Pan-Africanism. It featured contributions by some of the leading left African diasporic intellectuals in the world, including C.L.R. James, Kwame Nkrumah, the playwright Lorraine Hansberry, Communist Claudia Jones, and others. It was in his *Freedomways* essay that Baldwin asserted the claim which serves as an epigraph to this chapter: "It is not a question of whether they are going to give me my freedom. I am going to take my freedom."[59] The essay's call for a "metamorphosis" in social relations—Baldwin's euphemism for revolution—targeted at once capitalist inequality, a racist, indifferent state, and Cold War ideology for suppressing the question of black liberation for a minority, and social liberation for the many:

> We have begun to see what happens to a country when it is run according to the rules of a popularity contest; we have begun to see that we ourselves are far more dangerous for ourselves than Khrushchev or Castro. What we do not know about our black citizens is what we do not know about ourselves ... Nothing can save us—not all our money, nor all our bombs, nor all our guns—if we cannot achieve that long, long-delayed maturity.[60]

Meanwhile, FBI Director J. Edgar Hoover was turning the Red Scare lavender by putting Baldwin further in his crosshairs. In the bottom corner of a July 17, 1964, memorandum reporting that Baldwin was still possibly at work on *Blood Counters*, his threatened expose of the FBI (he was not), Hoover handwrote, "Isn't Baldwin a well-known pervert?"[61] Much has been made by historians of Hoover's vengeful closeted homosexuality, as well as the malicious closeted queerness of other notorious Cold War warriors like Joseph McCarthy's personal attorney Roy Cohn. These were the men who helped drive gay and lesbian civil servants out of the government, out of universities, out of work, sometimes to suicide or death. The FBI was in fact still obsessed with depictions of queer sex in Baldwin's novel *Another Country*, and now had the popular critical success of *The Fire Next Time* to elevate Baldwin further into the status of public enemy. In January of that year, Baldwin had also referred to heterosexual sex as "pure desperation" and attacked American homophobia in an interview in the *New York Post*.[62] Baldwin also continued to bait the FBI with his public politics, writing a *New York Post* essay about a week-long riot in Harlem precipitated by a white policeman shooting a 15-year-old African-American boy, James Powell. Baldwin focused in the essay on the rationality of ghetto dwellers' hatred for the cops, a theme of this 1966 essay "Report from Occupied Territory" cited earlier. Baldwin's singular status as a black public intellectual routinely assailing law enforcement cannot be underestimated in why the FBI continued to trail him, read his books, even pick through his garbage for clues to his politics. Baldwin himself was convinced the FBI was wiretapping his phone, a paranoia that was perfectly logical in the context of its ongoing practice of tapping the phones of prominent leaders like Martin Luther King, Jr. Perhaps the apotheosis of Baldwin's expressed contempt for the FBI came in a January 25, 1966 letter to David Leeming from Istanbul. Baldwin meditated in writing on whether the FBI might be reading his mail, "which is, alas, all too probable. I really don't give a shit about that miserable band of cock-suckers, and if they're reading my mail I hope that they read this (repeat: miserable, abject, despicable band of cock-suckers)."[63]

As the civil rights struggle grew, Baldwin's international reputation soared. On February 18, 1965, he debated arch conservative William F. Buckley at Cambridge University. Baldwin famously argued in his remarks that "the American dream is at the expense of the American Negro." He summarized his relationship to American popular culture by describing watching American movies as a child, not realizing that in the cowboy and Indian Western, "the Indian was you."[64] A mere three days after his debate, Malcolm X was assassinated at the Audubon Ballroom in Harlem. For Baldwin, Malcolm's death was an emotional sequel to the murder of his friend Medgar Evers. Malcolm's break with the Nation of Islam in 1964, his trip to Mecca, and his status as a pariah to the U.S. state had earned him considerable sympathy from Baldwin despite their political differences. Always generous with money, Baldwin sent a check for $100 to Malcolm's widow, Betty Shabazz. According to a letter to Baldwin from Alex Haley, she responded by saying "My estimation of Jimmy Baldwin is as high, if not higher, than for any man I know. It's sky high."[65]

Malcolm's death was also another spur to capture history. He undertook nearly immediately to produce a screen adaptation of his 1965 book *The Autobiography of Malcolm X*. In 1966, he came to an agreement with Columbia Studios to produce it. He worked diligently on the script through 1968, 1969, and 1970. The screenplay was finally completed and published in 1972. The finished text, *One Day, When I Was Lost*, to be discussed in Chapter 7, emphasized two primary themes of Malcolm's life that resonated with Baldwin's own: Malcolm's escape from a life of poverty and ghetto violence into political engagement, and his struggle with theology— Malcolm's with Islam, Baldwin's with Christianity. Baldwin's commitment to commemorate and popularize Malcolm's life did not cease there: after the assassination of Martin Luther

King, Jr. in 1968, he vowed to write a book about his relationship to three fallen friends and martyrs of the civil rights
and Black Power era: Medgar Evers, Malcolm, and King. The
book was to be called *Remember This House*. Baldwin never
wrote it, but the idea, and his notes towards it, would become
the inspiration and source for Raoul Peck's biographical film
about Baldwin, *I Am Not Your Negro*, released in 2016.

Baldwin's work and notoriety in the theater deepened considerably after the successful production of *Blues for Mister
Charlie*. Swedish film director Ingmar Bergman, who Baldwin
had met and interviewed in 1960, staged the play in Sweden.
Baldwin intended to attempt to make a film of the play, which
never materialized. On April 16, 1965, his play *The Amen
Corner* opened at the Barrymore Theater in New York. Another
production of it toured that summer in Europe and Israel.
Meanwhile, Baldwin continued to spend time in Istanbul,
where his friend Engin Cezzar helped convince him to try
his hand at directing. Eventually, he agreed to direct *Fortune
and Men's Eyes*, John Herbert's play about a 17-year-old man
arrested for drug use and his relationship in a youth reformatory to three queer cellmates. The play allowed Baldwin to
explore themes he had sketched out in his essay "The Male
Prison," about the carceral restrictions of love for men who
denied, or gave in to, repression of their queer sexual desires.
Baldwin, who complained in a 1965 letter to David Leeming of
being "terribly lonely" in Istanbul, described the play's theme
thusly in an interview, according to Magdalena Zaborowska:
"[The Play] symbolizes masculine loneliness in this century.
This is a universal problem for everyone everywhere in our
age."[66] In 1967, the play was staged in the U.S. at the Actors
Theater in New York, where it was considered transgressive
and shocking to mainstream theatergoers. The first Turkish
production under Baldwin's direction occurred in 1969. Bald-

win's commitment to the play was another indicator that queer themes were becoming more central to his public life and creative work. Zaborowska argues that queer and homosocial relationships in Istanbul—for some time Baldwin had a French lover there from Martinique named Alain—helped explain why books written there in total or in part, like *Another Country*, confronted sexual difference along with differences in other forms. She notes that Cass, the white woman from *Another Country*, thinks of the gay white man Eric as an exoticized other, "Turk, Spanish, Jew, Greek, Arabian."[67]

One of Baldwin's most explicit treatments of the interrelationship of race to sex was also published in 1965, the title story of his book of short stories *Going to Meet the Man*. In *Blues for Mister Charlie*, Baldwin had drawn on the history of miscegenation hysteria, lynching, and interracial sexual drama, including the Till case, as the basis for Lyle's killing of Richard Henry. A subplot to that story was Lyle's sexual use of and mastery over the bodies of vulnerable black women, what Lyle calls in reference to genitalia, "poontang." "Going To Meet the Man" makes graphic, corporeal, and explicit what Baldwin perceived as the psychosexual basis of white male racism. The story opens with Jesse, a deputy sheriff in a segregated southern town, failing to perform in bed after demanding sex from his wife, Grace. In the interlude after, he recounts a story of using a cattle prod on a black civil rights protester who continues to defy and curse him despite being severely beaten. The boy's resistance, and the relentless resistance of protesters, exhausts him—"Each day, each night, he felt worn out, aching, with their smell in his nostrils and filling his lungs, as though he were drowning—drowning in niggers."[68] As if to gather himself and his strength, he then lapses into a memory, nearly a reverie, of his father taking him to his first public lynching as a boy. The memory culminates with a vivid imaging of the knife that castrates the victim, his genitalia cut clean, and "a wound between what had been his legs."[69] That memory, combined with the memory of the beaten boy in his jail cell, arouses Jesse: "Something bubbled up in him, his nature again returned to him."[70] The story culminates grotesquely: "He thought of the morning, and grabbed her, laughing and crying, crying and laughing, and he whispered, as he stroked her, as he took her, 'Come on sugar, I'm going to do you like a nigger, just like a nigger, come on sugar, and love me just like you'd love a nigger.'"[71]

Baldwin's frequent contention that in the United States the African-American male is perceived in phallic terms is made a literal thematic in the story. Jesse's social power both represses and feeds off of the real and imaginary threat of black resistance to the social order. U.S. slavery's preclusion and prevention of black men from coupling with white women, white male power exercised as rape over black women, and the real interracial sexual desire that courses beneath these discursive axes is all conjoined in the story's equivalence of black castration and white consummation. The phallic "absence" of the lynching wound is the present power of white male sexuality in the story. As Baldwin put it in 1972, "it is absolutely certain that white men, who invented the nigger's big black prick, are still at the mercy of this nightmare, and are still, for the most part, doomed, in one way or another, to attempt to make this prick their own."[72]

*   *   *

As the U.S. prosecuted its war against Vietnam, U.S. imperialism continued to center itself in Baldwin's political development. In April of 1966, from Istanbul, he wrote a letter to Mimi Shofer of the Charter Group for a Pledge of Conscience in regards to his ongoing support for the Harlem Six in their efforts to get a new trial. "Every time I hear the Negro soldier praised for his valor in the jungles of South East Asia," he wrote, "I think of the jungles of Harlem and of how many men I knew perished before my eyes there; how that very same soldier, for that very same valor, is murdered in the streets of Mississippi and beaten in the streets of New York. Well. Before we free the South East Asians, let's free the Harlem Six."[73] In November of 1966, the philosopher and activist Bertrand Russell organized two simultaneous tribunals to protest U.S. violence in the war. Baldwin was one of 25 activists and intellectuals from 18 countries named to be original members of the tribunal. Others included Jean Paul-Sartre, Tariq Ali, writer Julio Cortázar, novelist Alice Walker, SNCC chairman Stokely Carmichael, and Simone de Beauvoir. Russell modeled the tribunal on the Nuremberg trials against the Nazis, intending to charge the administration of Lyndon Johnson, the U.S. President, with war crimes against the people of Vietnam.

Baldwin's statement for the tribunal was published in the Reader's Forum of *Freedomways*. The essay was one of Baldwin's most explicitly anti-imperialist and internationalist to date. Baldwin acknowledges the war as a "Western" war first fought by French colonizers then inherited by the U.S. He compares it to other ongoing Western imperial crimes—the English in South Africa and Rhodesia, the French in Algiers. The war in Vietnam, he notes, raises the question of whether in an age of Cold War superpowers small nations "will be allowed to work out their own destinies and live as they feel they should"—the theme of self-determination from Baldwin's earlier writings on Black Power.[74] The war also underscores the long history of colonialism and imperialism: "Why, for example, is Africa underpopulated, and why do the resources of, say, Sierra Leone, belong to Europe?"[75] Baldwin then analogizes U.S. crimes abroad with crimes at home:

Long, long before the Americans decided to liberate the Southeast Asians they decided to liberate me: my ancestors carried these scars to the grave, and so will I. A racist society can't but fight a racist war—that is the bitter truth. The assumptions acted on at home are also acted on abroad, and every American Negro knows this, for he, after the American Indian, was the first "Vietcong" victim. We were bombed first. How, then, can I believe a word you say, and what gives you the right to ask me to die for you?[76]

Baldwin closed the essay with a thundering condemnation of the United States government as what Martin Luther King, Jr. would call in 1967, in his speech "Beyond Vietnam," the "greatest purveyor of violence in the world today."[77] "The American idea of freedom," wrote Baldwin, "and still more the way this freedom is imposed, have made America the most terrifying nation in the world"; and, "The American endeavor in Vietnam is totally indefensible and totally doomed, and I wish to go on record as having no part of it. When the black population of America has a future, so will America have a future—not till then. And when the black population of the world has a future, so will the Western nations have a future—and not till then."[78]

Baldwin's commitment to an internationalist theory of Black Power—an idea that by 1967 he was calling a "political necessity"[79]—was tested by the emergence around 1966 of anti-semitism within black nationalist politics. Its primary catalyst was a February 1966 article in Daniel Watts's *Liberator*, for whom Baldwin had written and on whose advisory board he sat, titled "Semitism in the Black Ghetto" by Eddie Ellis. The article argued that a Jewish conspiracy existed to manipulate, dominate, and control black Americans and black politics. It charged, for example, that "Zionists" had used the writings of W.E.B. Du Bois to attack the black nationalist figure Marcus Garvey. This anti-semitism nested within a larger conspiratorial narrative of Jewish "betrayal" of African-Americans. One alleged betrayal was in the form of Jewish leftists and Communists during the 1930s and 1940s attempting to manipulate African-Americans into forfeiting their racial identity, or collective group solidarity, in the name of becoming Marxists. This was an argument of former Communist Harold Cruse's influential 1967 book *The Crisis of the Negro Intellectual*. A second current of anti-semitism was a hoary equivalence of Jews with capitalism and wealth. This idea infiltrated the SNCC, whose newsletter published "'Third World Round-up' The Palestine Problem: Test Your Knowledge." Among its 32 talking points was criticism of a U.S. government which had "constantly supported Israel and Zionism by sending military and financial aid," along with an allegation with blatantly anti-semitic overtones that Jewish wealth—the Rothschild's—"control much of Africa's mineral wealth."[80]

As the SNCC document attests, in some quarters of the black nationalist movement Zionism—a setter-colonial ideology that was the basis for the conquest of Palestine—was being equated with Judaism. A spur to this misinterpretation was Israel's Six-Day War of 1967 against Syria and Jordan, which resulted in the annexation of the Golan Heights, Gaza, and East Jerusalem. Concurrently, but separately, Israel's shifting ascent into a Western imperial power was beginning to fray even longstanding support among most African-Americans for the state of Israel. W.E.B. Du Bois, for example, an ardent supporter of its creation, began to shift his thinking when Israel joined with France and Britain in 1956 in an attempt to seize the Suez Canal.[81] Du Bois had himself once seen the early twentieth-century Zionist aspiration for a Jewish state as a possible model for African-American self-determination.

The challenge facing long-time critics of anti-semitism like Baldwin, then, was how to delineate a politics of black-Jewish solidarity while rejecting racism, imperialism, and anti-semitism in all of its forms. Towards this end he took two important steps. The first was resigning from the advisory board of *Liberator* in protest of its decision to publish Ellis's article. With his resignation, Baldwin also published an article in the Reader's Forum of *Freedomways* titled "Anti-Semitism and Black Power." The essay takes a backdoor into its argument, leading with a description of the contemporary United States as a "holocaust" in which many are dying. "We are a criminal nation, built on a lie."[82] Baldwin then argues that while blacks are suffering, it is the "system which created" the rich and powerful "which must be isolated, atomized, attacked, and destroyed":

> And I think we must be very clear-headed about this, for no people have ever been in a revolutionary situation so bizarre. It is a revolution which has all the aspects of a civil war; but at the same time, it is happening all over the globe, and America is fighting it all over the globe—using, by no means incidentally, vast numbers of its surplus and despised population ... if enough Vietnamese and black Americans are blown into eternity, the world will be made safe—for business.[83]

Baldwin invokes U.S. imperialism and its wars against liberation in South Africa and Cuba as a means of arguing for an interracial, internationalist solidarity against an anti-semitism which threatens to divide blacks and Jews. "If one accepts my basic assumption, which is that all men are brothers—

simply because all men share the same condition, however different the details of their lives may be—then it is perfectly possible ... that in re-creating ourselves, in saving ourselves, we can re-create and save many others ... The value of a human being is never indicated by the color of his skin." The *Liberator* article, and the threat of black anti-semitism, Baldwin concludes, only threatens to affirm the ideology of the enemy—white supremacy—and defer the "revolution" which might overturn it. About Daniel Watts and the *Liberator*, Baldwin writes, "Why, then, when we should be storming capitols, do they take refuge in the most ancient and barbaric of the Europeans myths? Do they want us to become better? Or do they want us, after all, carefully manipulating the color black, merely to become white?"[84]

Baldwin constructed a much deeper and considered essay on these same themes in the *New York Times Magazine* in April of 1967. Titled "Negroes Are Anti-Semitic Because They're Anti-White," the essay argues that Christianity and white supremacy were themselves the seed of anti-semitism in the West, and that African-Americans were susceptible to the influence of both: "The root of anti-Semitism among Negroes, is, ironically, the relationship of colored peoples—all over the globe—to the Christian world."[85] Capitalism, Baldwin argued, had exacerbated anti-semitism among African-Americans by placing Jews in an exploitative relationship to black communities like Harlem as shop owners and landlords. It is by accepting this exploitative relationship that Baldwin argues Jews become, in the eyes of African-Americans, "white." "Whiteness," in other words, is a social relationship of exploitation of people of color. The essay also argues that "The Jew's suffering is recognized as part of the moral history of the world and the Jew is recognized as a contributor to the world's history; that is not true for the blacks."[86] Baldwin cites as an example the creation of the state of Israel, and its celebration in the Western world, events he cannot imagine occurring for blacks. Baldwin concludes the essay with these two reflections on how black Americans generalize in their views of Jews:

> He is singled out by Negroes not because he acts differently from other White men, but because he doesn't. His major distinction is given him by that history of Christendom, which has so successfully victimized both Negroes and Jews. And he is playing in Harlem the role assigned him by Christians long ago: he is doing their dirty work.[87]

> The crisis taking place in the world, and in the minds and hearts of black men everywhere, is not produced by the star of David, but by the old, rugged, Roman cross on which Christendom's most celebrated Jew was murdered. And not by Jews.[88]

Baldwin's two essays were attempts to denounce and reject what he perceived as the explicit anti-semitism in the *Liberator* article. They were also blatant appeals for black-Jewish unity in the face of white supremacy and capitalist exploitation. The weakness of the essays is their universalizing tendency: in discussing only petty bourgeois Jews, Baldwin failed to demonstrate black-Jewish working-class unity as a continuing element of U.S. social life. By focusing narrowly on ghettos in the U.S., Baldwin also elided areas of civil rights organizing, or student life, and the left, where there was ongoing unity. To take one famous example, in 1964 James Chaney, Andrew Goodman, Michael Schwerner, civil rights activists, and voter registration organizers were murdered in Mississippi by Klansmen. Chaney was black, Goodman and Schwerner Jewish. Finally, the essay's abstraction of the category of "whiteness" into a broad metaphor of oppression skirted consideration of the unequal experiences of racism and exploitation for people who were nominally "white."

Today, we can understand Baldwin's essay as a major stepping stone in two areas of political urgency he helped to predict: the role of the state of Israel in the production of Western racism, imperialism, and ethnonationalism; and the "social constructedness" of race and racial identity, including for white Anglo-Saxon Protestants. If the world, as Baldwin once predicted, would never be "white" again in his time, it is partly because he not only predicted but helped to advance its withering away.

*　*　*

Every day in the Black Power era, the personal was political for James Baldwin. In the spring of 1967, his friend, former body-guard, and chaperone Tony Maynard was arrested in Hamburg, Germany and charged with the murder of a white U.S. Marine. The alleged episode had taken place during a street encounter in Greenwich Village. Maynard was poor, black, and had fled the country after a phony charge of car theft was made against him. In Germany, he was beaten by German police in prison. Baldwin immediately flew to Hamburg to be sure he had legal representation. For the next five years, Baldwin would be consumed with defending Maynard, raising money to assist with his defense, and writing about his case. His arrest, prison sentences, and two trials would become the basis for Baldwin's 1974 novel *If Beale Street Could Talk*, to be discussed in Chapter 6.

Baldwin was also drawn more literally into the Black Power movement by Stokely Carmichael. Carmichael was born in Trinidad and Tobago. After moving to Harlem as a child, he participated in the "Freedom Rides" organized by CORE in

1961 attempting to integrate interstate buses in the American South. In 1964, he became a field organizer in Mississippi for the SNCC. Baldwin first met Carmichael in March of 1965 when he participated in a march from Selma, Alabama to Montgomery, mainly in support of black voting rights. Carmichael had been recruited to help organize the march by James Forman. Both SNCC and CORE favored direct action tactics which at times conflicted with the goals of the Southern Christian Leadership Conference headed up by Martin Luther King, Jr. Carmichael also organized the Lowndes County Freedom Organization to register voters.

In 1966, Carmichael became chairman of SNCC. He was participating in a "March Against Fear" organized by James Meredith when he was arrested in Greenwood, Mississippi. After his release, he gave the speech where he coined the term "Black Power," which he described as "a call for black people in this country to unite, to recognize their heritage, to build a sense of community. It is a call for black people to define their own goals, to lead their own organizations."[89] In 1967, after stepping down as SNCC chair, Carmichael co-authored with Charles Hamilton the book *Black Power* which codified his thinking about the term. The book advocated opposition to the U.S. war in Vietnam, but was generally more reformist than revolutionary in its political orientation.

In February 1968, Baldwin wrote his own, more militant response to Carmichael's book, an essay simply titled "Black Power." As he had done since his 1963 speeches for CORE, Baldwin attempted to historicize the concept of Black Power, arguing that Carmichael "didn't coin it. He simply dug it up again from where it's been lying since the first slaves hit the gangplank."[90] The essay invoked earlier generations of radical black activists like Frederick Douglass and Paul Robeson to propose that all forms of black political self-activity constituted links in the chain of Black Power history: "when a black man, whose destiny and identity have always been controlled by others, decides and states that he will control his own destiny and rejects the identity given to him by others, he is talking revolution."[91] Baldwin also located the Black Power idea in its opposition to U.S. violence and imperialism:

> Let us attempt to face the fact that we are a racist society, racist to the very marrow, and we are fighting a racist war. No black man in chains in his own country, and watching the many deaths occurring around him every day, believes for a moment that America cares anything at all about the freedom of Asia. My own condition, as a black man in America, tells me what Americans really feel and really want, and tells me who they really are. And, therefore, every bombed village is my hometown.[92]

Baldwin's idea that the Vietnamese village is the ghetto was resonant with writings by the SNCC and the emerging Black Panther Party that black Americans were internally colonized subjects in the United States. That anti-colonial perspective, fostered for Baldwin in France by the Algerian War, nurtured by the war in Vietnam, would deepen and harden in Baldwin's thinking from 1968 and through the remainder of his life. We will explore its contours in subsequent chapters.

In 1965, Baldwin had begun another novel that was in many ways the culmination of a particular period of his life, from the time he lived in and left Harlem in the 1940s, to the moment of the arrival of Black Power. *Tell Me How Long the Train's Been Gone* was published in June of 1968. The book had taken a long time to write precisely because of Baldwin's numerous political commitments and engagements during the 1960s, and because events were constantly drawing his attention away from the book. "I seem to be writing my novel between—or rather, during—race riots," he wrote to his friend Eugene Lerner on August 9, 1966, "and it does not help my morale to live with the knowledge that I said it was going to happen."[93] The book was composed in parts in New York, San Francisco, and Istanbul. It is dedicated to three people who had become fixtures in Baldwin's emotional life: David Leeming, his literary aide and confidante; Engin Cezzar, the Turkish actor, and now close friend; and his younger brother David Baldwin. Of the three David Baldwin figures most prominently. At the center of the novel is a thinly veiled rendering of the Baldwin brothers' relationship, the closest one Baldwin had to any member of his family.

The book begins in 1945 in Harlem. Leo Proudhammer, the narrator and protagonist, is the son of a train porter, a "ruined Barbados peasant," his mother a seamstress in the garment district in New York. Leo's elder brother by seven years is Caleb. The novel begins *in media res*: Leo, middle aged, is a semi-successful stage actor, a lifelong aspiration fulfilled. In the book's first paragraph, he is stricken with a heart attack. As in many Baldwin novels, the book is structured so that past is present: we return to Leo's childhood years and its first major trauma, Caleb's arrest, imprisonment, and separation from his brother. That wound, or gap, is one Leo aspires to fill throughout the novel. We are alerted to its scope in the most breathtaking passage of queer love Baldwin had yet committed to paper, a description of Leo and Caleb, as youth, making love to each other. The episode is Leo's attempt to heal Caleb who has been traumatized physically and emotionally by his time in prison. The scene is both erotic and familial. "Brotherhood" in the novel is a totalizing relationship that transcends the limits of bourgeois morality, Christian doctrine, and sexual taboo. It is the most emotionally and physically complete experience of same-sex sex in Baldwin's writing:

> He held me and he kissed me and he murmured my name. I was full of attention, I was full of wonder. My brother had never, for me, had a body before. And in truth, I had never had a body before, either, though I carried it about with me and occasionally experimented with it ... More than anything on earth, that night, I wanted Caleb's joy. His joy was mine. When his breathing changed and his tremors began, I trembled too, with joy, with joy, with joy and pride, and we came together.[94]

This passage advanced Baldwin's public presentation of queer erotics past the closeted and anxious self-inflicted violence of *Giovanni's Room* and the destructive "taboo" of *Another Country*. Baldwin deploys the passage also as a foil to Leo's other romantic and sexual interest in the novel, Barbara, a white actress, with whom he shares professional intimacy, but nothing approaching the depth of his relationship to Caleb. Leo self-identifies in the book as "bisexual," a term Baldwin at times used to describe himself, and it is easy to perceive Leo as Baldwin's fictional avatar. Most evident of this is the fictionalization of Baldwin's experience with the Actors Studio in New York, recreated here as part of Proudhammer's theatrical ascent. Two of the teachers in the fictional workshop are modeled, argues David Leeming, on Lee Strasberg and Cheryl Crawford, with whom Baldwin worked. The former was famous for instilling "method" acting into his subjects, a process Baldwin disliked, and which is presented negatively in the novel. The character of the director, Konstantine Rafaeleto, is based on Baldwin's good friend Elia Kazan. Even the Jewish landlord in the novel, despised by the Proudhammer family, is according to Leeming modeled on a Ms. Rabinowitz who the Baldwin family despised.[95]

Baldwin uses the backdrop of Leo's life to mark out political themes resonant with his non-fiction writing of the 1940s and 1950s: police brutality, U.S. military violence (the dropping of bombs on Nagasaki and Hiroshima); McCarthyism; the crude commercialism of the American film and theater industries; racism in the theater business. The book counter-poses to these public traumas the central consolation of black family; the book's commitment to black love and black self-love are also firsts in Baldwin's fiction, and entirely different registers of the African-American family that we see in the autobiographical *Go Tell It On the Mountain*. This notion of black family is kin to the book's lionization of Black Power. Leo's ultimate love interest in the novel is a young black radical named Christopher who swoops into his late life bringing with him the accouterments, and the people, of the black freedom struggle. Here is a description:

> Every once in a while, some of Christopher's friends came by the house. All of his friends were black … I liked Christopher's friends very much, young, bright, eager, raggedy-assed, taking no shit from anyone; … They were younger than they thought there were, much: they might arrive in their Castro berets, their Castro beards, their parkas and hoods and sweaters and thin jeans or corduroys and heavy boots, and with their beautiful black kinky hair spinning around their heads like fire and prophecy … and with Camus or Fanon or Mao on their person, or with *Muhammad Speaks* under their arms.[96]

Christopher may well stand in for Stokely Carmichael, or any of the other young black militants of the period. Through the differences in the ages of Leo and Christopher, Baldwin writes himself into the relationship as an elder in the movement. Yet Christopher is also Baldwin's surrogate, speaking the self-same language of the movement as in Baldwin's essays like "Down at the Cross" and "Black Power." Here is Christopher addressing a wealthy white male character in the book:

> You had a good thing going for you. You'd done already killed off most of the Indians and you'd robbed them of their land and now you had all these blacks working for you for nothing and you don't want no black cat from Walla Walla being able to talk to no black cat from Boola Boola. If they could have talked to each other, they might have figured out a way of chopping off your heads, and getting rid of *you* … So you gave us Jesus. And told us it was the *Lord's* will that we should be toting the barges and lifting the bales while you all sat on your big, fat, white behinds and got rich.[97]

Black Christopher is Baldwin's prophetic mouthpiece in the novel. *Tell Me How Long the Train's Been Gone* is the autobiography of Baldwin's own transformation across time from Harlem no-name to middle-aging celebrity—he was 44 and at the peak of his notoriety by 1968— to Black Power intellectual laureate. Baldwin *was* more and more "talking revolution" by the time the curtain came down on his fourth novel. Yet even he could not have prophesied or predicted the next break in the political levee of his life and the life of the black freedom struggle.

6
Morbid Symptoms and Optimism of the Will: 1968–79

The crisis consists precisely in the fact that the old is dying and the new cannot be born; in this interregnum a great variety of morbid symptoms appear.[1]

Antonio Gramsci, *Selections from the Prison Notebooks*, 1930

An old world is dying, and a new one, kicking in the belly of its mother, time, announces that it is ready to be born.[2]

James Baldwin, *No Name in the Street*, 1972

I'm optimistic about the future, but not about the future of this civilization. I'm optimistic about the civilization which will replace this one.[3]

James Baldwin, interview with John Hall, 1970

I was, in some way, in those years, without entirely realizing it, the Great Black Hope of the Great White Father.[4]

James Baldwin, *No Name in the Street*, 1972

From 1968 to 1977, Baldwin underwent a re-evaluation of his personal and political life consonant with the revolutionary aspirations—and failures—of the Black Power era. As world historical movements against capitalism, the U.S. war in Vietnam, Western imperialism, and democratic crisis crested and fell, Baldwin attempted to draw political lessons to construct from them a more durable dissidence. From 1968 to 1973, Baldwin was pushed by a sympathetic affiliation with the Black Panther Party into a sharper critique of U.S. militarism and imperialism. The revolutionary sexual politics of the 1960s—one of its last and most potent chapters—were also life-altering. The emergence of black feminism, Third World feminism, and queer liberation politics again compelled Baldwin to rethink race and especially masculinity. In conversations with women intellectuals—especially poet Nikki Giovanni—and in response to public homophobic attacks by leaders in the movement, Baldwin was driven to a new awareness of gender dynamics, women's oppression, and the masculinist biases of the revolutionary left, including the black nationalist left, to which he had conjoined himself.

Baldwin's writing during this time is thus heavily marked by retrospection, self-reflection, and revision. His 1972 book *No Name in the Street* is his most dialectical account of his life: a revisiting of his years in Paris and the early 1960s through a newly radical, anti-imperialist perspective honed across the years during and after. Baldwin struggles in the book with massive emotional losses wrought by political assassinations and violent attacks on the civil rights and Black Power movements, recognizing even his own place in history as mediated by events beyond his control. Both of his major works of fiction during this period—*If Beale Street Could Talk* and his screenplay about the life of Malcolm X—draw harsh lessons about legacies of state repression, police violence, and the criminalization of black political dissents gleaned from the Black Power period. Thus, Baldwin oscillates wildly in his political mood of the 1970s, alternately denouncing the U.S. as a developing totalitarian state, while retaining a commitment to private political activism and solidarity with global anti-imperialist movements begun earlier, most especially the Palestinian liberation struggle. He also begins to build a refuge and retreat for the last third of his life in southern France, where declining health and sometime exhaustion resulted in a decreased pace of work. This period might then be considered Baldwin's reconfiguration and self-fashioning into an elder of black liberation and letters, determined to remain a radical political conscience, an optimist of the will, in the face of what he sometimes felt was a missed American revolution.

*   *   *

The year 1968 was, after 1963, the most important single political year in Baldwin's life, and in some ways its dark sequel. Where the latter was marked by Baldwin's entrée into the Student Nonviolent Coordinating Committee (SNCC) and support for the March on Washington, the former was shattered for Baldwin by Martin Luther King, Jr.'s assassination in Memphis on April 4, 1968. Baldwin was in Palm Springs, California, working on his screenplay adaptation of Malcolm X's *Autobiography*, when his brother David called to tell him that King had been shot. Baldwin had already developed complicated feelings about King's legacy: in *No Name in the Street*, he remembers agreeing with Malcolm X's assessment that the March on Washington should have been more militant and confrontational per the original plans for the event (Malcolm called it the "Farce on Washington"). At the same time, Baldwin recognized King as the "hope" of the movement, a hope that was extinguished with his assassination: "we've marched and petitioned for a decade, and now it's clear that there's no point in marching or petitioning. And what happens I don't know, but when they killed Martin they killed that hope. They didn't kill that dream, but they did kill that hope."[5]

Extraordinarily, two days after King's assassination, Black Panther Party member Bobby Hutton was murdered by police on the streets of Oakland, California. Baldwin now faced a logistical dilemma symbolic of a political one: which funeral should he attend? Baldwin had by April of 1968 moved into close political sympathy and personal affiliation with the Black Panther Party. The party had been formed in Oakland, California in 1966. On October 29, 1967, Baldwin had been formally introduced to the party via a personal meeting with founder Huey Newton in Oakland. From the start, Baldwin saw the Panthers as an historically necessary response to intolerable racial and economic conditions for African-Americans. "[T]he advent of the Panthers," he wrote in *No Name in the Street*, "was as inevitable as the arrival of the day in Montgomery, Alabama, when Mrs. Rosa Parks refused to stand up on that bus and give her seat to a white man."[6] For Baldwin, the Panthers' special appeal to black communities was their willingness to stand up to police violence by exploiting open-carry gun laws to build armed and mobilized self-defense cells that would monitor, and confront, ghetto police—a plague Baldwin had targeted in his writings since the 1940s. Baldwin also endorsed other elements of the Black Panther Party's agenda, including free school breakfasts and lunches, community schools, and healthcare programs for Oakland residents. These, he wrote, "are antidotes to the demoralization which is the scourge of the ghetto."[7]

Just as importantly, Baldwin saw the Panthers as a significant challenge to the repressive, imperialist power of the American state which had prosecuted the Vietnam War, and terrorized black communities with tactics of humiliation, surveillance, violence, and neglect:

Nothing more thoroughly reveals the actual intentions of this country, domestically and globally, than the ferocity of the repression, the storm of fire and blood which the Panthers have been forced to undergo merely for declaring themselves as men—men who want "land, bread, housing, education, clothing, justice and peace." The Panthers thus become the native Vietcong, the ghetto became the village in which the Vietcong were hidden, and in the ensuing search-and-destroy operations, everyone in the village became suspect.[8]

Baldwin was referring to several spokes at once in the wheel of the state's repressive apparatus. By 1972, when this passage was written, Black Panther Party leaders Fred Hampton and Mark Clark had been assassinated by Chicago police on December 4, 1969, aided by U.S. federal government surveillance and infiltration via the FBI COINTELPRO (Counterintelligence Program). By 1972, Black Panther Party leaders Eldridge Cleaver, Bobby Seale, and David Hilliard had already been incarcerated by the state. "The government," wrote Baldwin, "is absolutely determined to wipe the Black Panthers from the face of the earth: which is but another way of saying that it is absolutely determined to keep the nigger in his place."[9] Baldwin's comparison of the Panthers to the Vietcong echoed an analysis developed in 1967 and 1968 by the Black Panther Party and SNCC that African-American ghetto dwellers were internally colonized subjects: domestic victims of U.S. imperialism at home and abroad. Baldwin extended the implications of the argument further, drawing back to his long-time support for political national liberation and self-determination struggles:

any real commitment to black freedom in this country would have the effect of re-ordering all our priorities, and altering all our commitments, so that, for horrendous example, we would be supporting black freedom fighters in South Africa and Angola, and would not be allied with Portugal, would be closer to Cuba than we are to Spain, would be supporting the Arab nations instead of Israel, and would never have felt compelled to follow the French into Southeast Asia.[10]

The Panthers also revived and populated anew Baldwin's long-time, lingering faith in the possibility of socialism in the United States. Famously, the Panthers built their Oakland chapter in part by selling copies of Chairman Mao's *Little Red Book* at the University of California, Berkeley campus and using the money to buy guns. Panther study groups in Oakland and elsewhere included analysis of the readings of Marx, Mao, Che Guevara, and Frantz Fanon. In *No Name in the Street*, Baldwin professed a shared faith in the Panther version of a socialist U.S. "Huey believes, and I do, too, in the necessity of establishing a form of socialism in this country— what Bobby Seale would probably call a "Yankee Doodle type" socialism":

This means an indigenous socialism, formed by, and responding to, the real needs of the American people ... The necessity for a form of socialism is based on the observation that the world's present economic arrangements doom most of the world to misery; that the way of life dictated by these arrangements is both sterile and immoral; and finally, that there is no hope for peace in the world so long as these arrangements obtain.[11]

Baldwin here imperfectly weds his anti-colonial politics dating to the Algerian War against the French, to his even longer aspiration—dating to his 1940s anti-Stalinism—

for a socialism neither Washington nor Moscow: this is the most prescient meaning of his use of the term "indigenous." Indeed, influenced by the non-aligned movement of Third World countries, Baldwin referred to China in the 1970s as "the only faint hope that the Third World has. People in truncated revolts occurring all over the world can't look to Russia and America for aid."[12] This position, too, was influenced by Panther support for Maoism.

According to his FBI file, Baldwin spoke at a Black Panther Party meeting in Oakland in May of 1968, where he told the assembled that his next book would be titled *The Fire This Time*.[13] According to his biographer, David Leeming, Baldwin hosted a birthday party and fundraising rally for Huey Newton in Oakland after Newton was arrested in 1967 and charged with killing a police officer, giving rise to the popular slogan "Free Huey."[14] Baldwin had actually met Newton for the first time on the day of his arrest. Newton was initially convicted, but then freed after an appeals process determined that inappropriate deliberation procedures had been used during his trial.

Yet a lasting, important mark of Baldwin's association with the Panthers was also a brutal scar. Eldridge Cleaver, a former prison inmate convicted of rape, and minister of information for the Oakland Black Panther Party after his release, published his prison memoir and autobiography *Soul on Ice* in 1967. Cleaver had started writing the book while an inmate at Folsom Prison in California. *Soul on Ice* is a reactionary book in many ways, defending black male rape of white women as political rebellion, and positing a hare-brained theory of genetic mutation as an explanation for racial difference and racism. The book is also intensely homophobic, equating black male heterosexuality with healthy black nationalism, and queer black identity with betrayal of it. Assessing Baldwin's novels like

Giovanni's Room and *Another Country*, Cleaver argued in the book that the representation of queer relationships including white males (David or Eric, for example) was tantamount to race treason by Baldwin. As Cleaver wrote, "There is in James Baldwin's work the most grueling, agonizing, total hatred of the blacks, particularly of himself, and the most shameful, fanatical, fawning, sycophantic love of the whites that one can find in the writings of any black American writer of note in our time."[15] Cleaver also equates black male sexual desire for the white Other with a particular form of black emasculation, and betrayal of black national unity: "Many Negro homosexuals, acquiescing in this racial death-wish, are outraged because in their sickness they are unable to have a baby by a white man."[16]

Baldwin's first public written response to Cleaver came in his 1972 book *No Name in the Street*, where he wrote: "I felt that he [Cleaver] used my public reputation against me both naively and unjustly, and I also felt that I was confused in his mind with the unutterable debasement of the male—with all those faggots, punks, and sissies, the sight and sound of whom, in prison, must have made him vomit more than once." In a *Paris Review* interview published years later, Baldwin said, "My real difficulty with Cleaver, sadly, was visited on me by the kids who were following him, while he was calling me a faggot and the rest of it. I would come to a town to speak, Cleveland, let's say, and he would've been standing on the very same stage a couple of days earlier. I had to try to undo the damage I considered he was doing."[17]

Cleaver's attack on Baldwin was the most high-profile and public vilification of his sexuality to date. It has led over time to a popular misconception that the Black Panther Party was a uniformly homophobic organization. This is belied by the historical record. On August 15, 1970, for example, Huey Newton gave a speech on gay and lesbian liberation and women's rights. While slipping at times into clumsy heterosexual and heteronationalist stereotype, Newton defended queer sexuality, and argued about the Panthers, "We should try to form a working coalition with the gay liberation and women's liberation groups. We must always handle social forces in the most appropriate manner."[18]

On balance, we should read Cleaver's attack, and Baldwin's response, as the political cost of his lifelong battle to create space in public discourse and the black freedom struggle for black queer sexuality. The Black Power movement, like the civil rights struggle, was in its time dominated by male figures, masculinist projections of power, homosociality, and heteronationalist politics. Just as Bayard Rustin paid a price in the latter, Baldwin did in the former. Yet as recent scholarship by Donna Murch, Robyn Spencer, and others have shown, women within the Black Panther Party fought for gender equality via campaigns for contraception and free health care services, like pap smears, for women. Newton's speech aligning gay and lesbian politics with women's politics was both a sign of their mutual marginalization within the broader black freedom struggle, and their inevitable conjoining. It should not surprise us that the 1970s was a decade when black feminism emerged headed by black lesbian thinkers and writers, like Audre Lorde, many of them critical of homophobia and sexism in black nationalist politics.

Baldwin's careful, calculated reactions to Cleaver also demonstrate how he was personally constrained by heteronormativity within the movement in order to remain credible to it. Scholars have debated his opaque distinction between himself and what he calls "faggots, punks, and sissies." Are these Baldwin's characterizations, or his characterization of Cleaver's homophobic ideas? The attacks did cost Baldwin, both emotionally, and in his public presence. Cleaver gave fuel to the scurrilous representation of Baldwin as a "Martin Luther Queen." The attacks likely muted, or delayed, Baldwin's decision to proclaim queer sexuality as a political sexuality. Yet his openly gay presence within the Black Power movement, and the public weight he attained as a material and political supporter of groups like the SNCC and the Panthers, also likely contributed to Newton's decision to speak about the need for a movement addressing liberation across gender and sexual lines.

Baldwin's work with the Panthers was on a continuum with his reevaluation of political priorities triggered by events in late 1967 and early 1968, including King's assassination. In the summer of 1967, more than 150 race riots erupted across the U.S. in cities like Detroit, Newark, and Buffalo. In every instance, police repression played a role. Again, personal and public events were to converge for Baldwin: on the same day as Huey Newton was charged with murder in Oakland, Baldwin's dear friend and former bodyguard, Tony Maynard, was arrested in Hamburg, Germany, and charged with the murder of a seaman in New York City. As mentioned in Chapter 5, Baldwin immediately flew to Germany and hired attorneys to help prepare his defense. The case provided Baldwin with intimate, first-person confirmation of the legal system's racism. Even though there was evidence that the killer of the New York seaman was white, the courts ignored the evidence, pressing their case against Maynard. As Baldwin wrote about the case, "the question of justice is simply mocked when one considers that no attempt appears to have been made to discover the white assailant, and also by the fact that Tony has been asked to plead guilty and promised a light sentence if he would plead."[19] After an initial hung jury, Maynard was retried, and eventually exonerated, but only after a long prison term. Baldwin drew from the case a new, focused commitment to fighting the criminal justice system. "I do not claim that everyone in prison here is innocent," he wrote, "but I do claim that the law, as it operates, is guilty, and that the prisoners, therefore, are all unjustly imprisoned. Is it conceivable, after all, that any middle-class white boy—or, indeed, almost any white boy—would have been arrested on so grave a charge as murder, with such flimsy substantiation, and forced to spend … three years in prison?"[20]

The Maynard case, the Black Panther Party self-defense campaign, and the continued surveillance, arrest, and incarceration of leading members of the black freedom struggle led to several years of public activism for Baldwin against mass incarceration. In 1970, George Jackson, an inmate at Soledad Prison in California, was charged along with two other inmates with killing a prison guard. Prior to the charge, Jackson had become politically radicalized at Soledad Prison, co-founding the Maoist-Marxist prison group Black Guerilla Family. In 1971, he published a landmark book of the Black Power era, *Soledad Brother: The Prison Letters of George Jackson*, a testimonial of his path to radical politics in prison. In August of 1970, Jackson's younger brother, Jonathan, 17, entered a Marin County courthouse where George was on trial. Armed, he took the presiding judge in the case, the prosecutor, and three female jury members hostage. While they were fleeing the courthouse police gave pursuit, shooting at least one of the people in the car. The judge and several others were killed. Shortly thereafter, political activist, Communist Party member, and University of California, San Diego Professor Angela Davis was arrested and charged with conspiracy for having purchased the guns used in the courtroom takeover.

Baldwin perceived this mode of direct action by black radicals as a profound political escalation. "We're not on the edge of a racial war," he told David Frost in an interview published in 1970, "We're on the edge of a civil war."[21] Indeed, the increasing use of police force to repress and lock up political dissidents was a calculated strategy by the U.S. state spurred by the race rebellions of 1967 and 1968, when King was assassinated. In her groundbreaking 2012 book *The New Jim Crow*, scholar Michelle Alexander assigned this turn in U.S. politics to Richard Nixon's use of a rhetoric of "law and order" in his successful 1968 campaign for the presidency, and the implementation of new punitive laws empowering police like "no-knock" and "stop and frisk" meant to give police power to enter homes and shake down people of color on the streets.[22] Baldwin immediately saw these as a new form of racially specific oppression. "I know what a no-knock, stop-and-frisk law means. It means search and destroy. I know something about the history black people have endured and are still enduring in this place."[23]

Having identified the state as an oppressive force, Baldwin publicly sided with its new, notorious political prisoners. In 1970, he spoke at a meeting in support of Angela Davis and George Jackson at a Radical Actions Project meeting in Paris.[24] In November 1970, he published his now famous "An Open Letter to My Sister, Angela Davis," cited in the Introduction to this book, where he compares the incarceration of Davis and George Jackson to concentration camp internment, and U.S. prisons to Nazi camps. Six months later, on April 20, 1971, Baldwin spoke at a rally for black political prisoners held at the Central Hall in Westminster, England. The organizer for the rally was Angela Davis, free on bail at the time. More than 3,000 people attended. Baldwin used the UK setting to yoke together U.S. and British imperialism as symbols of wider Western domination, slavery, and exploitation: "this hall and this economy and the bank of the Holy Ghost which stands in

Rome were built on a principle which is politely called cheap labor":

> If we translate this from the high English into where I was born, it means that every dark child born—and this was the invention of civilization—was born to be used for the profit of white people. And this hall in which we stand is yet more important than the guns, the fleets, the bombs, because this hall represents the ways in which black people were taught to despise themselves.[25]

Baldwin's speech also directly implicated British colonialism—"We cannot afford ... all those prisoners in South Africa"—and railed against American leaders like President Richard Nixon and then California Governor (and future U.S. President) Ronald Reagan, who was responsible for firing Angela Davis from her university teaching position for her leftist politics. Baldwin also reminded the crowd that since Martin Luther King, Jr. died, a period of civil rights activity ended, and "will never come again," while urging them to build a new struggle for a new society.[26]

The assassinations of King and Hutton in April 1968 and the rebellions that followed also brought Baldwin to deeper, sympathetic reconsideration of direct action politics. On July 7, 1968, he spoke to the World Council of Churches in Sweden. Baldwin returned to a main theme of *The Fire Next Time* in his talk, namely "the actual historical confrontation between the non-white peoples of the world and the white peoples of the world, between the Christian Church and those people outside the Christian Church."[27] His speech quickly moved into a defense and analysis of Black Power, reminding his audience that SNCC organizer and later Black Panther Stokely Carmichael "began his life as a Christian" and spent years performing Christian deeds like feeding the hungry and marching non-violently until "a day came … when this young man grew weary of petitionizing" and turned to Black Power. Baldwin then zeroed in on his Christian audience: "it is astounding, and it says a great deal about Christendom, that whereas black power, the conjunction of the word 'black' with the word 'power', frightens everybody, no one in Christendom appears seriously to be frightened by the operation and the nature of white power."[28] Baldwin invoked South African apartheid, and Nazi Germany as also putatively "Christian" nations where white supremacy ruled. The essay is fueled by Baldwin's sense that especially after the death of Martin Luther King, Jr. black self-determination was the only path forward for African-Americans.

Not surprisingly, Baldwin's thickening identification with Black Power ideology also fostered a re-evaluation of the political contributions of Malcolm X. On February 20 of that year, two months before King's assassination, Baldwin accompanied Malcolm's widow Betty Shabazz to New York City to attend a memorial for the late leader. Baldwin was at the time heavily involved in writing his screenplay about the life of Malcolm. In a January 13, 1968 letter to Eugene Lerner he wrote, "Locking with the monster, Malcolm X, which is doing strange things to my nights and days."[29] The screenplay drew meticulously from the historical record, repeating verbatim key speeches from Malcolm's life. The text of the screenplay is entirely sympathetic, casting Malcolm as a Pan-African internationalist tempered by his famous 1964 trip to Mecca into an advocate for black self-determination as a path to self-determination for all people. Baldwin places Malcolm's speech after his trip to Mecca as the culminating political and dramatic moment of the narrative just before he is shot down at the Audubon:

I hope that once and for all, my Hajj to the Holy City of
Mecca has established our Muslim Mosque's authentic religious affiliation with the seven hundred and fifty million
Muslims of the orthodox Islamic world … Just as I wrote, I
shared true brotherly love with many white-complexioned
Muslims who never gave a single thought to the race, or
to the complexion, of another Muslim … and now that I
am back in America, my attitude here concerning white
people has to be governed by what my black brothers and
I experience here and what we witness here—in terms of
brotherhood. White people have believed for so long that
they were in some way superior that they may never be
able to overcome that sickness. I'll tell you this: our African
brothers are happy to know that we are waking from our long
sleep—after so-called Christian white America had taught
us to be ashamed of our African brothers and homeland![30]

Baldwin here turns Malcolm into a version of himself: advo-
cating interracial solidarity while fearful of the power of white
supremacy to negate it. The screenplay was part of a wholesale
recovery of Malcolm by Baldwin after 1968 as what eulogist
Ossie Davis famously called at his funeral the "Black, shining
prince" of the Black Power era.[31] Baldwin's favorable reconsideration of Malcolm's political development and evolution also
underwrote his self-reflective understanding that in opposing
Malcolm and the Nation of Islam so publicly in the early
1960s, he had become for the dominant culture the "Great
Black Hope of the Great White Father." Baldwin's reconsideration in the early 1970s was meant to inculcate black unity by
suturing Malcolm to his own legacy, and vice versa.

* * *

In December 1969, John Herbert's *Fortune and Men's Eyes*,
directed by Baldwin, opened in Istanbul. The play garnered

generally excellent reviews and special attention for being the first staged public representation of queer life in Turkey. Directing the play was somewhat cathartic for Baldwin after the attacks by Cleaver; he said, "Nor can anyone seriously claim to be shocked by being informed that love between men is among the many human possibilities."[32] Magdalena Zaborowska also notes that the character of Smitty in the play, the youth sentenced to the reformatory, "helped Baldwin to contextualize and revisit his struggles with the fathers of his earlier fictional characters."[33] The play also allowed Baldwin to collaborate with jazz musician Don Cherry, who composed the music, and to visit working-class territories of Turkey where the play toured. In other ways, Istanbul continued to be a productive, creative retreat for Baldwin. His friend Sedat Pakay made a short documentary film, *James Baldwin from Another Place*, in May 1970, and he worked diligently in Istanbul on both his Malcolm X screenplay, and *No Name in the Street*.

But Baldwin's health was also becoming erratic. In early 1970 he was ill with hepatitis. In October of that year he became ill again and was hospitalized in Paris. At the advice of his friend Mary Painter, he went to St. Paul-de-Vence in southern France, near Nice, to recuperate. That decision was life-changing. Baldwin fell in love with the quiet, countryside atmosphere of St. Paul-de-Vence. He purchased a large, rustic house on ten acres of land and hired Bernard Hassell to oversee the estate. From 1970 until the end of his life, that house would become Baldwin's permanent retreat. He would write there, host numerous guests, and hold his fiftieth birthday party in 1974. Zaborowska argues persuasively that Baldwin developed a physical and spiritual sense of "home" in St. Paul-de-Vence that was an antidote to his lifelong complaints about rootlessness, impermanence, and involuntary exile—as Baldwin saw it—from the United States.[34]

In the spring of 1970, Baldwin also visited New York
to record a conversation with the famous anthropologist
Margaret Mead. The discussion was extraordinary mainly for
a testy exchange over Palestine. Bolstered by rising public criticism of Zionism on the left, Baldwin used the interview to
make some of his sharpest public criticisms of Israel, asserting that "the creation of the State of Israel was one of the most
cynical achievements—really murderous, merciless, ugliest
and cynical achievements on the part of the Western nations."

"You have got to remember ... that I have been, in America,
the Arab at the hands of the Jews," he said.[35] Baldwin's comments
were a direct reflection of strong criticisms of Israeli militarism developed by groups like the Black Panthers and SNCC
after the 1967 Six-Day War, and their shift towards sympathetic identification with the Palestinian freedom struggle
as an anti-colonial movement for self-determination. This
perspective was also reflected in a November 1, 1970 advertisement in the *New York Times* titled "An Appeal by Black
Americans Against United States Support for the Zionist Government of Israel." The ad, signed by 56 African-Americans,
was in direct response to the slaughter in Jordan of thousands of Palestinians. The ad proclaimed that the slaughter
would not have been possible without the "encouragement,
armaments, and financial aid of the United States government."[36] It asserted that Israel, South Africa, and Rhodesia
were all settler-colonial states founded on the displacement
of indigenous populations, and compared the racist treatment
of African-Americans, Mexican-Americans, and Palestinian Arabs in the U.S. to Israel's mistreatment of its Palestinian
population. It noted South African support for Israel during
the Six-Day War. While Baldwin was not a signatory to the
letter, the interview with Mead confirmed his own developing analysis of Israel as a Zionist, apartheid state. This analysis

would become full-blown in *No Name in the Street*, cited earlier, where Baldwin equates the black freedom struggle to the struggle for Arab and Palestinian self-determination against Israeli settler-colonial rule, and the struggle of blacks against South African apartheid.

The interview with Mead was another index to Baldwin's increasing public visibility, especially in mainstream media. On November 4, 1971, Baldwin sat for a discussion with Black Arts Movement poet Nikki Giovanni for an episode of the television program *Soul*. Giovanni established herself as a beacon of Black Arts and an emerging black feminist within the arts by virtue of three remarkable books of poetry published between 1967 and 1970, including her first, *Black Feeling, Black Talk*. Giovanni was a regular guest on *Soul*, and helped contribute to its productions.

The conversation between Baldwin and Giovanni was published in 1973 as a book, titled *A Dialogue*. The conversation is a pointed exchange, sometimes debate, about gender roles in black America. Giovanni challenges Baldwin's defense of black masculinity under siege in the United States, arguing that it must be seen as imbricated with hierarchies of racial and gender oppression. Giovanni acknowledges racism against black men, but sees racism as contributing to both sexism and male domestic violence as a response to it. "So I don't like white people and I'm afraid of black men," she tells him.[37] In response to Baldwin's lament about his father's difficulty feeding multiple children, Giovanni argues, "to me the rent has nothing to do with the responsibility that you as a man have to assume with me as a woman."[38] Giovanni also uses the interview to proclaim black feminism as a paramount social movement with a special history and an urgent role to play in the present. "The only thing that's really changed since Martin Luther King, since '54, is the black woman."[39]

Baldwin is generally receptive to Giovanni's arguments but shows a hesitancy to decenter black men and masculinity in his analysis of the United States. Black women, he qualifies, have not so much changed as become more "visible."[40] The two find more common ground in their analysis of queer love, sexuality, and homophobia. Baldwin avers a comparison between the formation of racism and homophobia: "People invent categories in order to feel safe. White people invented black people to give white people identity … . Straight cats invented faggots so they can sleep with them without becoming faggots themselves." The result is a diminished capacity for love between men. Giovanni calls love a "tremendous responsibility" and Baldwin replies, "It's the only one to take, there isn't any other."[41]

More than ten years after this conversation, Baldwin would have a similar dialogue with pathbreaking black lesbian feminist Audre Lorde, to be discussed in Chapter 7. Matt Brim and other Baldwin scholars have noted that the Giovanni dialogue, in combination with Baldwin's male-centric novels and plays, both straight and gay, *does* indicate a general subordination in his work and political thought of women's oppression. Baldwin did reveal, though, simply by sitting down with Giovanni, a responsiveness to the new black feminist currents. Elsewhere in his writing on second-wave feminism of the 1970s Baldwin, learning from the example of Giovanni and others, excoriated the white, middle-class nature of the movement, anticipating the need for an autonomous black feminist current that history would fulfill. Baldwin also perceived the homophobia in mainstream feminism—National Organization of Women leader Betty Friedan's famous hostility to lesbians and lesbian politics as a "lavender menace," as leaving people like himself in the dustbin of history. Yet it is also possible—given our earlier analysis of characters like

Florence in *Go Tell It On the Mountain*, and Juanita in *Blues for Mister Charlie*—to read Baldwin's corpus of writings of the 1950s and 1960s as proto-black feminist. Indeed, by the 1980s, as we shall see, Baldwin had at least caught up, if not merged his politics, with mature women of color feminism.

In July 1972 *Intellectual Digest* published an interview with Baldwin conducted by Herbert Lottman. At the time of publication Baldwin had been living most of the previous year at his new home in St. Paul-de-Vence. Baldwin sat for multiple interviews published in 1972, the common themes of which were revolutions betrayed, deferred, or impending. In a television interview for Thames Television in the UK, for example, Baldwin noted Western support for the creation of Israel, but not for black revolution and self-determination: "You understand everything when white people stand up. You understand your revolution, but you don't understand ours, and that is because history makes you feel in some occult way that we are not like you."[42] In a two-part interview with *Muhammad Speaks*, Baldwin made his appeal for a "Yankee Doodle type socialism" cited earlier, and declared about capitalism, "It is not only a blatant injustice, but pure folly." In his interview with Lottman, Baldwin said, "I've already said I see a holocaust coming. That is the subject of my new book, *No Name in the Street*."[43]

In fact, *No Name in the Street* was Baldwin's anti-capitalist, anti-imperialist sequel to *The Fire Next Time*. Like that book, *No Name in the Street* invokes dark social prophecy, taking its title from the book of Job—"His remembrance shall perish from the earth and He shall have no name in the street." Both of the book's epigraphs suggest revolutionary compulsion and transformational imminence: "If I had-a my way | I'd tear this building down" from a slave song, and "Just a little while to stay here, Just a little while to stay" from a traditional. As noted earlier, the text declares Baldwin's opposition to the war in Vietnam, South African apartheid, and Israeli settler-colonialism; it asserts solidarity with Arab national liberation movements, Palestinian self-determination, and the Black Panther Party; it calls for and predicts a socialist future. The book's epilogue is literally an apocalyptic statement of a world "ready to be born":

> This book is not finished—can never be finished, by me ...
>
> People, even if they are so thoughtless as to be born black, do not come into this world merely to provide mink coats and diamonds for chattering, trivial, pale matrons, or genocidal opportunities for their unsexed, unloved, and, finally, despicable men—oh, pioneers!
>
> There will be bloody holding actions all over the world, for years to come: but the Western party is over, and the white man's sun has set. Period.[44]

Baldwin's revolutionary confidence bore testimony to the advance of the anti-Vietnam war movement in the U.S. and the establishment of cadres in organizations like the Black Panthers. These included his increasingly close friend Bobby Seale, with whom he shared a stage and planned to write a book—who appeared committed to a long-term anti-capitalist, anti-imperialist struggle. At the same time, his pronouncements about how the "revolution" might come about took on an increasingly adventurist cast. Asked by an interviewer for the French magazine *L'Express* in August of 1972, "You believe in the possible victory of the black minority," Baldwin replied "We represent around 10% of the American population. Without talking about starting a revolution, it is certainly enough to destroy society." Asked "In what way?" Baldwin replied, "It is easy for us, for example, to make the cities uninhabitable. It is the Blacks who form the bulk of the urban services."[45] Baldwin here seems to borrow from the playbook of defunct 1960s black nationalist groups like the Revolutionary Action Movement who had once dreamed of an urban guerilla war led by a black vanguard who could disrupt the grid of life in the United States as a first step towards interracial revolution. His prognosis also has a whiff of Maoist militarism fetishized by the Black Panthers, who once dreamed that power might come "from the barrel of a gun." In another interview from this same period Baldwin declared, "We are all Viet Cong!"[46]

Other signs from this period point to Baldwin vacillating between a sense of political foreclosure and personal marginalization brought about by world events. Baldwin was out of the United States much of the time between 1968 and 1972. His decision to spend more time in Turkey and France was an attempt to regather himself after traumas like the King assassination, and the personal attacks from the likes of Cleaver. David Leeming notes that in some quarters of the Black Power movement, Cleaver's portrait of Baldwin stuck and he was branded an "Uncle Tom." It is clear that the attacks hurt him and made him feel like a pariah. In *No Name in the Street*, his last book written mainly in Istanbul, he describes himself, painfully and uncharacteristically, as an "aging, lonely, sexually dubious, politically outrageous, unspeakably erratic freak."[47] Somewhere in this same period, Baldwin broke off a relationship with his lover, Alain. That event, and the Turkish military coup of March 1971, combined with his ailing health, may have advanced his decision to leave the country for good and buy his home that year in St. Paul-de-Vence. Meanwhile, in France, Baldwin was engaging in activity of a more personal nature: helping to care for example for an ailing Beauford Delaney, and writing a catalog tribute for a major retrospective of his work in Paris. He maintained ties and work in the U.S. with small projects, writing an introduction for *The Chasm*, a book about two experimental schools set up in New York in 1969 to try and improve learning for poor black children.

By late 1973, the U.S. political system was in crisis: U.S. President Richard Nixon had been exposed as helping to mastermind the break-in of the Democratic Party headquarters at the Watergate hotel in Washington, DC in order to try to win re-election in 1972. Nixon's landslide victory that year, and the resulting political scandal known as Watergate, were for Baldwin further evidence of the illegitimacy of the U.S. capitalist state. In an important interview with *The Black Scholar* in 1973, Baldwin drew on his memory of Nixon's 1968 repression of anti-war dissidents and commitment to police power to read Watergate as a symptom of racist, authoritarian rule in the U.S. Baldwin referred to the "law and order" Nixon regime as an effort "once again, to keep the nigger in his place," referring to the administration as the "Fourth Reich," a phrase he repeated in his characterization of the U.S. in his 1972 book *No Name in the Street*.[48] Baldwin's intimations of America as fascist was a politically dubious legacy of his proximity to the Black Panthers. As scholar Robyn Spencer notes, the Panthers were influenced by Georgi Dimitroff's "United Front Against Fascism" speech at the 1935 Comintern and held their own United Front Against Fascism Conference. They routinely used the term fascism to describe U.S. finance capital as an arm of U.S. imperialism. Signs of this analysis were evident in Baldwin's *Black Scholar* interview, which includes a reference to the U.S. CIA-backed coup against Salvador Allende in Chile just three months before the interview was published:

It is clear to anyone who thinks, and maybe even to the junkie who suffers, that the situation of black America is related to the situation of Mexicans, to all of Latin America. It's related to the military junta in Chile; with the misery of the people called the "have nots." It's not an act of God and it is not an accident ... . It is something which is necessary for the well being of the "master race" so that the poor of Latin America, or the poor of Vietnam, and me are in the same bag and are oppressed by the same people and for the same reason.[49]

Baldwin also used the interview to renew his criticism of Israel and its support by Western imperialist powers. One month after the Allende coup, the U.S. backed Israel in the "October War" as it was known by the Arab states, when Egypt and Syria attacked Israel trying to reclaim areas of Palestine—the Sinai Desert and Golan Heights—taken by Israel in the "Six-Day War" of 1967. Baldwin made perhaps his clearest public declaration to date of his criticism of Zionism and support for Palestinians:

There is a level at which one can say that the guilty conscience of the Christian western nations helped to create the state of Israel ... . In a certain sense, the state of Israel was created to keep the Arab in his place. It's a very cruel way to put it but that is the truth. In any case, it is not acceptable to me that the people who have been in refugee camps for the last twenty-five or thirty years have no equal rights to the land of Palestine, where Jews and Arabs have been together for so long. I am not myself deluded that either, in the case of Israel or in the case of Vietnam that the Western powers are fighting for anybody's freedom. They are fighting to protect their investments.[50]

The interview was also one of Baldwin's most explicitly anti-capitalist to date. Baldwin said, "The rise of capitalism and the rise of Christianity ... made genocide inevitable."[51] The heart of the problem for radicals, he averred, is "who owns the banks?"[52] "We are responsible to the *future*, and not to Chase Manhattan Bank."[53]

Finally, this interval of uncertain direction for the Black Power movement, Baldwin's prolonged time out of the country, and his increasingly strident political pronouncements helped to launch a narrative in the U.S. of what might be called James Baldwin's premature death. In August 1973, Baldwin was interviewed by *Time* magazine correspondent Henry Louis Gates, Jr. (later to become a major scholar of African-American literature) for the magazine. *Time*'s editor declined to print the story, declaring that Baldwin was "passé." Such declarations were their own morbid symptoms of a bourgeois establishment—including its Fourth Estate—desperate to declare the social and political rebellions of the 1960s "over." This moment is significant to Baldwin's legacy in two ways. It indicates first how much he had become a "figurehead" for—if not a leader in—public estimation of the shape and power of black liberation movements. At the same time, it signaled the beginnings of a real decline in mainstream attention to Baldwin (in an ironic bit of coincidental timing, in 1974 the FBI closed Baldwin's file and removed him from the Administrative Index, meaning he no longer qualified for surveillance).[54] This attempt to "disappear" Baldwin by mainstream society was its own version of cultural blacklisting that would help give the United States the leadership of figures like Ronald Reagan and the right-wing, Christian fundamentalist Moral Majority in the 1980s. As an openly queer, black, working-class, socialist writer, Baldwin was to become a "canary in the coal mine" of what would be called the "culture wars" in America ten years later, pitting conservative traditionalists against the upstart crows of feminism, ethnic studies, and queer studies. As we shall see in Chapter 7, Baldwin was well aware of these trends and would use them to frame his analysis of the U.S. in the final decade of his own life.

*   *   *

Baldwin carefully tracked every detail of Tony Maynard's legal status after his 1967 arrest, visiting him for hours at "The Tombs," the New York prison that held him, until his final acquittal and release in 1974. In between, he served as a literary and political "witness" to Maynard's case in *No Name in the Street*, declaiming, "if one really wishes to know how justice is administered in a country, one does not question the policemen, the lawyers, the judges, or the protected members of the middle class. One goes to the unprotected—those, precisely, who need the law's protection most!—and listen to their testimony."[55] As he had with the case of Medgar Evers, and Malcolm X, Baldwin decided that the best way to give voice to the voiceless martyred was through his creative writing. Much of 1971–73 he dedicated to writing, from his house in St. Paul-de-Vence, a fictionalized rendition of the Maynard case inspired by his real-life role as rapporteur on it. The finished book, published in 1974, was titled *If Beale Street Could Talk*.

Beale Street is a somber, simmering, angry novel. The book is quiet in tone, small in scale, more familial than social. It is a book about survival at the most minimal scale: the individual. It is also Baldwin's most damning single fictional indictment of the criminal justice system, a "northern" sequel to the southern injustices of *Blues for Mister Charlie*. The story centers on Fonny, a 22-year-old aspiring sculptor, and Tish, 19, the luminously intelligent narrator of the book and its controlling consciousness. The setting is early 1970s New

York. Tish and Fonny are very much in love, and planning to marry. Like many other Baldwin narratives, this one is told retrospectively after a trauma which structures the lives of all the book's characters. As the novel begins, Fonny has already been arrested and is in prison for a crime he did not commit, accused of raping a Puerto Rican woman named Victoria Rogers. Tish is three months pregnant with their child. The parents of both working-class families struggle to develop a defense for Fonny. They also differ in their reaction to the news that the couple will have a child.

The crucial symbolic episode in Baldwin's storyline is that Fonny has been framed by a racist white cop, who falsely testifies that he has seen Fonny running from the crime, testimony that coerces the victim into refusing to exonerate Fonny. Fonny is, in one sense, Tony Maynard, falsely accused. Like Maynard, neither Fonny's family nor Tish's has adequate financial means to mount a serious defense of their imprisoned son and son-in-law to be. Like Maynard, Fonny is in prison innocently—symbolically, in *Beale Street*, for the entire length of the novel. As did Baldwin for Maynard, the two families try desperately to work on behalf of the accused. Tish's mother, Sharon Rivers, travels to Puerto Rico—where Rogers goes to recover from the rape—to try to get her to change her testimony, but to no avail. For Baldwin, Rogers, an immigrant, a woman, is also a victim of a system that doesn't value her life except as an opportunity to incarcerate a young black man.

It is Tish who articulates Baldwin's sharpest expressions of the injustice done in the book. Fonny, the artist, is being punished because he dared to imagine a world for himself besides the one the world had planned. His real and existential difference as a black male artist in a racist, capitalist society foretells, anticipates, predicts his fate in the manner of police racial profiling, where guilt is assumed before innocence:

Fonny had found something that he could do, that he wanted to do, and this saved him from the death that was waiting to overtake the children of our age. Though the death took many forms, though people died early in many different ways, the death itself was very simple and the cause was simple, too: as simple as a plague: the kids had been told that they weren't worth shit and everything they saw around them proved it. They struggled, they struggled, but they fell, like flies, and they congregated on the garbage heap of their lives, like flies.[55]

The same passion which saved Fonny got him into trouble, and put him in jail. For, you see, he had found his center, his own center, inside him: and it showed. He wasn't anybody's nigger. And that's a crime, in this fucking free country. You're suppose to be *somebody's* nigger. And if you're nobody nigger, you're a bad nigger: and that's what the cops decided when Fonny moved downtown.[56]

Baldwin perceives Fonny and Tish as the aspirant genera-tion of the Black Power era who refuse to play the "nigger" any more. Here Baldwin traffics in one of the oldest motifs in African-American culture, the unruly black rebel, as exempli-fied in the figure of John Henry the defiant railroad worker. The story translates and passes down Baldwin's own escape from Harlem into his art, his attempt to transcend the fate of the "children" of his age, on to the next generation's efforts to break the historical cycle of entrapment. Yet Fonny's false arrest, and a racist police and judicial system, lock present into the past. Fonny is also, symbolically, the contemporary revolu-tionary hero as artist, artist as revolutionary (recalls Baldwin's assertion that the two are of the same cloth): Medgar, Malcolm, Paul Robeson, Beauford Delaney. Even Baldwin's metaphors are ripe with his own historical echoes: it was the image of people "falling like flies" that Baldwin had used to describe the plight of young black people in both Harlem and Vietnam in his essay "A Report From Occupied Territory" in 1966, and of Algerians killed by French police in *No Name in the Street*. American history, colonial history, imperial history, are rotten with the black dead.

As with *Blues for Mister Charlie*, there is no exit from systemic racist violence, economic inequality, and police brutality in *If Beale Street Could Talk*. The stories parallel in two other significant ways: the role of women as witness to injustice, and their capacity to reproduce the race. Juanita in *Blues* and Tish in *Beale Street* are the expressive voices of black suffering and protest. Both lose black male lovers. Juanita wishes to be pregnant with Richard's child to extend his legacy in the world, Tish is pregnant with Fonny's. Yet *Beale Street* carries pregnancy to term. The novel ends with Tish giving birth. The book's final paragraph symbolizes the connection Tish has drawn earlier in the novel between Fonny, still imprisoned, his desire to be an artist, and the baby's desire to be "free": "Fonny is working on the wood, on the stone, whistling, smiling. And, from far away, but coming nearer, the baby cries and cries and cries and cries and cries and cries and cries and cries, cries like it means to wake the dead."[57]

There is a possible echo in this final line of James Joyce's classic story "The Dead," with the difference of a possible resurrection—or political wake-up call—to the oppressed. In a 1972 interview, Baldwin told Herbert Lottman, "The book ends with the birth of the baby. *That's* what it's about, our responsibility to that baby." The "our" Baldwin implies is the broad social world. From a feminist perspective, the story naturalizes Tish's biological reproductive capacity as an intrinsic means of possible resistance—new life—while restricting her agency to maternity. As she is giving birth, she narrates, "And then I screamed, and my time had come."[58] But Baldwin does not narrate Tish into a future of her own making, or self-making. Her time is the "timeless" ritual of life—making another, not herself. We can perhaps see this as a form of imprisonment parallel to Fonny's—her description and his are set side by side on the book's final page. But Baldwin's insistence that it is the life of the baby which matters most diminishes the symbolic significance of her story. Even imprisoned, Fonny is working, making art, whistling, smiling. Tish is screaming, in pain, laboring for others' lives.

If Beale Street Could Talk draws its title from W.C. Handy's famous World War I-era blues tribute to Beale Street, the black musical center of Memphis, Tennessee. The street is home to beautiful women, home-grown food, stylish people and good times. The relevant lyric verse is:

If Beale Street could talk, if Beale Street could talk,
Married men would have to take their beds and walk,
Except one or two who never drink booze,
And the blind man on the corner singing "Beale Street
    Blues!"[59]

Beale Street is any street in black America—from Harlem to East St. Louis—where black people might take refuge and pleasure from a world of pain. Yet trouble waits around the corner on Beale Street. Handy's lyrics intone, "business never ceases 'till somebody gets killed," and "It's gonna take a sergeant for to make me go"—the latter a reference to a soldier not wanting to abandon his night out to fight a war for his country. In Baldwin's *Beale Street*, it is the cops who are described as "murder"[60] and the state which takes black men from the streets to prison. Baldwin works in allusions to a Billie Holiday song—"All my life is just despair | but I don't care"—and Marvin Gaye's anti-war, anti-racist protest song "What's Going On?" to both update his musical motif, and to point out through music and musical history the cyclicality of the blues and blues experience in black life.

Baldwin celebrated his fiftieth birthday with close friends and a party at St. Paul-de-Vence on August 1, 1974. He was at work simultaneously on two books: *The Devil Finds Work*, a collection of essays and reviews of American cinema, and *Little Man, Little Man: A Story of Childhood*. Both were radical departures for Baldwin. Each allowed Baldwin a prism, or keyhole, for interpreting his life in the United States. *The Devil Finds Work* is possible to consider as the first major work of African-American film criticism. The book surveys approximately 40 years of film history, from the 1930s to the 1970s, from the *Grapes of Wrath* to *The Exorcist*. Baldwin positions himself as a black-specific spectator onto film, instantiating what bell hooks calls a "black look" at the medium.[61] The act and practice of film-watching is thus made from the outset an intensely political activity: Baldwin's first chapter recalls Orilla Miller taking him to see film adaptations of Dickens— cited earlier—and is linked explicitly to his political education into the concepts of "revolution" and socialism. Also, film becomes, for Baldwin, the "language of our dreams," literally a porthole onto realms of life and lived experience that exceed the provincial confines of streets, or neighborhoods, like Harlem. Film for Baldwin is, like literature, a "bridge" to the human.

Baldwin singles out for critique landmark films addressing race. Most prominent among them is D.W. Griffith's 1915 film *The Birth of a Nation*. Based on a novel by white supremacist Thomas Dixon called *The Clansman*, the film attempts to create a new genre—the cinematic epic—to glorify the rise of the Ku Klux Klan in the United States. Then President Woodrow

Wilson declared after watching it that the film was "history written in lightning." For Baldwin, the film is a monument to American white supremacy: it is "really an elaborate justification of mass murder,"[62] most especially the violent killings and lynchings of African-Americans which is a subtext to the film's main storyline. Baldwin uses *Birth* to define a lineage of reactionary race films in the U.S.—*In the Heat of the Night*, for example, in which sympathy accrues for white supremacists—and to define counterpoint traditions of liberal race films (*The Defiant Ones*, *Guess Who's Coming to Dinner*) which tend to reiterate the sentimental, melodramatic, paternalistic race narratives akin to the "problem novels" of the 1940s Baldwin slew in "Everybody's Protest Novel."

Baldwin also analyzes unsystematically a handful of U.S. films which attempt to be more serious treatments of black life, like the film version of the life of Billie Holiday, *Lady Sings the Blues*. He finds most of these lacking. He is surprisingly dismissive of the so-called "Blaxploitation" films of the early 1970s written or directed by African-Americans—*Superfly*, *Shaft*, *Cleopatra Jones*—and even more serious efforts like *Sounder*. He admits to not having seen many of them, and dismisses them as primarily for-profit exercises which tend to make "black experience irrelevant and obsolete."[63] Baldwin laments that Hollywood cinema in particular has not attempted to adapt important works of African-American literature to the screen that might change this, like Booker T. Washington's *Up From Slavery*, Angelo Herndon's *Let Me Live*, Ralph Ellison's *Invisible Man*, Toni Morrison's *The Bluest Eye*, and George Jackson's *Soledad Brother.*[64]

Baldwin's "black look" at U.S. cinema ultimately expresses itself as a form of cultural studies. On the box office 1973 hit *The Exorcist*, Baldwin writes, "The mindless and hysterical banality of the evil presented ... is the most terrifying thing about the film":

> The Americans should certainly know more about evil than that; if they pretend otherwise, they are lying, and any black man, and not only blacks—many, many others, including white children—can call them on this lie; he who has been treated as the devil recognizes the devil when they meet ... The grapes of wrath are stored in the cotton fields and migrant shacks and ghettoes of this nation, and in the schools and prisons, and in the eyes and hearts and perceptions of the wretched everywhere, and in the ruined earth of Vietnam.[65]

The Devil Finds Work was not a big seller for Baldwin. In fact, its deviation from his normal skein of political writing became a new occasion for mainstream media to try to suppress and bury his—and national—history. A June 4, 1976 *New York Times* book review by Christopher Lehmann-Haupt inveighed, "So James Baldwin is still here, still pursuing us, a ghost of '60s past. Even though he long ago became unfashionable, long ago wore out his welcome even in the black revolution (because he dared to believe that whites and blacks could love each other despite everything) he goes on jumping up and down ... ."[66] Today, the book must be considered a minor landmark of black cultural criticism.

Baldwin's other departure book from 1976, *Little Man*, constellated themes and ideas on black childhood Baldwin had rehearsed in other places: his preface to the aforementioned book on black children and public schooling; his novel *Go Tell It On the Mountain*, and essays like "A Talk To Teachers" (1963) and "If Black English Isn't a Language, Then Tell Me What Is?" The book emerged from a promise: Baldwin had once told his young nephew Tejan that he would write a book about him. When Baldwin was in France helping to take care of his lifelong friend Beauford Delaney, he became reacquainted with Yoran Cazac, a French painter Delaney had introduced him to in Paris in 1959. Baldwin told Cazac he wanted to try a children's book and asked him to do the illustrations. The final book is dedicated to Delaney.

The story draws directly from Baldwin's life. He shared photographs of Tejan and his niece Aisha Karefa-Smart with Cazac to help him visualize the story. It is set in Harlem and features the lives of three children: TJ, based on Tejan; W.T., his seven-year-old friend, and Blinky, an eight-year-old girl. Another source was *The Black Book*, a compendium of photographs and visual artifacts of black life, compiled by Toni Morrison. The story itself is more a series of observations and vignettes than a plotted narrative, appropriate to the impressionist temporality of childhood. Soft palette watercolors of Harlem streetscapes produce a modest social realism from the point of view of children. Yet the story has jagged social events atypical of a traditional children's book. There are references to drug and alcohol addiction, police brutality, depression and aging, sex and biological reproduction. Nicholas Boggs also reads Blinky as a butch, non-binary girl refusing heteronormative roles in the story.[67] The book also centers on black pride: TJ's father reads the Nation of Islam newspaper *Muhammad Speaks* (which Baldwin once did an interview with). His parents tell him to be "proud of his people," and to read everything—glimpses of Baldwin's self-aspirations that were not necessarily passed on by his own parents. In this way, the book has the didactic function of children's writing specific to black lives.

Indeed, Baldwin wrote the book because he insisted that black childhood was an intensely political subject. He referred to the book as a "celebration of the self-esteem of black children."[68] In "If Black English Isn't a Language, Then Tell Me What Is?" Baldwin wrote "It is not the black child's language that is despised. It is his experience ... A child cannot be taught by anyone whose demand, essentially, is that the child repudiate his experience, and all that gives him sustenance, and enter a limbo in which he will no longer be black, and in which he knows he can never become white. black people have lost too many children that way."[69] More polemically, Baldwin had told public school teachers in 1963 that the purpose of education for black children should be training them to resist a world set to destroy them:

> Now if I were a teacher in this school, or any Negro school and I was dealing with Negro children, who were in my care only a few hours of every day and would then return to their homes and to the streets, children who have an apprehension of their future which with every hour grows grimmer and darker, I would try to make each child know that these things are the results of a criminal conspiracy to destroy him. I would teach him that if he intends to get to be a man, he must decide that he is stronger than this conspiracy and that he must never make his peace with it.[70]

Baldwin's book was of a piece with other radical new writing by black authors on childhood influenced by the Black Power and Black Arts Movements of the 1960s, including Julius Lester's *To Be a Slave* (1969), Alice Childress's *A Hero Ain't Nothing But a Sandwich* (1973), and Toni Morrison's groundbreaking first novel *The Bluest Eye* (1971). It also anticipates the mature treatment of urban childhood in works like Sandra Cisneros's *A House on Mango Street*. Baldwin's book did not sell well or remain in print long after its publication, but a sign of his recent renaissance was its republication in a handsome edition by Duke University Press in 2018. The new edition features a Foreword by Baldwin's nephew Tejan Karefa-Smart and an Afterword by Aisha Karefa-Smart.

Despite scattered proclamations of his irrelevance, Baldwin continued as public commentator and speaker on politics and remained a subject of interest for U.S. media, especially African-American media. In the summer of 1976, he spoke with members of the Women's Development Unit, a small group within the Rikers Island prison in New York, a continuation of his prison activism. He was the featured interview subject of the African-American magazine *Essence* in June of 1976. Baldwin used the interview to extol the short-lived 1974–75 Portuguese Revolution as further evidence of the "end of the Western world as we know it."[71] 1976 was also the year of the U.S. bicentennial, generally a nationalist, chauvinist pageant uncritically celebrating U.S. exceptionalism. Much like Frederick Douglass's famous "What to the Slave is the Fourth of July" speech of 1850, Baldwin typically dissented from the hegemonic fanfare in a *Los Angeles Times* editorial, attacking the celebration as an erasure of U.S. inequalities, especially its rampant poverty: "America's birthday present," he wrote, "on its two hundredth birthday, is to be the final banishment of the beast in the American playground."[72] Baldwin noted the high incidence of black, Chicano, Mexican, and Puerto Rican poverty and welfare, and vast expenditures on sending astronauts to the moon and militarization rather than eradicating poverty: "Man cannot live by nuclear warheads alone";[73] "It would seem to me," he wrote, "that the American social disaster is a tremendous burden on the American taxpayers. It is an investment on which his only return is chaos."[74]

Baldwin sharpened his national criticisms in a September 26, 1976 book review of Alex Haley's monumental bestselling book *Roots*, his semi-autobiographical tale of his family's African origins and forced migration to American slavery. Baldwin used the review to praise the book but also to cite the rising struggle against South African apartheid as a cautionary tale for a country celebrating its bicentennial with a blind eye to its own racist history. The South African example would draw even more of Baldwin's attention in the final decade of his life. Fittingly, Baldwin closed a decade of public dissidence on a case that hearkened back to the roots of the black freedom struggle. On February 8, 1971, ten black men were arrested and charged with burning down a grocery store in Wilmington, North Carolina. The ten included the Reverend Ben Chavis of the United Church of Christ. Chavis had been sent to Wilmington by the church when anger boiled over in the city around the closing of black public schools, segregation and racism directed against black residents, and the rise of marauding Ku Klux Klan gangs on the streets. Chavis and his comrades were actually meeting in the store when it was torched. The burning of the grocery store was a convenient excuse for the state to smash public protest. The Wilmington Ten were convicted and sentenced to a combined 282 years in jail.[75]

In 1976, Amnesty International took up the case, declaring the Wilmington Ten political prisoners. U.S. President Jimmy Carter, meanwhile, admonished the Soviet Union on holding its own political dissidents in jail, while ignoring Chavis and his imprisoned mates. Baldwin responded by taking up their case in "An Open Letter to Mr. Carter," comparing the imprisoned to civil rights protesters from an earlier era, like James Forman, and victims of southern racist violence like the four girls killed in the 1963 Birmingham church bombing. Baldwin appealed to Carter to intervene for their release: "I repeat, their situation is but a very small indication of the wretched in this country: the nonwhite, the Indian, the Puerto Rican, the Mexican, the Oriental."[76] While Carter remained indifferent, public protest and pressure eventually led to a 1980 reversal of the Wilmington Ten convictions when a key witness recanted their testimony, admitting they had been coerced by the state. In 2012, the governor of the state of North Carolina officially pardoned them.

Baldwin's role in the Wilmington Ten victory was small, but another indication that his public political voice was hardly silent, his role as a dissident and dissident writer not done. In 1977, Baldwin could not have known that he was about to enter the final leg of his life, one that would see the beginnings of an intense public grappling over his legacy, and a prolonged private dialogue between Baldwin's soul and self about the state of the world and his place in it.

7
Final Acts

Oh, towering Ronnie Reagan,
Wise and resigned lover of redwoods,
Deeply beloved, winning man-child of the yearning
  Republic,
From diaper to football field to Warner Brothers
  sound-stages,
Be thou our grinning, gently phallic, Big Boy of all the
  ages!

James Baldwin, "Staggerlee Wonders," 1985[1]

I hope that it is easier for the transgressor to become rec-
onciled with himself or herself than it was for many people
in my generation—and it was difficult for me. It is difficult
to be despised, in short. And if the so-called gay movement
can cause men and women, boys and girls, to come to some
kind of terms with themselves more speedily and with less
pain, then that's a very great advance.[2]

James Baldwin, interview with Richard Goldstein, 1984

Audre Lorde: I do not blame Black men; what I'm saying is,
we have to take a new look at the ways in which we fight our
joint oppression because if we don't, we're gonna be blowing
each other up. We have to begin to redefine the terms of
what woman is, what man is, how we relate to each other.
James Baldwin: But that demands redefining the terms of
the western world …

Audre Lorde: And both of us have to do it; both of us have
to do it …

> *Revolutionary Hope: A Conversation Between*
> *James Baldwin and Audre Lorde*, 1984[3]

Baldwin's final decade was lived in a world he both predicted
and hoped never to see. His black, queer, anti-capitalist,
anti-imperialist dissidence was confronted with a new sea of
political contradictions. On the one hand, a right-wing evan-
gelical U.S. state headed by a cowboy figurehead—Ronald
Reagan—Baldwin had already learned to hate for his pros-
ecution of radical friends in the 1960s while governor of
California. History seemed to be repeating itself as farce.
The Reagan regime brought with it a theologically driven
contempt for queer victims of a new medical plague—HIV/
AIDS. Baldwin would lose a lover to the disease not long
before his death. The confluence of a draconian and ruthless
"moral majority" exercising homophobic and racist state
power tipped Baldwin further into despair and rage over the
country of his birth. Reagan's cruelty was merely a symptom
of what Baldwin saw as the reconstitution of white supremacist ruling-class power in the United States newly hitched to
one of his most ancient political foes: the Christian church.
Never would his lifetime of fiery prophecy seem so fatally apt;
he would write some of his most scathing political commen-
taries as bulwarks, including a very public pronouncement of
support for the Palestinians.

At the same time, the long, pre-figurative roots of Baldwin's
own dissident orientation would furiously flower: the decades
of the 1970s and 1980s enabled the flourishing of black
feminism and queer politics, both of which swept Baldwin up
in their currents, overcoming his initial skepticism that either
feminism or gay and lesbian politics would become more

than white middle-class movements. In 1985, he published his modern manifesto of queer politics cited earlier, "Freaks and the American Ideal of Manhood." Both his 1970s novel *If Beale Street Could Talk* and his fictional finale—*Just Above My Head*—show Baldwin internalizing and manifesting new gender politics meant to challenge the hegemony of white, male power structures. *Just Above My Head* shed all earlier reluctance to center black queer love: the book's protagonist, and narrator, participates in the deepest renderings of black erotic intimacy Baldwin had written, aside from the noted passage in *Tell Me How Long the Train's Been Gone* discussed in Chapter 6. Baldwin also created a female avatar in the book— Julia—by which to express in profoundly gendered terms the destructive effects of patriarchal power and violence. These elements foreshadowed Baldwin's most important political conversation of the last decade of his life with black lesbian poet Audre Lorde, where Baldwin struggled to part forever with his lifelong attachment to black men—and black masculinity—as the center of his analysis of the world.

Between these acts of desktop fury, Baldwin, who never attended college, became an esteemed professor of literature and creative writing, supplementing his income as a visiting lecturer; continued his role as a political journalist and rapporteur in a final, non-fiction book; published his first and only book of poetry; fell ill, or exhausted; and finally developed cancer of the esophagus. He died in 1987 in his beloved St. Paul-de-Vence. And yet: the moment of his death heralded resurrection. Within days of his passing, the creation of many Baldwins, and Baldwin legacies, had begun. We will close our final chapter by charting these as threads from past to present.

* * *

In the spring of 1978, Baldwin taught a course in contemporary literature at Bowling Green College in Ohio. It was his first college teaching assignment and first long stay in the U.S. since 1969. He would return to teach at Bowling Green in the fall semesters of 1979 and 1981. The assignment began a period of public reward in higher education for his literary achievements: Baldwin would teach a class in 1979 at the University of California, Berkeley; give talks at UCLA and UC Santa Barbara; and in 1980 give lectures at Youngstown State and Wayne State Universities. In 1983–84, Baldwin began teaching in the Afro-American Studies department at the University of Massachusetts, Amherst. The Afro-American Studies department was one of the first in the United States, and one of the first to offer a PhD.

Baldwin thought of teaching as a political practice. His classroom was a place where he hoped political transformations might occur. Yet he also found the university "interpellated" by broader racial conditions in which it was embedded. At Bowling Green, where he was visiting writer-in-residence, a white student in a racially mixed class asked him, "Why does the white hate the nigger?" Caught off guard, Baldwin enabled a discussion wherein students "did not need me at all, except as a vaguely benign adult presence. They began talking to one another, and they were not talking about race. They were talking of their desire to know one another, their experience of the other … They were trying to become whole. They were trying to put themselves and their country together."[4] Baldwin drew from the class the lesson that, "The reality, the depth, and the persistence of the delusion of white supremacy in this country causes any real concept of education to be as remote, and as much to be feared, as change or freedom itself."[5]

More momentous than his teaching in 1978 was publication of Baldwin's sixth, and final, novel, *Just Above My Head*. This book continued Baldwin's concentrated attention in his late novels on the black family as a symbolic unit of black diaspora and black survival. The book sends its characters on a series of tours, or reverse migrations, from the American North to Africa, France, Korea, and the American South, regrouping them before and after to establish their fundamental historical unity. Similarly, the book takes place with time "out of joint" as a series of emotional flashbacks, and flash-forwards, to represent a communal challenge of surviving trauma and the memory of trauma: rape, incest, war, racism, addiction. In structure and telling, the novel is most like *Go Tell It On the Mountain* but with a much broader historical canvas, including America in World War II and the Cold War. Finally, the book is Baldwin's most musical work of fiction: from the title, an allusion to a black traditional, to its structuring epigraphs from gospel and blues, to its focus on the business of music, *Just Above My Head* queries the relationship between black lived experience and its musical manifestations. The novel is a complex gloss on this line from narrator and witness Hall Montana: "Niggers can sing gospel as no other people can because they aren't singing gospel—if you see what I mean. When a nigger quotes the Gospel, he is not quoting: he is telling you what happened to him today, and what is certainly going to happen to you tomorrow: it may be that it has already happened to you, and that you, poor soul, don't know it … Our suffering is our bridge to each other."[6]

In *Just Above My Head*, that "bridge" is constructed from the start when middle-age professional singer Arthur Montana collapses on the floor from a heart attack. The event is narrated by his brother, and sometime manager, Hall, who is also witness to his life. Like *Go Tell It On the Mountain* and *Tell Me How Long*, *Just Above My Head* is about brothers, and in this way is a loosely veiled autobiography: Baldwin's real-life brother David to whom he was closest was a part-time professional singer who, like Arthur, toured the American South, David in support of the Henry Wallace campaign of 1948, Arthur in support of the civil rights movement. But the latter is symbolically a distant background to the ongoing racial and sexual traumas endured by Baldwin's main characters.

For Arthur, that trauma is the pressure of trying to succeed as a black artist while simultaneously negotiating and accepting his queer identity. He is in every way Baldwin's most fully realized black and openly queer character: after an initial confusing, traumatizing sexual encounter that awakens his sexuality, he moves through several meaningful gay relationships with a close friend, Crunch; a Frenchman, Guy; and finally Jimmy (Baldwin's partial avatar) who is fiercely loyal and fiercely confident of his own gay identity. Baldwin frequently links the erotic pleasure of song and singing for Arthur to his queer pleasure. The book unleashes and celebrates the libidinal connection—or "bridge"—between the black body, spirituality, and music intimated by the life of John Grimes in *Go Tell It On the Mountain*.

Baldwin also represents queer sex as a path to black healing. Red, a friend of Hall and Arthur's, is thrown into heroin addiction. In one of the most tender scenes in Baldwin's writing—akin to the brotherly sexual love in *Tell Me How Long*, Red and Hall masturbate each other in order to ease other's pain, to build a "bridge." Hall may be bisexual, or gay: the scene surpasses in intimacy and emotional reward his "married" relationship to Ruth Granger, a good woman with whom Hall has settled as the novel begins. The book clearly proposes that queer sexuality is an elevated pathway to love, a practice of love, as Baldwin often insisted. Characters "go the way their blood beats" in the book as Baldwin described it in his 1985 interview with Richard Goldstein.

Hovering over all of the action of the novel are two forms of rapacious violence, one sponsored by the state, one by patri-archal power. Hall is a veteran of the Korean War, which he survives. But the ancillary power of the U.S. "military-industrial complex" is felt by Red, who is imprisoned, and becomes an addict; and Peanut, who is murdered. More central to the novel still, its central structuring trauma, is Julia's repeated incestuous rape by her minister father. That violence breaks her, sends her to a life as a prostitute, and nearly destroys her. She "heals" via a symbolic trip to Africa and restorative love from Hall, with whom she has a temporary relationship. Bald-win's book reflects for the first time in his work the centrality of black women's lives and their wide range of sufferings in U.S. society. At the same time, Julia's recovery is central to the construction of a fragile utopian peace achieved by the main characters of the book near its end, when Julia, Jimmy, Arthur, and Hall are reunited. Hall imagines their peace in musical terms recalling a dream of Arthur's singing these gospel lyrics: "Oh, my loving brother, when the world's on fire, don't you want God's bosom to be your pillow?"[7] But the dream is a dream, and Hall wakes up to tears on his pillow. The novel comes full circle to an assertion that suffering is a bridge between black people who survive it by maintaining ties of kinship and history. Music in the book provides that real and metaphorical bridge. As Baldwin put it in a 1979 essay on the topic, "Music is our witness, and our ally. The 'beat' is the con-fession which recognizes, changes, and conquers time. Then, history becomes a garment we can wear, and share, and not a cloak in which to hide: and time becomes a friend."[8]

On March 26, 1979, Beauford Delaney died in Paris. Baldwin, who had tended to and monitored his condition throughout the period of his decline, went into seclusion at his home in St. Paul-de-Vence. The death of his closest artistic mentor put him in a further reflective mood. On June 30, 1979, he sent a letter to his literary agent, Jay Acton, proposing to write a book about the lives of Medgar Evers, Malcolm X, and Martin Luther King, Jr. Provisionally titled *Remember This House*, the book was to be a "journey" as Baldwin described it, limned by intimations of his own mortality: "And I will be fifty-five (yes! Fiftyfive!) in a month." As to the book, it would cover the lives of the three men from 1955 to 1968, and underscore their political martyrdom. Baldwin proposed, "I want these three lives to bang against and reveal each other, as, in truth, they did ... and use their dreadful journey as a means of instructing the people whom they loved so much, who betrayed them, and for whom they gave their lives."[9] Baldwin conceived the project as an opportunity to return to the South to interview witnesses and survivors, like Coretta Scott King. But teaching and other commitments short-circuited the project, which never got past the proposal phase.

Meanwhile, on August 15, 1979, U.S. United Nations Ambassador Andrew Young, a veteran of the civil rights movement and former adviser to Martin Luther King, Jr., resigned his position. Young left after he was publically attacked for meeting privately with Zehdi Labib Terzi, the observer at the United Nations for the Palestinian Liberation Organization. Young wanted to discuss an upcoming report from the United Nations recommending a Palestinian state. The meeting brought Young under fire because officially the U.S. had agreed to Israel that it would not meet with the Palestine Liberation Organization. The report of the meeting, illegally obtained by Mossad, was leaked to *Newsweek* magazine. Young, under fire, resigned.

Baldwin responded with a September 29, 1979 *Nation* essay titled, "Open Letter to the Born Again." The essay is in many ways the apotheosis of his thinking on the question of the

Arab, and the Palestinian, in the contemporary world, and also an important document on the history of Zionism in the West. In it, Baldwin is both furious in his denunciation of Western anti-semitism, and unbound in his open solidarity with Palestinian self-determination as a break in Western history's manifest destiny. Baldwin also links his own break with Christian fundamentalism to Christianity's own role in the persecution and betrayal of Jews. More pointedly, he aligns Carter's dismissal of Young with imperial gerrymandering in the Middle East dating to the Balfour Declaration and the history of "broken promises" known by both Jews and Palestinians. Notes Baldwin, "The Zionists—as distinguished from the people known as Jews—using, as someone put it, the 'available political machinery,' i.e. colonialism, e.g. the British Empire—promised the British that, if the territory were given to them, the British Empire would be safe forever."[10] Here, Baldwin closes in on his essay's theme, "betrayal," noting the priority of Western colonial, not Jewish, interests in the Zionist project, and importantly the fact that, "The Palestinians have been paying for the British colonial policy of 'divide and rule' and for Europe's guilty Christian conscience for more than thirty years."[11] There is, Baldwin writes, "no hope" of peace in the Middle East without "dealing with the Palestinians." The essay also compares Israel to South Africa, a comparison that the anti-apartheid movement of the 1970s had well established, and which Baldwin himself had previously cited. Written not long after the collapse of the Shah of Iran's regime in the face of the Iranian revolution, Baldwin notes that the collapse "not only revealed the depth of the pious Carter's concern for 'human rights,' it also revealed who supplied oil to Israel, and to whom Israel supplied arms. It happened to be, to spell it out, white South Africa."[12]

With "Open Letter to the Born Again," Baldwin renounces both Christian Zionism, and settler-colonial Zionism, as secret sharers in the domination of the Afro-Arab world. For Baldwin, Andrew Young is a Palestinian Christ on the international cross of Anglo-American Middle East imperialism, one who has become a "hero, betrayed by cowards."[13] Baldwin's stringent stance against both anti-semitism and what we would now call Islamophobia in the essay effectively calls out the West's own peculiar history of Orientalist disdain for the Jew in days past, and the Arab in days present. Likewise, the essay's rhizomatic history of Western "broken promises,"—of 40 acres and a mule to the slave, of abandoned state treaties to the Indian, of Balfour to the Jews, of Palestinian dispossession—draws together into a singular totality a composite portrait of what Baldwin once called, self-referentially, "bastards of the west."

Baldwin's corrosive assessment of the Carter administration was not new—he had referred in a 1978 essay to the state of the union as "catastrophic,"[14] and described the ballyhooed oil shortages in the U.S. as a healthy sign of economic self-determination by the Arab states. "The energy crisis is a matter of bankruptcy in the western world. The bankruptcy of the western world is simply the end of the possibilities of plunder."[15] And, "what you call the 'energy crisis' means that I am no longer forced to sell what I produce, to you, and your prices"[16]—a reference to the oil and petroleum cartel OPEC (the Organization of the Petroleum Exporting Countries) created by the Middle Eastern oil-producing states. Baldwin's first foray into commentary on what would become the reactionary reign of Ronald Reagan, who defeated Carter in November 1980, came in a February 1980 speech at Wayne State University, some nine months before his election. Baldwin grouped Reagan with UK Prime Minster Margaret

Thatcher as symbols of white, Western capitalist supremacy. "White is a metaphor for power," said Baldwin, "and that is simply a way of describing Chase Manhattan Bank."[17] In a separate essay published on November 1, 1980, just days before the presidential election, Baldwin recalled living in California during Reagan's reign as governor: "The time of the Black Panther harassment, the beginning (and the end) of the Soledad Brothers, the persecution, and trial, of Angela Davis ... but what I really found unspeakable about the man was his contempt, his brutal contempt, for the poor."[18]

Baldwin's observations could not have been more prescient: in 1981, one year into office, Reagan fired 11,000 federal unionized air traffic controllers for striking, a watershed blow to the American labor movement which found a parallel in the UK in Margaret Thatcher's withering destruction of the 1984 miners' strike. Reagan also made enormous budget cuts to social welfare, famously demonizing poor African-American women as "welfare queens" cheating the system and siphoning off public funds. Reagan also ruthlessly exploited his Hollywood career as an actor preceding his political one, quoting lines from Clint Eastwood movies—"Make My Day"—to indicate his virile toughness. Baldwin's mock-heroic tribute to Reagan which is an epigraph to this chapter lasered in on this feature, "queering" Reagan's tough-guy masculinity in a tribute to his own arguments in his earlier essay on André Gide about the "prison" of male sexuality. In the poem, "Big Boy" refers to the grinning, forever boyish male figure used as a logo on a famous chain of restaurants, but the words double here as an ironic totem of normative—i.e. healthy—heterosexuality. Embedded in the poem is also a critique of that sexuality as a building block of American exceptionalism and manifest destiny—Reagan is paired in the stanza with a parodic image of John Wayne hunting Indians. The poem articulates a central argument of Baldwin's seminal "Freaks and the American Ideal of Manhood," published the same year as the poem, and indisputably a Reagan-era text:

> The American ideal, then, of sexuality appears to be rooted in the American ideal of masculinity. This idea has created cowboys and Indians, good guys and bad guys, punks and studs, tough guys and softies, butch and faggot, black and white. It is an ideal so paralytically infantile that it is virtually forbidden—as an unpatriotic act—that the American boy evolve into the complexity of manhood.[19]

Ronald Reagan was indeed, for Baldwin, America's "Big Boy."

* * *

In July 1979, Edward Hope Smith, a 14-year-old African-American from Atlanta, went missing, and turned up dead. He had been shot. Not long after, two more young black men were found murdered. The killing continued: between the summer of 1979 and the spring of 1981, 29 young black men, all from poor sections of Atlanta, were found murdered. The story gained national attention only when aggrieved black mothers of the dead went public to lament the fate of their children. Ronald Reagan, silent until then, suddenly called it "one of the most tragic situations that has ever confronted an American community."[20] Celebrities like Frank Sinatra and the Jackson Five poured into Atlanta to raise funds to help look for suspects in the killings, but there were none. Racist, homophobic panic filled the vacuum: local and national media began peddling stories of "organized homosexual activity" being responsible for the kidnap and rape of the boys. Other stories, without evidence, suggested a "black homosexual" killer was responsible.

Baldwin followed the story closely from France. Coincidentally, in 1980 he was commissioned by the *New Yorker* magazine to travel to Atlanta to write a story about the city as an emblem of the so-called "New South," a designation used by city elders, including its black leadership, to mark progress and distance between a post- and pre-civil rights era, and the increasing prosperity of Atlanta's burgeoning black middle class. Baldwin did travel to Atlanta in 1980 with English filmmaker Dick Fontaine and African-American actress Pat Hartley as part of a documentary film completed and released in 1982 called *I Heard it Through the Grapevine*. He used the trip as an opportunity to research the killings first hand. Baldwin felt drawn to the Atlanta murder stories by several things. He considered the mass killing of black children—and its underreporting—symptomatic of the violent neglect he had assigned the United States throughout his life towards black youth. He also had some literary roots in the city—recall his essay "Journey to Atlanta" from his first book *Notes of a Native Son*, and his first visit there in 1957 as part of his efforts to report on the black freedom struggle.

In December 1981, Baldwin published an article in *Playboy* magazine about the serial murders titled, "Atlanta: The Evidence of Things Not Seen." The article interpreted the mass killings of black children as evidence of a *lack* of racial progress in the United States. "Forget everything you may have heard, or may wish to believe, concerning the New South," he wrote.[21] As he had in his first report about the city years before, Baldwin zeroed in on the persistence of poverty and racism, despite apparent signs of material prosperity and upward mobility for Atlanta blacks. "The black middle class of Atlanta believes itself to be the oldest and noblest in the South—which means the nation—and it probably is; and who cares? I mean, who gives a flying fuck about all this genteel house-nigger ancestry if it cannot save our children or clarify a town?"[22]

In June of 1981, Wayne B. Williams, a 23-year-old African-American from Atlanta, was arrested. A month earlier, Williams had been pulled over after a police officer reportedly heard a splash in a nearby river he was driving past. Two days later, the murdered body of Nathaniel Cater was found floating downriver. Williams was charged with the murder—and that of one other adult—based on carpet fibers and dog hairs, and Williams's failure on a polygraph test when interviewed about the Cater case. He was eventually convicted. However, police then claimed Williams was also responsible for at least 24 of the unsolved 30 child murders, and designated those "solved" or "closed," while offering virtually no evidence of his guilt.[23]

Baldwin's lifelong suspicions of unfair police treatment of African-Americans was doubled-down upon by events in Atlanta. The Williams case became for him a new bell-wether of southern injustice, and a modern-day version of the Emmett Till case, with both the victims of murder and the suspect of the killings assuming a version of Till's role as vulnerable to mob justice. Baldwin moved rapidly to develop his initial *Playboy* article into a book, poring over details of the case, Williams's life and arrest, and the local and national response. He put his opening argument to the book as follows: "Either the accused is being tried for twenty-eight murders or for two. If he is *not* being tried for twenty-eight murders, it can only be, after all, for lack of evidence. How, then, does it happen—legally—that a man charged with *two* murders can be tried for twenty-eight?"[24] And: "He is not, literally or legally, *accused* of being a mass murderer: but he is the only suspect, and he is *assumed* to be a mass murderer."[25]

Baldwin understands Williams's legal fate as a form of racial profiling and police complicity with the destruction of black lives. In Baldwin's mind, even if guilty, Williams is a version of Fonny from *If Beale Street Could Talk*, or Tony Maynard. Baldwin also understands Williams's fate as a result of homophobic panic. About media speculation that Williams was gay, Baldwin writes, "It is unlikely, as well as irrelevant, that he is homosexual. He is, far more probably, not sexual at all: he never learned to love himself."[26] For Baldwin, Williams is an example of a sexually traumatized subject who "may never grow up" because of the prevailing hegemony of a traumatized homophobic society.[27] At another point in the book, Baldwin "queers" media reports that the young boys may have been seduced into a "homosexual ring." "In any case, the place to which a male child may go for sexual release is not likely to be the place from which he does not return—rumor spreads quickly in the streets."[28]

Baldwin also reads the Williams case as a parable of the Reagan era. "One may add, for I would like to have this on my record, that the Reagan vote was an anti-black/black vote—absolutely."[29] The roster of underreported dead black boys and the rush to condemn and convict Williams are also figments of other American atrocities—manifest destiny, Hiroshima—and a slippery slope to broader authoritarian currents: "This is untidy," he writes of Williams's treatment. "It also establishes a precedent, a precedent that may lead us, with our consent, to the barbed wire and the gas oven."[30]

Between the time of Baldwin's first interest in the Atlanta child murders in 1979, and publication of his book on the case in 1985, the dungeon of gay life in America shook. On June 5, 1981, the Centers for Disease Control and Prevention's newsletter *Morbidity and Mortality Weekly* announced that five men in Los Angeles had been diagnosed with Pneumocystis carinii pneumonia and that two had died. All five were homosexual. These were the first public reports announcing the onset of acquired immune deficiency syndrome, or HIV/AIDS. Between 1981 and 1987, more than 50,000 people in the U.S. would be diagnosed, a full 25 percent of them African-American, nearly double the demographic percentage in the general population. Of that number, nearly 17,000 died.[31]

Baldwin's references to the railroading of Wayne Williams and the dead boys of Atlanta as a figurative American genocide, coupled with his rage against Reagan-era racism, should be understood intertextually as figments of the emergent AIDS crisis. In 1982, Reagan's press spokesperson, Larry Speakes made headlines when he and other media members laughed at a reference to HIV as a "gay plague," this at a time when the Reagan administration response to the crisis was non-existent. Indeed, much of the energy and creativity of the direct action queer activist group ACT UP (AIDS Coalition to Unleash Power), the policy-driven New York's Gay Men's Health Crisis, and broader AIDS activism in the early 1980s U.S. was making demands for federal attention—and financial commitment—to fighting the disease. AIDS activists pointed out that failing major commitments of resources to fight the disease, the federal government was a mere spectator to genocide. In *Evidence of Things Not Seen*, Baldwin closes the text with a melancholy memory of Buddy, a young gay man he knew in Harlem at 14, outcast from his community because of his sexuality. The last time Baldwin sees him before he disappears from the community, he is looking ill and haggard. "Very shortly afterward, he died, I was told, of TB, tuberculosis."[32] Baldwin muses: "For while there is no guarantee that the community could have, as a friend of mine puts it, 'kissed the hurt away,' his sense of being valued might have made the split-second difference between choosing life and choosing death. All of our lives really hang on some such tiny thread and it is very dangerous not to know this."[33]

Tuberculosis was the most common presenting illness of HIV sufferers from the inception of the disease, the World Health Organization reporting that persons with HIV were, and are, 16–27 times more likely to develop TB than those without. In 1984, one year before he published *Evidence of Things Not Seen*, *Village Voice* journalist Richard Goldstein recalls interviewing Baldwin, who was asking questions about the AIDS epidemic, such as how it was transmitted and what its effects were. At least one of the answers found its way obliquely into Baldwin's "genocide" book of the Reagan era.

*   *   *

Baldwin's greatest political and personal challenge of the 1980s was articulating his relationship to burgeoning movements for gender and LGBTQ equality. Many scholars have expressed regret or disappointment that Baldwin did not use his social power to assume a leading role in both. His failure to do so owes to several things at once that careful reading of the record of his last seven years throws into relief.

For example, in a 1980 interview with Wolfgang Binder, Baldwin was asked to assess both the feminist and gay rights movements. The interview came roughly ten years after the beginnings of both movements; at least publically, Baldwin had been reticent about participating in either. Baldwin's response was telling of the reasons why: "The Women's Liberation Movement is a little like the Gay Movement in that it is essentially a white middle-class phenomenon, which doesn't have any real organic connection with the black situation on any level whatever ... The dangers my sisters face, my mother faced, have nothing to do with what Women's Liberation thinks it is about, nothing at all."[34]

Baldwin was referring in the main to the white, heter-onormative leadership of organizations like the National Organization for Women and perhaps to early, predominantly white and middle-class gay rights organizations like the Mattachine Society. However, his characterization also elides the important role of trans and queer people of color like Sylvia Rivera and Marsha P. Johnson in seminal events like the Stonewall Rebellion in New York of 1969—which Baldwin never wrote about—or even the role of key non-white activists like Audre Lorde in the National March on Washington for Gay and Lesbian Rights in 1979. Part of Baldwin's ignorance stemmed from being out of the country in France much of the 1970s, but part was simply a failure to reckon with facts on the ground of shifting social movements in the U.S. One reason for his inattention may have been Baldwin's stated incapacity to reconcile the simultaneity of racism and homophobia in his own political life and work. In 1984, he famously told George Plimpton that he had made David, the protagonist of *Giovanni's Room*, white rather than black because "I could not handle both propositions in the same book."[35] Baldwin's reaction to what he perceived as racism in the LGBTQ movement also contributed to his position that sexual oppression was secondary, if not subordinate, to racial oppression. As he put it in an interview with Richard Goldstein in 1984, "A black gay person who is a sexual conundrum to society is already, long before the question of sexuality comes into it, menaced and marked because he's black or she's black. The sexual question comes after the question of color."[36] Perhaps concurrently, scholar Matt Brim has noted that despite real-life friendships with many women of color, and lesbians of color—Nikki Giovanni, Lorraine Hansberry, Audre Lorde—black lesbians are entirely absent from Baldwin's creative writing corpus. They simply do not exist.[37]

Thus Baldwin's steps towards an engagement with and recognition of the intersection of race and sexual/gender oppression are noteworthy. In 1982, for example, he spoke on the topic of "Race, Racism and the Gay Community" to the National Association of Black and White Men Together, an interracial queer organization founded in 1980.[38] In his 1981 *Playboy* article on the Wayne Williams case, and his subsequent work on the book *Evidence of Things Unseen*, Baldwin also drew together an analysis of how racism and homophobia were conjoining to create public panic. But it was his interview with Audre Lorde cited earlier that left the clearest public record of Baldwin's struggle to develop a comprehension of what black feminism of the period was defining as a radical, intersectional approach to politics. Important founding statements of this perspective were the Combahee River Collective's statement from 1980 which argued,

The most general statement of our politics at the present time would be that we are actively committed to struggling against racial, sexual, heterosexual, and class oppression, and see as our particular task the development of integrated analysis and practice based upon the fact that the major systems of oppression are interlocking. The synthesis of these oppressions creates the conditions of our lives. As Black women we see Black feminism as the logical political movement to combat the manifold and simultaneous oppressions that all women of color face.[39]

A second seminal document of intersectional black feminism was the 1981 literary anthology *This Bridge Called My Back*, edited by Cherríe Moraga and Gloria Anzaldúa. That book was the first to combine in collective form writing by leading lesbian women of color. Lorde was a contributor.

In their dialogue together, Lorde presses Baldwin constantly to develop something like an intersectional understanding of black women's lives. In response to Baldwin's claim that black people are America's "nightmare," Lorde replies,

Even worse than the nightmare is the blank. And black women are the blank. I don't want to break all this down, then have to stop at the wall of male/female division. When we admit and deal with difference; when we deal with the deep bitterness; when we deal with the horror of even our different nightmares; when we turn them and look at them, it's like looking at death: hard but possible.[40]

Lorde's emphasis on "difference" is meant to incite Baldwin to differentiate oppression by factoring in gender: "We need to acknowledge those power differences between us and see where they lead us. An enormous amount of energy is being taken up with either denying the power differences between black men and women or fighting over power differences between black men and women or killing each other off behind them."

Lorde continues, pressing Baldwin further to gender race:

It's vital that we deal constantly with racism, and with white racism among black people—that we recognize this as a legitimate area of inquiry. We must also examine the ways that we have absorbed sexism and heterosexism. These are the norms in this dragon we have been born into—and we need to examine these distortions with the same kind of openness and dedication that we examine racism.

I do not blame black men for what they are. I'm asking them to move beyond. I do not blame black men; what I'm saying is, we have to take a new look at the ways in which we fight our joint oppression because if we don't, we're gonna be blowing each other up. We have to begin to redefine the terms of what woman is, what man is, how we relate to each other.[41]

Baldwin was sufficiently inspired by Lorde's analysis that when he republished his manifesto on queer sexuality and "ideals" of American manhood he retitled the essay "Here Be Dragons" after Lorde's metaphor of heteronormativity. The influence is also seen in Baldwin's attempts to "redefine the terms of what woman is, what man is, how we relate to each other." This is evident in Baldwin's conclusion: "we are all androgynous … each of us, helplessly and forever, contains the other—male in female, female in male, white in black and black in white. We are a part of each other."[42]

How did this retheorization of sexuality play out in practice in Baldwin's later life? Here the record is mixed. Baldwin's most extensive statement on LGBTQ politics in the 1980s remains his 1984 interview with Richard Goldstein. Baldwin is generationally suspect of an LGBTQ movement whose language and tactics exceed his political vocabulary. Asked by Goldstein if he feels like a stranger in gay America, Baldwin says, "The word 'gay' has always rubbed me the wrong way. I never understood what was meant by it."[43] Asked if he felt a responsibility to the current gay social movement, Baldwin insists that for him sexuality had always been a more private than public matter, and that his responsibility lay mainly in being a witness, not participant. Asked if he felt optimistic about the possibility of building a "coalition" in support of gay and lesbian rights, Baldwin reverts to a language of universalism:

It's simply that the whole question has entered my mind another way. I know a great many white people, men and women, straight and gay, whatever, who are unlike the majority of their countrymen. On what basis we could form a coalition is still an open question. The idea of basing it on sexual preference strikes me as somewhat dubious, strikes me as being less than a firm foundation. It seems to me that a coalition has to be based on the grounds of human dignity. Anyway, what connects us, speaking about the private life, is mainly unspoken.[44]

Here, time seemed out of joint, too. Baldwin's impulse towards a non-identity-based movement of political values was a remnant of his earlier, radical humanism that had made him shy away from party membership on the left; indeed, in the interview with Goldstein he avers that he is not one to join a "club," citing his earlier, very brief stint as a socialist as an example. Baldwin also acknowledges that his marching days are over, even as a new movement is rising. In part, this was chronology overtaking him: less than a year after his interview with Goldstein, Baldwin would be admitted to the hospital with exhaustion, the beginnings of a marked downward slide in his health until the time of his death in 1987. Finally, Baldwin appears to try to preserve the bourgeois sphere of the "private" just as the LGBTQ movement was exposing and detonating that realm as the closet.

At the same time, Baldwin's insistence that homosexuality is not a "noun" but in effect a practice denotes sexuality as what Foucault would call "discursive." Baldwin's suspicions about both sexual names and camps comprehends heteronormativity itself less as repression and more as discursive power. Asked by Goldstein "Why do you think homophobia falls so often on the right of the political spectrum?" Baldwin replies:

It's a way of controlling people. Nobody really cares who goes to bed with whom, finally, I mean, the State doesn't really care, the church doesn't really care. They care that you should be frightened of what you do. As long as you feel guilty about it, the State can rule you. It's a way of exerting control over the universe, by terrifying people.[45]

The shadow of the Christian church that hung over Baldwin's preadolescent desires now hung as a wider scimitar wielded by a "moral majority" of the Reagan era bent on transmuting scripture into raw political power.

Baldwin's last significant public conversation showed the lingering relevance of support by the U.S. state for Israel and the perils of his own criticism of Israeli settler-colonialism. On February 28, 1984, Baldwin spoke on the campus of the University of Massachusetts, Amherst. The subject of his talk was "Blacks and Jews." The previous month, the topic had risen to public attention when presidential candidate Jesse Jackson, a long-time civil rights activist, was heard using the word "Hymietown" to refer to New York City. "Hymie" is a derogatory slur for Jews. Jackson was widely attacked for the remark as anti-semitic.

Baldwin's remarks at the university were both personal and global. He recalled that in high school his best friends were Jewish because of his empathy for their treatment by the Nazis. Turning to the state of Israel, Baldwin repeated his argument from "An Open Letter to the Born Again" that the nation "came into existence as a means of protecting Western interests at the age of the Middle East."[46] Baldwin then noted the "incipient attack" on Jesse Jackson as an anti-semite, saying "I think I know Jesse well enough to say that that seems to me exceedingly unlikely. But what does impress me is the uses to which this anecdote is being put."[47]

In discussion with students after his remarks, Baldwin elaborated that he felt the attack on Jackson was "an attempt to set us at another division, obviously an attempt to discredit Jackson, but to prevent the possibility of a certain kind of coalition. Not only between blacks and Jews but ... The importance of Jesse's campaign, I thought, was perhaps to create a possibility of a coalition between people who stopped voting quite some time ago."[48] Baldwin was referring to the so-called "Rainbow Coalition" built by Jackson of non-white, previously disenfranchised, mainly poor voters who had been the target of his campaign. Baldwin also said the attack on Jackson could have the effect of muting discussion of important global political issues, such as Israel's shipment of arms to South Africa.

After the event, University of Massachusetts Professor Julius Lester, a one-time activist with the Student Nonviolent Coordinating Committee and speechwriter for Stokely Carmichael, who had since converted to Judaism, wrote in his book *Lovesong* about Baldwin's remarks at the event, "I know he is not an anti-Semite, but his remarks in class were anti-Semitic, and he does not realize it."[49] After colleagues in the Afro-American Studies program defended Baldwin, Lester left it to work in the university's program of Judaic Studies. Meanwhile, Jackson's Hymietown remark seriously damaged a campaign that, while he was not expected to win, had been the most successful presidential campaign to date by an African-American. Baldwin never commented publically on Lester's attacks on him.

* * *

In 1985, Baldwin's published and some unpublished essays were gathered in a single volume titled *The Price of the Ticket*. The book was significant for both looking backward, retrospectively and in a monumental manner, at the whole of

Baldwin's life, and forward, to the beginnings of the process of his memory and commemoration. By 1985, Baldwin's literary production had become relatively meager. He was tired, winding down, traveling less, and camping out mainly at St. Paul-de-Vence. The lover he had lost to AIDS, according to David Leeming, died with him there, his ashes scattered around the property's garden.

Baldwin was committed to two writing projects in these closing years of his life. The first, begun years earlier, was titled *No Papers for Muhammad*. According to Baldwin biographers James Campbell and David Leeming, the novel was to be based on Baldwin's own frightening encounter with French immigration authorities—one perhaps fictionalized in David's near apprehension by the police in "Les Evade's" discussed earlier—and on the case of an Arab friend deported to Algeria. Baldwin never completed the novel. However, important kernels and seedlings from it did manifest themselves in what became his final creative project, a play entitled *The Welcome Table*. Magdalena Zaborowska, in her superb book on Baldwin's Turkish decade, refers to Baldwin's *The Welcome Table* as a "last testament" to major life themes, including exile, erotics, and the multiple identities of the diasporic black subject.[50] It is also, as Joseph Vogel noted, the only place in his creative writing where Baldwin made reference to the AIDS/HIV crisis.

The play begins when Peter David, an American journalist, arrives in Paris. He has come to France to interview Edith Hemings, a famous singer and actress. The action then moves to Hemings's home in southern France—a stand-in for Baldwin's St. Paul-de-Vence property, where Hemings is hosting a birthday party for the 93-year-old Algerian exile Madame LaFarge. The play is a dinner party, Chekhovian in nature, with an assorted cast, many of them with non-fictional roots in Baldwin's life. Hemings is a composite of female artists

Baldwin had known, including Eartha Kitt and Nina Simone.[51] LaFarge is based on Jeanne Faure, a French-Algerian in exile from her land of birth and from whom Baldwin purchased his home; Peter is likely based on Henry Louis Gates, Jr., the Harvard African-American Studies professor—then journalist—who had interviewed Baldwin for *Time* magazine; Daniel, a former Black Panther attempting to become a playwright, a loose mock-up of Stokely Carmichael and Baldwin himself; Rob, Edith's "protégé and lover," and Mark, a Jewish man, also Mark's lover; and Muhammad, inspired by Baldwin's gardener, and the protagonist of his unfinished novel.

Baldwin's primary theme is described by the author thusly: "Forays, frontiers, and flags are useless. Nobody can go home anymore." While the play offers a sequence of characters permanently displaced by politics, war, sexual crisis, gender traumas, it is the figure of Muhammad, the play's servant, whose "unwelcomeness" at the *Welcome Table* is Baldwin's deepest figuration of dispossession. Indeed, Muhammad's location in the "rambling stone house" which contains the play's actions is marked frequently as a literal outsider: he spends significant time in the garden, enters the dramatic action almost always as an instrumental attendant, and provides a literal denouement to the action by leaving the house (and the stage) when he drives the erstwhile matriarch and original owner of the house, Madame LaFarge, away into the night. The symbolic double departure of the fallen expatriate from Algiers—driven out of the country first by the national liberation struggle, and second by Muhammad's escort—is shorthand for the play's theme of decline and fall: from colonial grandeur, from theatrical careers, from revolutionary movements, from houses and homes. At a broader level, the text is a playful, sardonic signifier for a terminus, and crossroads, in the West's history of revolutions, from Paris

1789, to Algiers 1954. This is captured in the symbolism of the 93-year-old LaFarge's birthday, possibly her last, which all have come to commemorate, and in this exchange between Muhammad and Peter David, a black American journalist, about Muhammad and Edith's working relationship in Algiers:

> Mohammed: "In my country—when she was home, there—she never serves us cake."
> Peter: "You ever hear of a French Queen, called Marie Antoinette?"
> Mohammed: "She was—beheaded?"
> Peter: "She ran out of cake."[52]

In *The Welcome Table*, the presence of journalist Peter David—along with Daniel, an ex-Black Panther now in exile—also provides Baldwin with an opportunity to explore the symbiotic relationship between African-Americans confronting American racism and empire at home (Baldwin began the play in 1967 during the time of the Vietnam War and a year after the Black Panther Party chapter was founded in Oakland), and the corresponding conditions in France for exiles like himself. Baldwin's decision to end the play with Muhammad driving Madame LaFarge out of the house, and the play, bespeaks the text's anxious, cyclical post-colonial thematic about the declension of Western empires. Their overturning is echoed by signs and symptoms of the erosion of the "other" Western hegemon in the play's French setting—the U.S.—whose dominance as described totters under challenges by militants like the Panthers, imperial overreach suggested via allusion to U.S. political crimes in Guatemala (the 1954 coup), Chile (Allende, 1973), and both South Africa and Palestine, briefly referenced in the text. Thus the play examines what might be called imperial fatigue, the ennui of "rootless cosmopolitanism" and exile as conditions generated by historical processes of national conquest, imperial domination, anti-colonial resistance, and displacement. As Regina, Edith's oldest friend, puts it," I hope to God I never see another flag, as long as I live. I would like to burn them all—burn every pass-port."[53] In so saying, the play's other aging grand dame expresses an ambivalence about the inevitability of *statelessness*.

Which returns us to Muhammad: he is *The Welcome Table*'s subaltern nomad, waiting in the wings of modernity's rituals of self-aggrandizement for, well, cake. As such, Muhammad embodies statelessness as a condition of lack, of national unbelonging, the condition of being, as Baldwin put it in the title of his final, unpublished, and incomplete novel about Muhammad himself, without papers. Indeed, according to James Campbell and David Leeming, the novel *No Papers for Muhammad* was to be Baldwin's book based on his own frightening encounter with French immigration authorities. Campbell also notes that the novel was to capture Baldwin's "personal conundrum" that his residency in Turkey coincided with the "first waves of Turkish immigrants flooding into Germany and Switzerland," a conundrum exacerbated by Baldwin's recognition of himself as "the oppressor" as he put it in an interview, in his relationship to his own Algerian gardener.[54] This paper trail around *No Papers* then serves as an ineffable coda to Baldwin's confession from *No Name in the Street* about his relationship as an African-American to the Arab world: "as I began to discern what their history had made of them, I began to suspect, somewhat painfully, what my history had made of me." Clearly Baldwin saw in his X-ray examination of the Afro-Arab condition the skeleton not just of Western history but the master–slave dialectic played out on the backs of he who the former Black Panther Daniel calls, in *The Welcome Table*, "My Algerian brother."[55]

Besides the Arab question, HIV/AIDS is the other shadow hovering over Baldwin's final work. Edith raises the specter of the disease in Act 1 when she tells her lover Rob, "There's a man going 'round taking names, you know," a reference, Joseph Vogel notes, to death in a Lead Belly song, but here specific to HIV: "You're talking about the plague?" says Rob, "because of Mark?"—Rob's other romantic interest, but not a sexual partner. Edith complains, "You don't know where Mark's been, who he's been with."[56] Rob draws from the discussion a lesson about his loyalty to her: "For me, it just means that we are going to have to take seriously—what we always claimed to take seriously—our responsibility for each other."[57]

Baldwin was literally dying as he wrote *The Welcome Table*. All through 1986 he had been weakening, suffering from a sore throat. In early 1987, he was diagnosed with cancer of the esophagus. As he grew weaker, he was cared for by his brother David, and visiting relatives and friends. He died at his home at St. Paul-de-Vence on December 1, 1987, with David, his one-time lover Lucien Happersberger, and his household attendant, Hassell, by his side.

Baldwin once wrote, "Not everything that is faced can be changed, but nothing can be changed until it is faced."[58] It is noteworthy that in his final major piece of writing, Baldwin at last faced the crisis of HIV, a dying man serving as witness to it. It is a fitting final act of political conscience from Baldwin, who aimed constantly to create and set right a new history from the ashes of its—and his—contradictions.

Postscript:
Baldwin's Queer Legacies

For Jimmy was God's revolutionary black mouth.
Amiri Baraka, eulogy at James Baldwin's funeral[1]

On December 8, 1987 more than 5,000 people swelled the gothic interior of the Cathedral of St. John the Divine in New York to pay their last respects to James Baldwin. The event inaugurated what might be called the first phase of Baldwin's posthumous legacy. Global literary figures ascended the podium to canonize Baldwin as the most important literary voice of the U.S. civil rights era. Baldwin was ordained as the writer who had most inspired what had become by the 1980s a renaissance of African-American writing, perhaps best symbolized by Toni Morrison's anointment the year following Baldwin's death as the first African-American woman to win the Nobel Prize in Literature. In her remarks at the service at St. John the Divine, Morrison praised Baldwin for his "courage" to name white supremacy as a subject for the black writer. Other authors who came forth in tribute included Baldwin's friend William Styron, poet and novelist Maya Angelou, poet Amiri Baraka, novelist Mary McCarthy, and Nigerian novelist Chinua Achebe. Baldwin's first "legacy," then, captured in a tribute volume published in 1989, was as nominal mentor for both black and white writers in the post-war period seeking a means to wed political commitments to literary production, and to use literature as a pulpit or platform to tell original stories about the black diaspora. Baldwin's death and commemoration also coincided with a general rebirth, or in some cases discovery, of African-American writing by colleges and universities. Baldwin's work, somewhat neglected during the period of his so-called "decline" in the 1970s and 1980s, began a gradual reversal of fortune.

What was not much discussed at St. John the Divine was Baldwin's sexuality. Despite the fact that he had opened the door onto his queer life more and more in the 1980s, especially in his interviews with Audre Lorde and Richard Goldstein, Baldwin remained at the time of his death a vaguely closeted figure. This began to change in 1999, when scholar Dwight McBride published the edited volume *James Baldwin Now!* The book included several essays directly examining queer themes and moments in Baldwin's life and writing. The book heralded and captured two aspects of black gay life changing at once in the U.S.: a recognition in the public arena of the sometimes "invisible" lives of African-American gay men, and the institutional beginnings of what is now called Black Queer Studies. Both of these events were by-products of the AIDS/HIV crisis of the 1980s and 1990s, and the specifically devastating effects of that on the lives of black men (and women). Despite his belatedness in addressing the AIDS crisis, Baldwin was to become an avatar for both of these developments. Groundbreaking scholarship has followed in recent years by scholars like Marlon Ross, Dwight McBride, E. Patrick Johnson, Roderick Ferguson, Maurice Wallace, Robert Reid-Pharr, and Matt Brim. It is safe to say now that Baldwin has helped to queer African-American Studies and American literary history, and that neither will ever be the same again.

We are now in the third significant phase of Baldwin's legacy, the Baldwin of Black Lives Matter. As noted in our Introduction, Ta-Nehesi Coates's 2015 book *Between the World and Me*, directly inspired by Baldwin's *The Fire Next*

Time, and a bestselling meditation on police violence against African-Americans, was singularly responsible for the redis-covery of Baldwin by the Black Lives Matter movement. This is appropriate. It was after all Baldwin who insisted that the artist and the revolutionary were sisters under the skin, both with a special responsibility to society. A whole new genera-tion of readers is now coming to Baldwin not just to help them understand and study the world, but to change it.

At the same time, the repopularization of Baldwin reflects fundamental unchanging currents in the conditions of African-Americans in the U.S. Rampant economic inequali-ties between blacks and non-blacks; disproportionate rates of imprisonment; chronic urban poverty. Under Donald Trump, black Americans saw themselves marginalized further by the normalization of white nationalism and white suprem-acist ideas that have resulted in new far-right mobilizations, targeted killings of blacks, Jews, and Muslims, and the demon-ization of immigrants. Baldwin would not have been surprised by any of these developments, but he would certainly have called them by their name, and fought them. Those tasks now fall to the next generation who may create a legacy to match the one he left us.

Notes

Preface to the Paperback Edition

1. Kelly Jensen. "Why Read a Book When You Can Just Ban It? Inside Florida's Clay County School District." *Book Riot*. November 10, 2022. https://bookriot.com/clay-county-district-schools-book-bans/
2. "10 Banned Books That Are Crucial to Black Culture." *Afro: The Black Media Authority*. February 6, 2022. https://afro.com/10-banned-books-that-are-crucial-to-black-culture/.
3. Elaine Hegwood Bowen. "'James Baldwin Abroad' Program Captures Iconic Novelist and Activist in Paris, London and Istanbul." *Chicago Crusader*. January 5, 2023. https://chicagocrusader.com/james-baldwin-abroad-program-captures-iconic-novelist-and-activist-in-paris-london-and-istanbul/
4. Tim Murphy. "A Fascinating 1984 Talk Between James Baldwin and Audre Lorde Will Be Reenacted in NYC on Feb. 6th." *The Body*. January 23, 2023. www.thebody.com/article/baldwin-lorde-talk-reenacted

Introduction: James Baldwin—A Revolutionary for Our Time

1. Interview with James Baldwin. IKOR/CVK Television. February 17, 1972. Box 5, Folder 12. James Baldwin Papers, 1936–92. Schomburg Center for Research in Black Culture, New York Public Library.
2. James Baldwin. Letter to Mary Garin-Painter. Box 2, Folder 4. Walter O. Evans Collection of James Baldwin. 1953–87. James Baldwin Photographs and Papers. Beinecke Rare Book and Manuscript Library, Yale University.
3. James Baldwin, "From Nationalism, Colonialism, and the United States: One Minute to Twelve—A Forum," in *The Cross*

of Redemption: Uncollected Writings. Ed. Randall Kenan. New York: Vintage Books, 2010, p. 14.

4. Orilla Miller interview with Lynn Scott. Videotape. James Baldwin Photographs and Papers. Beinecke Rare Book and Manuscript Library, Yale University.

5. Herb Boyd, *Baldwin's Harlem.* New York: Atria Books, 2008, p. 1.

6. Ibid., p.18.

7. James Baldwin, "An Open Letter to My Sister Miss Angela Davis." *New York Review of Books.* January 7, 1971. www.nybooks.com/articles/1971/01/07/an-open-letter-to-my-sister-miss-angela-davis/.

8. James A. Dievler, "Sexual Exiles: James Baldwin and Another Country" in *James Baldwin Now.* Ed. Dwight A. McBride. New York: New York University Press, 1999, p. 162.

9. Magdalena J. Zaborowska, *James Baldwin's Turkish Decade: Erotics of Exile.* Durham, NC: Duke University Press, 2009.

10. James Baldwin. Letter to Orilla Miller. Box 1, Folder 1. James Baldwin Photographs and Papers. Beinecke Rare Book and Manuscript Library, Yale University.

11. James Baldwin, *No Name in the Street.* New York: Vintage, 1972, p. 197.

12. James Baldwin, "Stranger in the Village" in *James Baldwin: Collected Essays.* Ed. Toni Morrison. New York: Library of America, 1998, p. 129.

13. Eddie Glaude, "James Baldwin and the Trap of Our History." Time Magazine. August 18, 2016. http://time.com/4457112/james-baldwin-eddie-glaude.

14. Ta-Nehisi Coates, *Between the World and Me.* New York: Spiegel & Grau, 2015.

15. *I Am Not Your Negro.* D. Raoul Peck, 2016, Velvet Film, Inc. See also *I Am Not Your Negro.* New York: Vintage International, 2017; Jesmyn Ward (ed.), *The Fire This Time: A New Generation Speaks About Race.* New York: Scribner, 2016; Teju Cole, *Known and Strange Things.* New York: Random House, 2016; Michael Eric Dyson, *What Truth Sounds Like: Robert F. Kennedy, James Baldwin and Our Unfinished Conversation About Race.* New York: St. Martin's Press, 2018; Alice Mikal Craven and William

E. Dow, (eds.), associate editor Yoko Nakamura, *Of Latitudes Unknown: James Baldwin's Radical Imagination*. London: Bloomsbury, forthcoming.

16. James Baldwin, "A Report from Occupied Territory." *The Nation*. July 11, 1966. www.thenation.com/article/report-occupied-territory/.

17. Among these books of note are Matt Brim, *James Baldwin and the Queer Imagination*. Ann Arbor: University of Michigan Press, 2014; Robert Reid-Pharr, *Once You Go Black: Choice, Desire, and the Black American Intellectual*. New York: New York University Press, 2007; Marlon Ross, *Manning the Race: Reforming Black Men in the Jim Crow Era*. New York: New York University Press, 2004; E. Patrick Johnson, Mae G. Henderson, Sharon Patricia Holland, and Cathy Cohen (eds.), *Black Queer Studies: A Critical Anthology.*. Durham: Duke University Press, 2004; E. Patrick Johnson (ed.), *No Tea, No Shade: New Writings in Black Queer Studies*. Durham: Duke University Press, 2016; Roderick Ferguson, *Aberrations in Black: Towards a Queer of Color Critique*. Minneapolis: University of Minnesota Press, 2003; Maurice Wallace, *Constructing the Black Masculine: Identity and Ideality in African American Men's Literature and Culture, 1775–1995*. Durham: Duke University Press, 2002.

18. See Joseph Vogel, *James Baldwin and the 1980s: Witnessing the Reagan Era*. Urbana-Champaign: University of Illinois Press, 2018.

19. See Ed Pavlić, *Who Can Afford to Improvise? James Baldwin and Black Music, the Lyric and the Listeners*. New York: Fordham University Press, 2015.

20. See Zaborowksa, *James Baldwin's Turkish Decade*. See also Paul Gilroy, *The Black Atlantic: Modernity and Double Consciousness*. Cambridge: Harvard University Press, 1993.

21. See "Black for Palestine." www.blackforpalestine.com.

22. See Keith Feldman, *A Shadow Over Palestine: The Imperial Life of Race in America*. Minneapolis: University of Minnesota Press, 2017; and Alex Lubin, *Geographies of Liberation: The Making of an Afro-Arab Political Imaginary*. Durham: University of North Carolina Press, 2014.

23. See William J. Maxwell (ed.), *James Baldwin: The FBI File*. New York: Arcade Publishing, 2017.

Chapter 1. Baptism by Fire: Childhood and Youth, 1924–42

1. James Baldwin, "Autobiographical Notes" in *James Baldwin Collected Essays*. Ed. Toni Morrison. New York: The Library of America, 1998, p. 7.
2. James Baldwin. Unpublished essay. Box 1, Folder 4. James Baldwin Papers. New York Public Library, Schomburg Center for Research in Black Culture.
3. James Baldwin, "Fifth Avenue Uptown: A Letter from Harlem" in *James Baldwin Collected Essays*. Ed. Toni Morrison. New York: The Library of America, 1998, p. 176.
4. Herb Boyd, *Baldwin's Harlem*. New York: Atria Books, 2008, p. 4.
5. Joe Walker, "A Television Conversation: James Baldwin" in *Conversations with James Baldwin*. Ed. Fred L. Standley and Louis H. Pratt. Jackson: University Press of Mississippi, 1989, p. 123.
6. See Claude McKay, "If We Must Die." www.poetryfoundation.org/poems/44694/if-we-must-die.
7. *Souls of Black Folk* was the title of the groundbreaking collection of writing published in 1903 by W.E.B. Du Bois. The book's title refers to many things, including the tradition in African-American history of writing, music, and religion to sustain and characterize survival and resistance. See W.E.B. Du Bois, *Souls of Black Folk*. New York: Dover Press, 1994.
8. James Baldwin in *James Baldwin Nikki Giovanni: A Dialogue*. New York: Lippincott Books, 1973, 32.
9. James Baldwin. Interview with Richard Barron, October 23, 1963. Box 5, Folder 2. James Baldwin Papers. New York Public Library, Schomburg Center for Research in Black Culture, p. 8, 9.
10. *Take This Hammer*. Bay Area Television Archive. https://diva.sfsu.edu/collections/sfbatv/bundles/187041.
11. James Baldwin. Interview with Richard Barron, 77.

12. James Baldwin, "The Harlem Ghetto" in *James Baldwin Collected Essays.* Ed. Toni Morrison. New York: The Library of America, 1998, p. 48.

13. James Baldwin, *Go Tell It On the Mountain.* New York: Vintage International, 1952, 1980, p. 3.

14. James Baldwin, "Letter from a Region of My Mind" in *James Baldwin Collected Essays.* Ed. Toni Morrison. New York: The Library of America, 1998, p. 306.

15. James Baldwin, "Synposis: Crying Holy." No date. Box 127, Folder 1. James Baldwin Early Manuscripts and Paper, 1941–45. Beinecke Library, Yale University, p. 1.

16. Ibid., p. 1.

17. Ibid., p. 2.

18. Ibid., p. 2.

19. Ibid., p. 3.

20. James Baldwin. Interview with Richared Barron, p. 20.

21. James Baldwin, "Synposis: Crying Holy," p. 4.

22. James Baldwin. Interview with Arthur Crossman. 1986. Unpublished. Box 5, Folder 1. James Baldwin Papers. New York Public Library, Schomburg Center for Research in Black Culture, p. 18.

23. James Baldwin. Interview with Richard Barron, p. 70.

24. James Baldwin. Interview with Arthur Crossman, p.1.

25. James Baldwin. Interview with Richard Barron, p. 31.

26. James Baldwin, Interview with Arthur Crossman, p. 34.

27. Boyd, *Harlem*, p. 12.

28. Ibid., p. 18.

29. Orilla Miller interview with Lynn Scott. Video. James Baldwin Papers and Manuscripts. Beinecke Library, Yale University.

30. Ibid.

31. James Baldwin, *The Devil Finds Work* in *James Baldwin Collected Essays.* Ed. Toni Morrison. New York: The Library of America, 1998, p. 483.

32. Ibid., p. 486.

33. See Michael Denning, *The Cultural Front: The Laboring of American Culture in the Twentieth Century.* New York: Verso, 2011.

34. Baldwin, *Devil*, p. 504.

35. Ibid., p. 503.

36. Ibid., p. 488.
37. Douglas Field, *All Those Strangers: The Art and Lives of James Baldwin*. Oxford: Oxford University Press, 2015, p. 14.
38. Baldwin, *Devil*, p. 481.
39. *The Price of the Ticket*. Video. California Newsreel. http://james baldwinproject.org/AboutUsDistrib.html.
40. James Baldwin. Letter to Orilla Winfield. December 27, 1984. Box 1, Folder 1. James Baldwin Papers. Beinecke Library, Yale University.
41. James Campbell, *Talking at the Gates: A Life of James Baldwin*. New York: Viking, 1991, p. 21.
42. Ibid., p. 13.
43. James Baldwin. James Baldwin Early Manuscript and Papers, 1941–45. Box 1, Folder 18.
44. James Baldwin. Letter to Abel Meeropol. Box 3b, Folder 2. James Baldwin Papers. New York Public Library, Schomburg Center for Research in Black Culture.
45. James Baldwin, "The Price of the Ticket" in *James Baldwin Collected Essays*. Ed. Toni Morrison. New York: The Library of America, 1998, p. 830.
46. Ibid., p. 830.
47. Ibid., p. 832.
48. James Baldwin, "On the Painter Beauford Delaney" in *James Baldwin Collected Essays*. Ed. Toni Morrison. New York: The Library of America, 1998, p. 720.
49. James Baldwin, "The Creative Process" in *James Baldwin Collected Essays*. Ed. Toni Morrison. New York: The Library of America, 1998, p. 670.
50. James Baldwin, "On the Painter," p. 721.
51. James Baldwin, *No Name in the Street* in *James Baldwin Collected Essays*. Ed. Toni Morrison. New York: The Library of America, 1998, p. 540.
52. James Baldwin, "The Price of the Ticket" in *James Baldwin Collected Essays*. Ed. Toni Morrison. New York: The Library of America, 1998, p. 831.
53. Ibid., p. 831.
54. James Baldwin, "Synopsis: Crying Holy." Box 127, Folder 1. James Baldwin Early Manuscripts and Papers. Beinecke Library, Yale University, p. 3.

55. James Baldwin, "A Talk to Teachers" in *James Baldwin Collected Essays*. Ed. Toni Morrison. New York: The Library of America, 1998, p. 685.

56. Ibid., p. 685.

Chapter 2. Dissidence, Disillusionment, Resistance: 1942–48

1. Wilmer T. Stone. Letter of Recommendation for James Baldwin to the Editor of the *Amsterdam News*. October 16, 1941. Box 2, Folder 45. James Baldwin Early Manuscripts and Papers, 1941–45. Beinecke Library, Yale University.

2. James Baldwin. Letter to Tom Martin. September 2, 1944. Box 2, Folder 43. James Baldwin Early Manuscripts and Papers, 1941–45. Beinecke Library, Yale University.

3. James Baldwin. Review of Stuart Engstrand's *The Sling and the Arrow* in *The Cross of Redemption: Uncollected Writings*. Ed. Randall Kenan. New York: Vintage International, 2010, 304.

4. James Baldwin. Letter to Tom Martin. September 2, 1944. Box 2, Folder 43. James Baldwin Early Manuscripts and Papers, 1941–45. Beinecke Library, Yale University.

5. There are many good accounts of the Double Victory campaign and the Black Press and attempts by the federal government to repress it. See Patrick Washburn, *A Question of Sedition: The Federal Government's Investigation of the Black Press During World War II*. New York: Oxford University Press, 1986.

6. James Baldwin. *Notes of a Native Son* in *James Baldwin: Collected Essays*. Ed. Toni Morrison. New York: The Library of America, 1998, pp. 68–69.

7. Ibid., p. 69.

8. Ibid., p. 69.

9. Ibid., p. 70.

10. Ibid., p. 71.

11. Ibid., p. 71.

12. Ibid., p. 72.

13. Ibid., p. 72.

14. Ibid., p. 70.

15. Alan Wald. *American Night: The Literary Left in the Era of the Cold War*. Charlotte: University of North Carolina Press, 2012, p. 132.

16. "Award 20 Scholarships To Young Writers." *Daily Worker*. January 19, 1942, p. 7.

17. Baldwin, *Notes*, p. 67.

18. Ibid., p. 64.

19. Ibid., p. 65.

20. Ibid., p. 63.

21. Ibid., pp. 81, 82.

22. Ibid., p. 83.

23. Ibid., p. 84.

24. James Campbell. *Talking at the Gates: A Life of James Baldwin*. New York: Viking, 1991. p. 31.

25. On the milieu indicated here, see Robert J. Fitrakis, *The Idea of Democratic Socialism in America and the Decline of the Socialist Party*. Columbus, OH: CICJ Books, 2007; George Breitman, Paul Le Blanc, and Alan Wald, *Trotskyism in the United States, Historical Essays and Reconsiderations*. Chicago: Haymarket Books, 2016; Alan Wald, *The New York Intellectuals: The Rise and Decline of the Anti-Stalinist Left from the 1930s to the 1980s*. Chapel Hill: University of North Carolina Press, 1987.

26. James Baldwin quoted in Douglas Field, *All Those Strangers: The Art and Lives of James Baldwin*. Oxford: Oxford University Press, 2015. p. 13.

27. James Baldwin, "Letter to Orilla Winfield." 1955 undated. James Baldwin Correspondence with Orilla Winfield, 1955–90. Box 1, Folder 1. James Baldwin Papers. Beinecke Library. Yale University.

28. "The Art of Fiction: LXXVIII: James Baldwin." Interview of James Baldwin by Jordan Elgrably and George Plimpton in *Conversations with James Baldwin*. Ed. Fred. L. Standley and Louis H. Pratt. Jackson: University Press of Mississippi, 1989. p. 237.

29. "'Go the Way Your Blood Beats': An Interview with James Baldwin by Richard Goldstein." *The Village Voice*. June 26, 1984 in *James Baldwin: The Last Interview and Other Conversations*. Brooklyn: Melville House, 2014. p. 60.

30. *Challenge!* May 1944. Box 4, Folder 65. James Baldwin Early Manuscripts and Papers, 1941–45. Beinecke Library, Yale University.

31. Douglas Field, *All Those Strangers*, p. 15.

32. Campbell, *Talking*, p. 33.

33. Dan La Botz, "James Baldwin, Stan Weir, and Socialism." *New Politics.* May 3, 2017. http://newpol.org/content/james-baldwin-stan-weir-and-socialism.

34. James Baldwin, "Interview with Francois Bondy." *Transition* 12 1964, 15. Box 5, Folder 4. James Baldwin Papers. New York Public Library. Schomburg Center for Research in Black Culture, 15.

35. Joe Walker, "Exclusive Interview with James Baldwin" in *Conversations with James Baldwin*. Ed. Fred. L. Standley and Louis H. Pratt. Jackson: University Press of Mississippi, 1989. p. 131.

36. James Baldwin, "The Harlem Ghetto" in *James Baldwin: Collected Essays*. Ed. Toni Morrison. New York: The Library of America, 1998. p. 45.

37. James did take note of Baldwin. In 1948, James wrote to his wife: "That Jimmy Baldwin writes well. We must invite him to the party." "Jimmy Baldwin, the outcast little Negro switch and Bohemian *writes*—he is as different from Howe as genuine orange-juice is to the stuff in cans." See C.L.R. James, *Special Delivery: The Letters of C.L.R. James to Constance Webb 1939–1948*. Ed. Anna Grimshaw. Oxford: Blackwell, 1996, pp. 355, 372. In 1964, James wrote, "James Baldwin, popularly regarded at home as well as abroad as the effective spokesman against the century of old persecution of Negro Americans, has unequivocally stated that the problem is not a problem of black skin—it is a sickness in American civilization itself, which has expressed and expresses itself in the persecution of the Negro population." See C.L.R. James, "Lenin and the Problem" in *The C.L.R. James Reader*. Ed. Anna Grimshaw. Oxford: Blackwell, 1992, p. 331. It is likely that James's use of the term "switch" to describe Baldwin was in its time a homophobic slur.

38. *James Baldwin, Nikki Giovanni: A Dialogue*. New York: Lippincott, 1973, p. 64.

39. *Why?* Vol. 1, No. 8, March 1943. Box 4, Folder 67. James Baldwin Early Manuscripts and Papers, 1941–45. Beinecke Library, Yale University.
40. "The Veteran Problem: He'll Be Bitter." *New York Post.* February 28, 1945. Box 4, Folder 57. James Baldwin Early Manuscripts and Papers, 1941–45. Beinecke Library, Yale University.
41. Diva Agostinelli and Rebecca DeWitt, "A 79-Year-Old Woman Who Bowls: An Interview with Diva Agostinelli." The Anarchist Library. https://theanarchistlibrary.org/library/diva-agostinelli-and-rebecca-dewitt-a-79-year-old-woman-who-bowls.
42. Tom Martin. Letter to James Baldwin. June 14, 1944. Box 2, Folder 35. James Baldwin Early Manuscripts and Papers, 1941–45. Beinecke Library, Yale University.
43. James Baldwin. Draft of Letter to Tom Martin. September 2, 1944. Box 2, Folder 43. James Baldwin Early Manuscripts and Papers, 1941–45. Beinecke Library, Yale University.
44. Ibid.
45. Ibid.
46. James Baldwin. Unfinished letter to Sheldon Beigel. Box 2, Folder 28. James Baldwin Early Manuscripts and Papers, 1941–45. Beinecke Library, Yale University.
47. James Baldwin. Letter to Jackson MacLow. December 16, 1944. Box 2, Folder 34. James Baldwin Early Manuscripts and Papers, 1941–45. Beinecke Library, Yale University.
48. Tax Documents 1944. Box 4, Folder 68. James Baldwin Early Manuscripts and Papers, 1941–45. Beinecke Library, Yale University.
49. United States Office of War Information letter. January 3, 1945. Box 2, Folder 39. James Baldwin Early Manuscripts and Papers, 1941–45. Beinecke Library, Yale University.
50. James Baldwin, "Freaks and the American Ideal of Manhood" in *James Baldwin: Collected Essays.* Ed. Toni Morrison. New York: The Library of America, 1998. p. 818.
51. Ibid., p.821.
52. Ibid., p.819.
53. David Leeming. *James Baldwin: A Biography.* New York: Alfred Knopf, 1994, p. 115.
54. Ibid., p. 127.

55. James Baldwin. Undated draft letter to Dan "l". Box 2, Folder 44. James Baldwin Early Manuscripts and Papers, 1941–45. Beinecke Library, Yale University.

56. Leeming, *James Baldwin*, p. 46.

57. James Baldwin. Review of "*Best Short Stories* by Maxim Gorky." Originally published as "Maxim Gorki As Artist." *The Nation*, April 12, 1947. Reprinted in *The Cross of Redemption: Uncollected Writings*. Ed. Randall Kenan. New York: Vintage, 2010. p. 291.

58. Ibid., p. 293.

59. Ibid., p. 293.

60. James Baldwin, "The Artist's Struggle for Integrity." Orig. published in *Freedomways*, 1963. Reprinted in *The Cross of Redemption: Uncollected Writings*. Ed. Randall Kenan. New York: Vintage, 2010, p. 53.

61. *James Baldwin Nikki Giovanni: A Dialogue*. New York: Lippincott, 1973, p. 74.

62. James Baldwin, "Why I Stopped Hating Shakespeare." Originally published in *The Observer*, April 19, 1964. Reprinted in *The Cross of Redemption: Uncollected Writings*. Ed. Randall Kenan. New York: Vintage, 2010, p. 68.

63. James Baldwin review of *Mother* by Maxim Gorky. Originally published as "Battle Hymn" in New Leader, Nov. 29, 1947. Reprinted in *The Cross of Redemption: Uncollected Writings*. Ed. Randall Kenan. New York: Vintage, 2010. p. 296.

64. James Baldwin. *The Devil Finds Work* in *James Baldwin: Collected Essays*. Ed. Toni Morrison. New York: The Library of America, 1998, p. 512.

65. Douglas Field. *All Those Strangers*, p. 17.

66. Leon Trotsky, "Class and Art." www.marxists.org/archive/trotsky/1924/05/art.htm

67. Andre Breton and Leon Trotsky, "Manifesto: Towards a Free Revolutionary Art." www.generation-online.org/c/fcsurrealism1.htm

68. James Baldwin. Letter to Sol Stein in *James Baldwin and Sol Stein: Native Sons*. New York: One World, 2005, p. 98.

69. Quoted in Field, *All Those Strangers*, p. 20.

70. James Baldwin, "The Harlem Ghetto" in *James Baldwin: Collected Essays*. Ed. Toni Morrison. New York: The Library of America, 1998, p. 51.

71. James Baldwin. Outline for "Unto the Dying Lamb." Box 58, Folder 1. James Baldwin Papers. New York Public Library. Schomburg Center for Research in Black Culture, p. 3.

72. Ibid., p. 2.

73. Ibid., p. 3.

74. James Baldwin. Review of *The Sling and the Arrow* by Stuart Engstrand. Originally published as "Without Grisly Gaiety" in *New Leader*, September 20, 1947. Republished in *The Cross of Redemption: Uncollected Writings*. Ed. Randall Kenan. New York: Vintage, 2010, p. 304.

75. "Go the Way Your Blood Beats: An Interview with James Baldwin." Richard Goldstein. *The Village Voice*. June 26, 1984. Reprinted in *James Baldwin: The Last Interview and Others Conversations*. Brooklyn: Melville House, 2014, p. 62.

76. James Baldwin, "The Male Prison" in *James Baldwin: Collected Essays*. Ed. Toni Morrison. New York: The Library of America, 1998, p. 235.

77. Baldwin, "Freaks."

78. Baldwin, Review of "Slings," p. 304.

79. James Baldwin, "Nursery Rhyme." *New Masses*. May 21, 1945, p. 10.

80. Wald, *American Night*, p. 133.

81. Karl Marx. *The Eighteenth Brumaire of Louis Bonaparte*. www.marxists.org/archive/marx/works/1852/18th-brumaire/.

Chapter 3. Political Exile and Survival: 1948–57

1. *James Baldwin, Nikki Giovanni: A Dialogue*. New York: Lippincott, 1973, p. 78.

2. James Baldwin. Letter to Mary Painter, January 7, 1954. Box 2, Folder 1. James Baldwin Photographs and Papers. Beinecke Rare Book and Manuscript Library. Yale University.

3. "*The Black Scholar* Interviews James Baldwin." *The Black Scholar*, 5 (December 1973–January 1974), 33–42. Reprinted in

Conversations with James Baldwin. Ed. Fred Standley and Louis H. Pratt. Jackson: University Press of Mississippi, 1989, p. 152.

4. James Baldwin, "Stranger in the Village" in *James Baldwin Collected Essays.* Ed. Toni Morrison. New York: Library of America, 1998, p. 129.

5. James Baldwin, "The Image of the Negro" in *James Baldwin Collected Essays.* Ed. Toni Morrison. New York: Library of America, 1998, p. 587.

6. Ibid., p. 582.

7. "James Baldwin, an Interview." Wolfgang Binder. Originally published in *Revista/Review Interamericana,* 10 (Fall 1980), 326–41. Republished in *Conversations with James Baldwin.* Ed. Fred Standley and Louis H. Pratt. Jackson: University Press of Mississippi, 1989, p. 202.

8. James Baldwin. Undated letter to Orilla Winfield, 1955. James Baldwin Correspondence with Orilla Winfield, 1955–90. Box 1, Folder 1. James Baldwin Photographs and Papers. Beinecke Rare Book and Manuscript Library. Yale University.

9. James Baldwin, *No Name in the Street.* New York: Vintage, 1972, p. 29.

10. James Baldwin. Box 29. "The Amen Corner." Folder 1. James Baldwin Paper. New York Public Library. Schomburg Center for Research in Black Culture, p. 3.

11. James Baldwin, "A Question of Identity" in *James Baldwin Collected Essays.* Ed. Toni Morrison. New York: Library of America, 1998, p. 100.

12. James Baldwin, "Autobiographical Notes" in *James Baldwin Collected Essays.* Ed. Toni Morrison. New York: Library of America, 1998, p. 7–8.

13. James Baldwin, "Stranger in the Village" in *James Baldwin Collected Essays.* Ed. Toni Morrison. New York: Library of America, 1998, p. 129.

14. James Baldwin. Letter to Mary Garin-Painter. January 7, 1954. Walter O. Evans Collection of James Baldwin, 1953–87, Box 2, Folder 1. James Baldwin. Photographs and Papers. Beinecke Rare Book and Manuscript Library. Yale University.

15. James Baldwin. Undated letter to Mary Garin-Painter. 1955. Box 2, Folder 1. Walter O. Evans Collection of James Baldwin,

1953–87. James Baldwin. Photographs and Papers. Beinecke Rare Book and Manuscript Library. Yale University.

16. David Leeming, *James Baldwin: A Biography*. New York: Alfred Knopf, 1994, p. 50.

17. "An Interview with James Baldwin." David C. Estes. First published in *New Orleans Review* 13 (Fall 1986), 59–64. Republished in *Conversations with James Baldwin*. Ed. Fred L. Standley and Louis H. Pratt. Jackson: University Press of Mississippi, 1989, p. 276.

18. James Baldwin, "Everybody's Protest Novel" in *James Baldwin Collected Essays*. Ed. Toni Morrison. New York: Library of America, 1998, p. 18.

19. "Interview," Estes, p. 276.

20. Baldwin, "Everybody's," p. 18.

21. Ibid., p. 18.

22. "James Baldwin: An Interview," Binder, p. 203.

23. Quoted In Jurgen E. Grandt, "Into a Darker Past: James Baldwin's 'Giovanni's Room' and the Anxiety of Authenticity." *CLA Journal*, Vol. 54, No. 3. (March 2011), p. 269.

24. Leeming, *Biography*, 67.

25. James Baldwin, "Equal in Paris" in *James Baldwin Collected Essays*. Ed. Toni Morrison. New York: Library of America, 1998, pp. 106–07.

26. Baldwin, "Question," p. 98.

27. Baldwin, "Equal," p. 111.

28. Baldwin, "Equal," p. 116.

29. James Baldwin, "The Price of the Ticket" in *James Baldwin Collected Essays*. Ed. Toni Morrison. New York: Library of America, 1998, p. 835.

30. Baldwin, *No Name*, p. 38.

31. Ibid., p. 38.

32. James Baldwin Papers 1936–92. Box 13, Folder 2. New York Public Library. Schomburg Center for Research in Black Culture.

33. Robert Warshaw, "Letter to James Baldwin." March 28, 1950. Box 58, Folder 1. James Baldwin Papers 1936–92. New York Public Library. Schomburg Center for Research in Black Culture.

34. James Baldwin, "Stranger in the Village" in *James Baldwin Collected Essays*. Ed. Toni Morrison. New York: Library of America, 1998, p. 119.

35. Ibid., p. 121.

36. Ibid., p. 122.

37. Ibid., p. 124.

38. Ibid., p. 129.

39. James Baldwin, "Journey to Atlanta" in *James Baldwin Collected Essays*. Ed. Toni Morrison. New York: Library of America, 1998, p. 55.

40. Baldwin, *No Name*, p. 25.

41. James Baldwin, "Outline for a Novel: I, John." Box 12, Folder 2. James Baldwin Papers 1936–92. New York Public Library. Schomburg Center for Research in Black Culture, p. 1.

42. Ibid., p. 3.

43. Ibid., pp. 3–4.

44. James Baldwin, *Go Tell It On the Mountain*. New York: Vintage Books, 1981, p. 23.

45. Trudier Harris, *Black Women in the Fiction of James Baldwin*. Knoxville: University of Tennessee Press, 1985, p. 5.

46. Baldwin, *Go Tell It*, 82.

47. Ibid., p. 182.

48. Ibid., pp. 262–63.

49. Ibid., p. 259.

50. Ed Pavlić. *Who Can Afford to Improvise? James Baldwin and Black Music, the Lyric and the Listener*. New York: Fordham University Press, 2016, p. 4.

51. Babacar M'Baye, "African Retentions in *Go Tell It On the Mountain*" in James Baldwin's *Go Tell It On the Mountain: Historical and Critical Essays*. Ed. Carol E. Henderson. New York: Peter Lang, 2006, p. 42.

52. James Baldwin, "Many Thousands Gone" in *James Baldwin Collected Essays*. Ed. Toni Morrison. New York: Library of America, 1998, p. 25.

53. James Baldwin. Letter to Mary Garin-Painter. May 20, 1955. Box 2, Folder 1. Walter O. Evans Collection of James Baldwin, 1953–87. James Baldwin. Photographs and Papers. Beinecke Rare Book and Manuscript Library. Yale University.

54. James Baldwin. Letter to Mary Garin-Painter. January 7, 1954. Box 2, Folder 1. Walter O. Evans Collection of James Baldwin, 1953–87. James Baldwin. Photographs and Papers. Beinecke Rare Book and Manuscript Library. Yale University.

55. James Baldwin. Undated letter to Mary Garin-Painter. 1955. Box 2, Folder 1. Walter O. Evans Collection of James Baldwin, 1953–87. James Baldwin. Photographs and Papers. Beinecke Rare Book and Manuscript Library. Yale University.

56. James Baldwin. Undated letter to Mary Garin-Painter. 1956. Box 2, Folder 4. Walter O. Evans Collection of James Baldwin, 1953–87. James Baldwin. Photographs and Papers. Beinecke Rare Book and Manuscript Library. Yale University.

57. James Baldwin. Undated Letter to Mary Garin-Painter. October 1955. Box 2, Folder. Walter O. Evans Collection of James Baldwin, 1953–87. James Baldwin. Photographs and Papers. Beinecke Rare Book and Manuscript Library. Yale University.

58. Leeming, *Biography*, p. 123.

59. Ibid., p. 131.

60. James Baldwin. Letter to Mary Garin-Painter. April 2, 1956. Box 2, Folder 4. Walter O. Evans Collection of James Baldwin, 1953–87. James Baldwin. Photographs and Papers. Beinecke Rare Book and Manuscript Library. Yale University.

61. James Baldwin. Transcript of Interview with Arthur Crossman. Unpublished. Box 5, Folder 1. James Baldwin Papers 1936–92. New York Public Library. Schomburg Center for Research in Black Culture, p. 12.

62. James Baldwin. Letter to Mary Garin-Painter. Undated. October 1955. Box 2, Folder 1. Walter O. Evans Collection of James Baldwin, 1953–87. James Baldwin. Photographs and Papers. Beinecke Rare Book and Manuscript Library. Yale University.

63. Box 29, "The Amen Corner," Folder 1. James Baldwin Papers 1936–92. New York Public Library. Schomburg Center for Research in Black Culture.

64. James Baldwin, *The Amen Corner*. New York: Vintage International, 1996, p. xvi.

65. James Baldwin. Letter to Mary Garin-Painter. May 20, 1955. Box 2, Folder 1. Walter O. Evans Collection of James Baldwin,

1953–87. James Baldwin. Photographs and Papers. Beinecke Rare Book and Manuscript Library. Yale University.

66. James Baldwin. Letter "Dea Sam" Undated. Box 16, Folder 4. James Baldwin Papers 1936–92. New York Public Library. Schomburg Center for Research in Black Culture.

67. Ibid.

68. Ibid.

69. "Go the Way Your Blood Beats." An Interview with James Baldwin. Interview by Richard Goldstein. *The Village Voice.* June 26, 1984. Republished in *James Baldwin: The Last Interview and Other Conversations.* Brooklyn: Melville House, 2014, p. 61.

70. See Roderick A. Ferguson, "The Parvenu Baldwin and the Other Side of Redemption: Modernity, Race, Sexuality, and the Cold War" in *James Baldwin Now.* Ed. Dwight A. McBride. New York: New York University Press, 1999, pp. 233–64. See also Robert F. Reid-Pharr. *Once You Go Black: Choice, Desire and the Black American Intellectual.* New York: New York University Press, 2007.

71. James Baldwin. *Giovanni's Room.* New York: Vintage International, 2013, p. 1.

72. Leeming, *Biography*, p. 125.

73. James Baldwin, "The Male Prison" in *James Baldwin Collected Essays.* Ed. Toni Morrison. New York: Library of America, 1998, p. 235. Scholars have noted that Baldwin's plot line in *Giovanni's Room* was inspired in part by the case of Lucien Carr, a beatnik writer who as a youth killed David Kamerrer in New York City in 1944. Carr claimed that Kamerrer had made sexual advances.

74. Baldwin, *Giovanni's*, p. 54.

75. Ibid., p. 233.

76. Ibid., p. 223.

77. James Baldwin. Letter "Dea Sam" Undated. Box 16, Folder 4. James Baldwin Papers 1936–92. New York Public Library. Schomburg Center for Research in Black Culture.

78. James Baldwin. Letter to Mary Garin-Painter. March 25, 1955. Box 2, Folder 1. Walter O. Evans Collection of James Baldwin, 1953–87. James Baldwin. Photographs and Papers. Beinecke Rare Book and Manuscript Library. Yale University.

79. Baldwin, *Giovanni's*, p. 120.

80. Ibid., p. 166.

81. Eve Kosofsky Sedgwick, *Epistemology of the Closet*. Berkeley: University of California Press, 2008, p. 74.

82. See Judith Butler, "Performative Acts and Gender Constitution: An Essay in Phenomenology and Feminist Theory." *Theater Journal*, Vol. 40, No. 4 (December 1988), p. 519.

83. Baldwin, "Autobiographical," p. 8

84. Ibid., p. 9.

85. See Francis Stonor Saunders, *Who Paid the Piper: The CIA and the Cultural Cold War*. London: Granta Books, 2000.

86. James Baldwin. Letter to Mary Garin-Painter. May 20, 1955. Box 2, Folder 1. Walter O. Evans Collection of James Baldwin, 1953–87. James Baldwin. Photographs and Papers. Beinecke Rare Book and Manuscript Library. Yale University.

87. James Baldwin, "Princes and Powers" in *James Baldwin Collected Essays*. Ed. Toni Morrison. New York: Library of America, 1998, p. 158.

88. Ibid., p. 153.

89. Ibid., p. 145.

90. Ibid., p. 146.

91. Ibid., p. 147.

92. Ibid., p. 146.

93. Ibid., p. 154.

94. Ibid., p. 155.

Chapter 4. Paying His Dues: 1957–63

1. "Conversation: Ida Lewis and James Baldwin." Ida Lewis. First published in *Essence*, 16 (October 1970). Reprinted in *Conversations with James Baldwin*. Ed. Fred L. Standley and Louis H. Pratt. Jackson: University Press of Mississippi, 1989, p. 84.

2. James Baldwin. Letter to Mary Garin-Painter. May 26, 1960. Walter O. Evans Collection of James Baldwin, 1953–87. James Baldwin. Photographs and Papers. Beinecke Rare Book and Manuscript Library. Yale University.

3. U.S. Government Memorandum. May 29, 1963. In *James Baldwin: The FBI File*. Ed. William J. Maxwell. New York: Arcade Publishing, 2017, p. 1017.

4. "An Interview with James Baldwin." Studs Terkel. First published in Almanac, WFMT, Chicago. December 29, 1961. Republished in *James Baldwin: The Last Interview*. New York: Melville House, 2014, p. 20.

5. James Baldwin. Letter to Mary Garin-Painter. October 18, 1957. Box 2, Folder 5. Walter O. Evans Collection of James Baldwin, 1953–87. James Baldwin. Photographs and Papers. Beinecke Rare Book and Manuscript Library. Yale University.

6. James Baldwin. Undated Letter to Mary Garin-Painter. Box 2, Folder 6. Walter O. Evans Collection of James Baldwin, 1953–87. James Baldwin. Photographs and Papers. Beinecke Rare Book and Manuscript Library. Yale University.

7. James Baldwin, *No Name in the Street*. New York: Vintage International, 2000, p. 50.

8. Ed Pavlić, "Why James Baldwin Went to the South and What It Meant to Him." *Literary Hub*. June 29, 2018. https://lithub.com/why-james-baldwin-went-to-the-south-and-what-it-meant-to-him/.

9. Baldwin, *No Name*, 50. Ed Pavlić has written two revealing essays about Baldwin's southern journeys and their motivations. See Ed Pavlić, "Beyond Simplicity Part I: Towards James Baldwin's Letter from the Birmingham Motel" in *Brick*, 101, Summer 2018, pp. 42–52 and "Beyond Simplicity: The Journey Towards James Baldwin's Letter from the Birmingham Motel" in *Brick*, 102, Winter 2019, pp. 100–13.

10. Ibid., p. 60.

11. James Baldwin. Letter to Mary Garin-Painter. October 28, 1957. Box 2, Folder 5. Walter O. Evans Collection of James Baldwin, 1953–87. James Baldwin. Photographs and Papers. Beinecke Rare Book and Manuscript Library. Yale University.

12. James Baldwin, *Nobody Know My Name* in *James Baldwin Collected Essays*. Ed. Toni Morrison. New York: The Library of America, 1998, p. 206.

13. Ibid., p. 207.

14. Ibid., p. 207.

15. James Baldwin, "A Fly in Buttermilk" in *James Baldwin Collected Essays*. Ed. Toni Morrison. New York: The Library of America, 1998, p. 191.

16. James Baldwin, "Faulkner and Desegregation" in *James Baldwin Collected Essays*. Ed. Toni Morrison. New York: The Library of America, 1998, p. 211.

17. Baldwin, *Nobody*, p. 208.

18. James Baldwin. Letter to Mary Garin-Painter. October 18, 1957. Box 2, Folder 5. Walter O. Evans Collection of James Baldwin, 1953–87. James Baldwin. Photographs and Papers. Beinecke Rare Book and Manuscript Library. Yale University.

19. Ibid.

20. James Baldwin. Letter to Mary Garin-Painter. October 28, 1957. Box 2, Folder 5. Walter O. Evans Collection of James Baldwin, 1953–87. James Baldwin. Photographs and Papers. Beinecke Rare Book and Manuscript Library. Yale University.

21. Ibid.

22. James Baldwin. Letter to Mary Garin-Painter. December 26, 1957. Walter O. Evans Collection of James Baldwin, 1953–87. James Baldwin. Photographs and Papers. Beinecke Rare Book and Manuscript Library. Yale University.

23. Ibid.

24. Ibid.

25. James Baldwin, "Paris, 1958, Several Typescripts Some Handwritten Pages." Box 44, Folder 1. James Baldwin Papers 1936–92. New York Public Library. Schomburg Center for Research in Black Culture, pp. 2–3.

26. Ibid., p. 14.

27. Ibid., p. 16.

28. Ibid., pp. 2–3.

29. Ibid., p. 16.

30. Ibid., pp. 13, 14, 16.

31. James Baldwin, "Les Evade's." Box 56, Folder 11. James Baldwin Papers 1936–92. New York Public Library. Schomburg Center for Research in Black Culture.

32. Ibid.

33. James Baldwin, "Paris, 1958." Box 44, Folder 1, p. 14.

34. Baldwin, *No Name*, 44.

35. David Leeming. *James Baldwin: A Biography*. New York: Alfred Knopf, p. 156.
36. Ibid., p. 168.
37. James Baldwin. Letter to Mary Garin-Painter. Undated. Box 2, Folder 6. Walter O. Evans Collection of James Baldwin, 1953–87. James Baldwin. Photographs and Papers. Beinecke Rare Book and Manuscript Library. Yale University.
38. James Baldwin. Letter to Mary Garin-Painter. Undated. August, 1959. Box 2, Folder 5. Walter O. Evans Collection of James Baldwin, 1953–87. James Baldwin. Photographs and Papers. Beinecke Rare Book and Manuscript Library. Yale University.
39. James Baldwin, "They Can't Turn Back." *Mademoiselle*. 1960. www.historyisaweapon.com/defcon1/baldwincantturnback.html.
40. Ibid.
41. Ibid.
42. James Baldwin. Letter to Martin Luther King, Jr. Undated. 1960. https://kinginstitute.stanford.edu/king-papers/documents/james-baldwin.
43. James Baldwin, "The Dangerous Road Before Martin Luther King" in *James Baldwin Collected Essays*. Ed. Toni Morrison. New York: The Library of America, 1998, p. 638.
44. Ibid., p. 639.
45. Ibid., p. 657.
46. James Baldwin, "East River, Downtown: Postscript to a Letter from Harlem" in *James Baldwin Collected Essays*. Ed. Toni Morrison. New York: The Library of America, 1998, p. 183. The essay was originally published in the *New York Times Magazine*, March 12, 1961, with the title "A Negro Assays the Negro Mood."
47. James Baldwin. Letter to Mary Garin-Painter. May 26, 1960. Box 2, Folder 6. Walter O. Evans Collection of James Baldwin, 1953–87. James Baldwin. Photographs and Papers. Beinecke Rare Book and Manuscript Library. Yale University.
48. James Baldwin, "The Fire Next Time" in *James Baldwin Collected Essays*. Ed. Toni Morrison. New York: The Library of America, 1998, p. 327.
49. "The Hate That Hate Produced." WNTA-TV. July 13–17, 1959. www.youtube.com/watch?v=BsYWD2EqavQ.

50. "The Black Muslims in America." Transcription. *The Open Mind*. April 23, 1961. Box 5, Folder 3. James Baldwin Papers 1936–92. New York Public Library. Schomburg Center for Research in Black Culture, p. 7.

51. Ibid., p. 8.

52. Ibid., p. 9.

53. Ibid., p. 53.

54. Ibid., p. 54.

55. Herb Boyd. *Baldwin's Harlem: A Biography of James Baldwin*. New York: Atria Books, 2008, p. 77.

56. (SANE) 1961–64. Box 6, Folder 4. James Baldwin Papers 1936–92. New York Public Library. Schomburg Center for Research in Black Culture.

57. *James Baldwin: The FBI File*. Ed. William J. Maxwell. New York: Arcade Publishing, 2017, p. 1015.

58. James Baldwin, "From Nationalism, Colonialism, and the United States: One Minute to Twelve—A Forum" in *The Cross of Redemption: Uncollected Writings*. Ed. Randall Kenan. New York: Vintage International, 2010, p. 17.

59. Ibid., p. 14.

60. Ibid., p. 15.

61. Ibid., p. 18.

62. Maxwell, *FBI*, p. 1017.

63. James Campbell, *Talking at the Gates: A Life of James Baldwin*. New York: Viking, 1991, p. 152.

64. Leeming, *Biography*, p. 193.

65. James Baldwin, *No Name in the Street*. New York: Vintage International, 2007, p. 42.

66. An important primary source for understanding the development of Trotskyism's response to the formation of the state of Israel are Tony Cliff's (born Ygael Gluckstein) essays written from Palestine between 1938 and 1946: www.marxists.org/archive/cliff/index.htm.

67. James Baldwin. Letter to Mary Garin-Painter. October 7, 1961. Walter O. Evans Collection of James Baldwin, 1953–87. James Baldwin. Photographs and Papers. Beinecke Rare Book and Manuscript Library. Yale University.

68. Quoted in Keith Feldman, *A Shadow Over Palestine: The Imperial Life of Race in America.* Minneapolis: University of Minnesota Press, 2017, p. ix.

69. Ibid., p. viii.

70. Magdalena Zaborowska, *James Baldwin's Turkish Decade: Erotics of Exile.* Durham: Duke University Press, 2009, p. 8.

71. Ibid., p. 17.

72. Ibid., p. 6.

73. Ibid., p. 16.

74. Ibid., p. 85.

75. James Baldwin. Letter to Mary Garin-Painter. October 7, 1961. Box 2, Folder 7. Walter O. Evans Collection of James Baldwin, 1953–87. James Baldwin. Photographs and Papers. Beinecke Rare Book and Manuscript Library. Yale University.

76. James Baldwin, *Another Country.* New York: Dell Publishing, 1960.

77. Ibid., p. 66.

78. Ibid., p. 77.

79. Ibid., p. 76.

80. James Baldwin, "Freaks and the American Ideal of Manhood" in *James Baldwin Collected Essays.* Ed. Toni Morrison. New York: The Library of America, 1998, p. 815.

81. Ibid., p. 821.

82. Ibid., pp. 828–29.

83. Baldwin, *Another Country*, p. 278.

84. See Judith Butler, "Performative Acts and Gender Constitution: An Essay in Phenomenology and Feminist Theory." *Theater Journal*, Vol. 40, No. 4 (December 1988), pp. 519–531. See also her book *Gender Trouble: Feminism and the Subversion of Identity.* New York: Routledge, 2006.

85. "Race, Hate, Sex, and Colour: A Conversation with James Baldwin and Colin MacInness." James Mossman. First published in *Encounter*, 25 (July 1965), pp. 55–60. Republished in *Conversations with James Baldwin.* Ed. Fred L. Standley and Louis H. Pratt. Jackson: University Press of Mississippi, 1989, p. 54.

86. Maxwell, FBI, pp. 46–47.

87. Leeming, *Biography*, p. 216.

Chapter 5. Baldwin and Black Power : 1963–68

1. Stokely Carmichael, "Black Power." October 29, 1966. http://voic-esofdemocracy.umd.edu/carmichael-black-power-speech-text/.
2. "James Baldwin Breaks His Silence." Interview with Cep Dergisi. First published in *Atlas*, 13 (March 1967), pp. 47–49. Republished in *Conversations with James Baldwin*. Ed. Fred L. Standley and Louis H. Prass. Jackson: University Press of Mississippi, 1989, p. 61.
3. James Baldwin, "What Price Freedom?" in *James Baldwin: The Cross of Redemption*. New York: Vintage International, 2010, p. 85.
4. James Baldwin in *Collected Essays*. Ed. Toni Morrison. New York: Library of America, 1998. p. 337.
5. Congress National Convention Community Relations Document. 1963. www.crmvet.org/docs/63_core_conv_corel.pdf.
6. Quoted in Davis W. Houck, "Who's the Nigger Now? Rhetoric and Identity in James Baldwin's Revolution From Within." *James Baldwin Review*, Vol. 3, 2017, pp. 118–19. www.researchgate.net/publication/320231833_Who%27s_the_Nigger_Now_Rhetoric_and_Identity_in_James_Baldwin%27s_Revolution_from_Within
7. Ibid., p. 121.
8. James Baldwin in *Collected Essays*. Ed. Toni Morrison. New York: Library of America, 1998, p. 285.
9. Ibid., p. 291.
10. Ibid., p. 293.
11. Ibid., p. 293.
12. Ibid., p. 300.
13. Ibid., p. 304–05.
14. Ibid., p. 307.
15. Ibid., p. 313.
16. Ibid., p. 317.
17. Ibid., p. 328.
18. Ibid., p. 310.
19. Ibid., p. 330.
20. Ibid., p. 340.

21. Karl Marx. *Capital* Volume 1. www.marxists.org/archive/marx/works/1867-c1/.

22. E. San Juan, Jr., "James Baldwin's Allegory of Black Self-Determination" in *The Discourse of Multiplicity—The Meeting-Point of Popular Culture*. Ed. Tsuneo Kurachi, Shoichi Maeda and Yuichi Midzumoe. Tokyo: Taga-Shippan, 1995, p. 13.

23. Baldwin, *Collected Essays*, p. 345.

24. Ibid., p. 346.

25. James Baldwin, "Sweet Lorraine" in *Collected Essays*. Ed. Toni Morrison. New York: Library of America, 1998, 760.

26. Quoted in *James Baldwin: The FBI File*. Ed. William J. Maxwell. New York: Arcade Publishing, p. 61.

27. Ibid., p. 66.

28. Ibid., p. 80. In "The Dangerous Road Before Martin Luther King," Baldwin commented: "He [King] lost much moral credit, for example, in the eyes of the young, when he allowed Adam Clayton Powell to force the resignation of his (King's) extremely able organizer and lieutenant, Bayard Rustin." See James Baldwin, *Collected Essays*, ed. by Toni Morrison (New York: Library of America/Random House, 1998), p. 656.

29. Ibid., p. 1018.

30. Ibid., p. 1018.

31. Baldwin, "What Price," p. 83.

32. James Baldwin. *Blues for Mister Charlie*. New York: Vintage International, 1992, p. xv.

33. Ibid., p. 2.

34. Ibid., p. 74.

35. James Baldwin. Interview with Francois Bondy. *Transition* 12, 1964. Box 5, Folder 4. James Baldwin Papers 1936–92. New York Public Library. Schomburg Center for Research in Black Culture, p. 11.

36. James Baldwin. Box 58, Folder 17. James Baldwin Papers 1936–92. New York Public Library. Schomburg Center for Research in Black Culture.

37. James Baldwin, "Statement on Birmingham. Typescript Sept. 16, 1963." Box 44, Folder 14. James Baldwin Papers 1936–92. New York Public Library. Schomburg Center for Research in Black Culture.

38. Baldwin, "What Price Freedom?" p. 83.

39. James Baldwin, "Birmingham." Introduction, Outline. Box 58, Folder 18. James Baldwin Papers 1936–92. New York Public Library. Schomburg Center for Research in Black Culture.

40. Maxwell, *FBI*, p. 1936.

41. Ibid., p. 90.

42. James Baldwin, "We Can Change the Country" in *James Baldwin: The Cross of Redemption*. New York: Vintage International, 2010, p. 59.

43. Ibid., p. 61.

44. Ibid., p. 64.

45. Ibid., p. 62.

46. Ibid., p. 63.

47. Unpublished interview with Charles Childs. Box 5, Folder 7. James Baldwin Papers 1936–92. New York Public Library. Schomburg Center for Research in Black Culture, p. 14.

48. Ibid., p. 15.

49. Ibid., p. 16.

50. Ibid., p. 15.

51. See Dan La Botz, "James Baldwin, Stan Weir, and Socialism" in *New Politics*. May 3, 2017. http://newpol.org/content/james-baldwin-stan-weir-and-socialism. For Baldwin on whiteness see *The Price of the Ticket*. Dir. Karen Thorsen. 1989.

52. James E. Jackson, "James Baldwin Indicts the System" in *The Worker*, October 1, 1963, p. 2.

53. Ibid., p. 2.

54. Quoted in Howard Zinn, *You Can't Be Neutral on a Moving Train*. www.howardzinn.org/freedom-day-selma-1963/.

55. There is much reporting and scholarship on the so-called "Central Park jogger" case. For a good interview see "City Releases Trove of Documents in Central Park Jogger Case." *New York Times*. July 20, 2018. www.nytimes.com/2018/07/20/nyregion/documents-from-the-central-park-jogger-case-are-released.html.

56. James Baldwin, "A Report From Occupied Territory" in *Collected Essays*. Ed. Toni Morrison. New York: Library of America, 1998, p. 734.

57. Ibid., p. 738.

58. Richard Avedon and James Baldwin, *Nothing Personal*. New York: Taschen Books, 2017.

59. Baldwin, "What Price Freedom?" p. 85.

60. Ibid., p. 87.

61. Baldwin, *FBI*, p. 1258.

62. Ibid., p. 1258.

63. James Baldwin. Letter to David Adams Leeming. January 25, 1966. Box 2, Folder 8. James Baldwin Photographs and Papers. Beinecke Rare Book and Manuscript Library.

64. "James Baldwin Debates William F. Buckley." www.youtube.com/watch?v=oFeoS41xe7w.

65. Alex Haley. Letter to James Baldwin. May 7, 1967. Box 3, Folder 19. James Baldwin Papers 1936–92. New York Public Library. Schomburg Center for Research in Black Culture.

66. Magdalena Zaborowska, *James Baldwin's Turkish Decade: Erotics of Exile*. Durham: Duke University Press, 2009, p. 148.

67. Ibid., p. 135.

68. James Baldwin, "Going to Meet the Man" in *Going to Meet the Man*. New York: Vintage International, 1993, p. 236.

69. Ibid., p. 248.

70. Ibid., p. 249.

71. Ibid., p. 249.

72. James Baldwin. *No Name in the Street*. New York: Vintage International, 2000, p. 63.

73. "Harlem Six." Box 6, Folder 3. James Baldwin Papers 1936–92. New York Public Library. Schomburg Center for Research in Black Culture.

74. James Baldwin, "The International War Crimes Tribunal" in *James Baldwin: The Cross of Redemption*. New York: Vintage International, 2010, p. 246.

75. Ibid., p. 248.

76. Ibid., p. 248.

77. Martin Luther King, Jr, "Beyond Vietnam." Speech. April 4, 1967. https://kinginstitute.stanford.edu/encyclopedia/beyond-vietnam.

78. Baldwin, "International," pp. 247, 248.

79. James Baldwin, "Anti-Semitism and Black Power" in *James Baldwin: The Cross of Redemption.* New York: Vintage International, 2010, p. 252.

80. Alex Lubin, *Geographies of Liberation: The Making of an Afro-Arab Political Imaginary.* Chapel Hill: University or North Carolina Press, 2014, p. 118.

81. While there are many accounts of Du Bois's shifting perspective on Israel (including his own, as in his poem "Suez"), an especially trenchant analysis is provided in Vaughn Rasberry, *Race and the Totalitarian Century: Geopolitics in the Black Literary Imagination.* Cambridge: Harvard University Press, 2016.

82. Baldwin, "Anti-Semitism and Black Power," p. 252.

83. Ibid., p. 252.

84. Ibid., pp. 252–53.

85. James Baldwin, "Negroes Are Anti-Semitic Because They're Anti-White" in *Collected Essays.* Ed. Toni Morrison. New York: Library of America, 1998, p. 741.

86. Ibid., p. 742.

87. Ibid., p. 746.

88. Ibid., p. 748.

89. Carmichael, "Black Power."

90. James Baldwin, "Black Power" in *James Baldwin: The Cross of Redemption.* New York: Vintage International, 2010, p. 99.

91. Ibid., p. 100.

92. Ibid., p. 104.

93. James Baldwin. Letter to Eugene Lerner. August 9, 1966. Box 2, Folder 9. James Baldwin Photographs and Papers. Beinecke Rare Book and Manuscript Library.

94. James Baldwin. *Tell Me How Long the Train's Been Gone.* New York: Vintage International, 1968, p. 211.

95. Leeming, *Biography,* p. 280.

96. Baldwin, *Tell Me,* 454.

97. Ibid., p. 464.

Chapter 6. Morbid Symptoms and Optimism of the Will: 1968–79

1. Antonio Gramsci, *Selections from the Prison Notebooks of Antonio Gramsci.* London: Lawrence and Wishart, 1971.

2. James Baldwin, *No Name in the Street*. New York: Vintage International, 1972, p. 196.

3. "James Baldwin Interviewed." First published in *Transatlantic Review*, 37–38 (Autumn–Winter 1970–71), pp. 5–14. Reprinted in *Conversations with James Baldwin*. Ed. Fred L. Standley and Louis H. Pratt. Jackson: University Press of Mississippi, 1989, p. 102.

4. Baldwin, *No Name*, p. 74.

5. "Baldwin Interviewed," Hall, 102.

6. Baldwin, *No Name*, p. 164.

7. Ibid., p. 166.

8. Ibid., p. 167.

9. Ibid., p. 168.

10. Ibid., p. 170.

11. Ibid., p. 175.

12. "Exclusive Interview with James Baldwin." Joe Walker. First published in *Muhammad Speaks*, 11–12 (September–October 1972). Republished in *Conversations with James Baldwin*. Ed. Fred L. Standley and Louis H. Pratt. Jackson: University Press of Mississippi, p. 136.

13. Quoted in James Campbell, "Jimmy is Everywhere." *Times Literary Supplement*. March 7, 2018. www.the-tls.co.uk/articles/public/james-baldwin-fbi-files/.

14. David Leeming, *James Baldwin: A Biography*. New York: Alfred Knopf, 1994, p. 293.

15. Eldridge Cleaver, *Soul on Ice*. New York: Dell, p. 124.

16. Quoted in Henry Louis Gates, Jr., "The Fire This Time." *New Republic*. June 1, 1992. https://newrepublic.com/article/114134/fire-last-time

17. See Baldwin, *No Name*, p. 173 and "The Art of Fiction LXXVII: James Baldwin." Interview by Jordan Elgrably and George Plimpton. First published in *The Paris Review*, 26 (Spring 1984), pp. 49–92. Republished in *Conversations with James Baldwin*. Ed. Fred L. Standley and Louis H. Pratt. Jackson: University Press of Mississippi, 1989, p. 252.

18. Huey P. Newton on gay, women's liberation. *Worker's World*. May 16, 2012.

19. Baldwin, *No Name*, p. 144.

20. Ibid., p. 148.

21. "Are We on the Edge of Civil War?" Interview with David Frost. First published in *The Americans*. New York: Stein and Day, 1970, pp. 145–50. Republished in *Conversations with James Baldwin*. Ed. Fred L. Standley and Louis H. Pratt. Jackson: University Press of Mississippi, 1989, p. 95.

22. See Michelle Alexander, *The New Jim Crow: Mass Incarceration in the Age of Color Blindness*. New York: The New Press, 2012.

23. "Are We," Frost, p. 95.

24. Leeming, *Biography*, p. 311.

25. James Baldwin, "Speech from the Soledad Rally" in *James Baldwin: The Cross of Redemption*. New York: Vintage International, 2010, p. 122.

26. Ibid., p. 123.

27. James Baldwin, "White Racism or World Community?" in *James Baldwin: Collected Essays*. New York: Vintage International, 1998, p. 749.

28. Ibid., p. 753.

29. James Baldwin. Letter to Eugene Lerner. January 13, 1968. Box 2, Folder 9. James Baldwin Photographs and Papers. Beinecke Rare Book and Manuscript Library. Yale University.

30. James Baldwin, *One Day When I Was Lost: A Scenario Based on Alex Haley's "The Autobiography of Malcolm X."* New York: The Dial Press, 1973, p. 256.

31. Ossie Davis, "Eulogy Delivered by Ossie Davis at the Funeral for Malcolm X." February 27, 1965. http://malcolmx.com/eulogy/.

32. Magdalena Zaborowska, *James Baldwin's Turkish Decade: Erotics of Exile*. Durham: Duke University Press, 2009, p. 175.

33. Ibid., p. 178.

34. See Magdalena Zaborowska, *Me and My House: James Baldwin's Last Decade in France*. Durham: Duke University Press, 2018.

35. James Baldwin and Margaret Mead, *A Rap on Race*. Philadelphia: Lippincott, 1971, p. 193.

36. "An Appeal by Black Americans Against United States Support for the Zionist Government of Israel." *New York Times*. November 1, 1970. www.blackleftunity.org/blackliberationarchive.htm.

37. James Baldwin and Nikki Giovanni. *A Dialogue*. New York: Lippincott, 1973, p. 45.

38. Ibid., p. 65.
39. Ibid., p. 67.
40. Ibid., p. 67.
41. Ibid., p. 94.
42. "It's Hard to be James Baldwin." Interview with Herbert R. Lottman. First published in *Intellectual Digest*, 2 (July 1972), pp. 67–68. Republished in *Conversations with James Baldwin*. Ed. Fred L. Standley and Louis H. Pratt. Jackson: University Press of Mississippi, 1989, p. 121.
43. Ibid., p. 111.
44. Baldwin, *No Name*, pp. 196–97.
45. James Baldwin *The FBI File*. Ed. William J. Maxwell. New York: Arcade Publishing, 2017, p. 1002.
46. Leeming, *Biography*, p. 308.
47. Baldwin, *No Name*, p. 18.
48. "*The Black Scholar* Interviews James Baldwin." First published in *The Black Scholar*, 5 (December 1973–January 1974), pp. 33–42. Republished in *Conversations with James Baldwin*. Ed. Fred L. Standley and Louis H. Pratt. Jackson: University Press of Mississippi, 1989, p. 145. See also Baldwin, *No Name in the Street*, p. 184.
49. Ibid., p. 148.
50. Ibid., p. 149.
51. Ibid., p. 150.
52. Ibid., p. 146.
53. Ibid., p. 150.
54. Maxwell, *FBI*, p. 1045.
55. James Baldwin, *If Beale Street Could Talk*. New York: Vintage International, 2002, p. 36.
56. Ibid., p. 57.
57. Ibid., p. 197.
58. Lottman, "Hard," p. 109.
59. "Beale Street Blues" lyrics. www.lyricsfreak.com/l/louis+armstrong/beale+street+blues_20826531.html.
60. Baldwin, *Beale*, p. 135.
61. See bell hooks, *Black Looks: Race and Representation*. Boston: Sound End Press, 1992.

62. James Baldwin, *The Devil Finds Work* in *James Baldwin: Collected Essays*. New York: Vintage International, 1998, p. 511.

63. Ibid., p. 555.

64. Ibid., p. 555.

65. Ibid., p. 572.

66. Christopher Lehmann-Haupt, "Review of *The Devil Finds Work*." *New York Times*. June 4, 1976. Box 37, Folder 8. James Baldwin Photographs and Manuscripts. New York Public Library. Schomburg Center for Research in Black Culture.

67. See James Baldwin and Yoran Cazac, *Little Man Little Man: A Story of Childhood*. Durham, NC: Duke University Press, 2018, p. xviii. See also Nicholas Boggs, "Baldwin and Yoran Cazac's 'Child's Story for Adults'" in *The Cambridge Companion to James Baldwin*. Ed. Michele Elam. Cambridge: Cambridge University Press, 2015, pp. 118–34.

68. Baldwin, *Little Man*, p. xv.

69. Ibid., p. xvii.

70. James Baldwin, "A Talk to Teachers" in *James Baldwin: Collected Essays*. New York: Vintage International, 1998, p. 685.

71. "James Baldwin Comes Home", interview with Jewell Handy Gresham. First published in *Essence*, 7 (June 1976), pp. 54–5, 80, 82, 85. Republished in *Conversations with James Baldwin*. Ed. Fred L. Standley and Louis H. Pratt. Jackson: University Press of Mississippi, 1989, p. 166.

72. James Baldwin, "A Challenge to Bicentennial Candidates" in *James Baldwin: The Cross of Redemption*. New York: Vintage International, 2010, p. 127.

73. Ibid., p. 128.

74. Ibid., p. 129.

75. James Baldwin, "How One Black Man Came to Be an American" in *James Baldwin: Collected Essays*. New York: Vintage International, 1998, p. 762.

76. James Baldwin, "An Open Letter to Mr. Carter" in *James Baldwin: Collected Essays*. New York: Vintage International, 1998, p. 769.

Chapter 7. Final Acts

1. James Baldwin, *Jimmy's Blues and Other Poems*. Boston: Beacon Press, 2014, p. 5.

2. "Go The Way Your Blood Beats." *Village Voice*, June 26, 1984. Republished in *James Baldwin: The Last Interview*. Brooklyn: Melville House, 2014, p. 72.

3. "Revolutionary Hope: A Conversation Between James Baldwin and Audre Lorde." *Essence Magazine*, 1984. http://theculture. forharriet.com/2014/03/revolutionary-hope-conversation-between.html.

4. James Baldwin, "Dark Days" in *Collected Essays*. New York: The Library of America, 1998, p. 798.

5. Ibid., p. 798.

6. James Baldwin, *Just Above My Head*. New York: Delta, 1979, p.110.

7. Ibid., p. 584.

8. James Baldwin, "Of the Sorrow Songs: The Cross of Redemption" in *The Cross of Redemption: Uncollected Writings*. Ed. Randall Kenan. New York: Vintage International, 2010, p. 153.

9. *I Am Not Your Negro*. New York: Vintage International, 2017, p. 6.

10. James Baldwin, "Open Letter to the Born Again" in *Collected Essays*. New York: The Library of America, 1998, p. 785.

11. Ibid., p. 786.

12. Ibid., pp. 786–87.

13. Ibid., p. 787.

14. James Baldwin, "The News from All the Northern Cities Is, to Understate it, Grim; the State of the Union Is Catastrophic" in *The Cross of Redemption: Uncollected Writings*. Ed. Randall Kenan. New York: Vintage International, 2010, p. 131.

15. "James Baldwin: An Interview." Wolfgang Binder. First published in *Revista/Review Interamericana*, 10 (Fall 1980), pp. 326–41. Republished in *Conversations with James Baldwin*. Ed. Fred L. Standley and Louis H. Pratt. Jackson: University Press of Mississippi, 1989, p. 184.

16. James Baldwin, "Black English: A Dishonest Argument" in *The Cross of Redemption: Uncollected Writings*. Ed. Randall Kenan. New York: Vintage International, 2010, p. 159.

17. Ibid., p. 178.

18. James Baldwin, "Notes on the House of Bondage" in *Collected Essays*. New York: The Library of America, 1998, p. 804.

19. James Baldwin, "Freaks and the American Ideal of Manhood" in *Collected Essays*. New York: The Library of America, 1998, p. 815.

20. Joseph Vogel, *James Baldwin and the 1980s: Witnessing the Reagan Era*. Urban: University of Illinois Press, 2019, p. 119.

21. Ibid., p. 124.

22. Ibid., p. 124.

23. Ibid., p. 131.

24. James Baldwin, *The Evidence of Things Not Seen*. New York: Henry Holt, 1995, p. 12.

25. Ibid., p. 9.

26. Ibid., p. 19.

27. Ibid., p. 19.

28. Ibid., p. 78.

29. Ibid., p. 79.

30. Ibid., p. 98.

31. Centers for Disease Control and Prevention, "Morbidity and Mortality Weekly Report." June 1, 2001. Vol. 50, No. 21. www.cdc.gov/mmwr/PDF/wk/mm5021.pdf.

32. Baldwin, *Evidence*, p. 122.

33. Ibid., p. 123.

34. Binder, "James Baldwin," p. 197.

35. "The Art of Fiction LXXVII: James Baldwin." Jordan Elgrably and George Plimpton. First published in *The Paris Review*, 26 (spring 1984), pp. 49–82. Republished in *Conversations with James Baldwin*. Ed. Fred L. Standley and Louis H. Pratt. Jackson: University Press of Mississippi, 1989, p. 239.

36. Goldstein, "Go," pp. 66–67.

37. See Matt Brim, *James Baldwin and the Queer Imagination*. Ann Arbor: University of Michigan Press, 2014, especially "The Queer Imagination and the Male Conundrum," pp. 152–76.

38. David Leeming, *James Baldwin: A Biography*. New York: Alfred Knopf, 1994, p. 239.

39. "The Combahee River Collective Statement" in *How We Get Free: Black Feminism and the Combahee River Collective*. Ed. Keeanga-Yamahtta Taylor. Chicago: Haymarket Books, 2017.

40. James Baldwin and Audre Lorde, "Revolutionary Hope." http://mocada-museum.tumblr.com/post/73421979421/revolutionary-hope-a-conversation-between-james.

41. Ibid.

42. Baldwin, "Freaks," p. 828.

43. Goldstein, "Go," p. 59.

44. Ibid., p. 68.

45. Ibid., p. 65.

46. James Baldwin, "Black and Jews" in *The Cross of Redemption: Uncollected Writings*. Ed. Randall Kenan. New York: Vintage International, 2010, p. 174.

47. Ibid., p. 175.

48. Ibid., p. 177.

49. "Action at Massachusetts University Raises Censorship Cry." *The New York Times*. May 29, 1988. www.nytimes.com/1988/05/29/us/action-at-massachusetts-u-raises-censorship-cry.html.

50. See Magdalena Zaborowska, *James Baldwin's Turkish Decade: The Erotics of Exile*. Durham: Duke University Press, 2009, p. xxiv.

51. Ibid., p. 251.

52. James Baldwin, "The Welcome Table." Box 138. James Baldwin Papers, 1936–92. New York Public Library. Schomburg Center for Research in Black Culture, p. 75.

53. Ibid., p. 37.

54. Quoted in James Campbell, *Talking at the Gates: A Life of James Baldwin*. New York: Viking, 1991, p. 271.

55. Ibid., p. 249.

56. Vogel, *James Baldwin*, p. 79.

57. Ibid., p. 80.

58. James Baldwin, "As Much Truth As One Can Bear" in *The Cross of Redemption: Uncollected Writings*. Ed. Randall Kenan. New York: Vintage International, 2010, p. 42.

Postscript: Baldwin's Queer Legacies

1. Amiri Baraka, "Jimmy!" in *James Baldwin: The Legacy*. Ed. Quincy Troupe. New York: Touchstone Boos, 1989, p. 134.

Acknowledgments

In 1987 I was teaching freshman writing at Hunter College in New York City. Every term, I would teach James Baldwin's essay "Fifth Avenue, Uptown: A Letter from Harlem." Because we were not far from Harlem, and because my students were so much like a young Baldwin—working-class immigrants, migrants, or diasporic subjects living for the city—the essay was always a huge hit. Everyone wanted to write their own version of the piece. Especially, everyone wanted to find a way to express in their own words Baldwin's slow, burning rage towards abusive state power. In 1983, young, Black graffiti artist Michael Stewart had been murdered by New York City Transit Police for painting on a subway wall. In 1984, 66-year-old Eleanor Bumpurs, a Black woman, was shot dead in her Bronx apartment by New York City police who were evicting her. "The only way to police a ghetto is to be oppressive," wrote Baldwin in "Letter from Harlem." The presence of the police "is an insult, and it would be, even if they spent their entire day feeding gumdrops to children."

Fast forward to February, 2012. Seventeen-year-old Trayvon Martin is shot to death by George Zimmerman in Sanford, Florida, carrying a bag of Skittles candy. Black Lives Matter returns people to where their collective hopes are always most animated—the street. At my campus in Indiana, 500 people march. Two years later, in June, 2014, Eric Garner is murdered by cops in Staten Island. In August, Michael Brown is killed by police in Ferguson. Our students and faculty stage a "die-in," tying up traffic, reading poetry in intersections, wagering with their bodies that change must come.

It was these dissenting lives that brought me back to "A Letter from Harlem," and back to Baldwin. In the Fall of 2016, I offered a graduate seminar called "James Baldwin and the Global Black Freedom Struggle." Students in that seminar— Andrea Adomako, Yu Dou, Ruqayyah Perkins-Wiliams, Kylie Regan and Megan Williams—dove into Baldwin's thought, deploying his ideas, reassembling them, in order to make sense of the social movement of Black Lives Matter, gender and sexuality in *Another Country* and *Giovanni's Room*, feminism (or not?) in *Blues for Mister Charlie*. Together, these students helped envision new relationships between what Edward Said—himself a student and admirer of Baldwin's work—called the world, the text and the critic. This project owes in part to their vision.

Fortuitously, as I was planning my Baldwin seminar, Alice Craven and Wiliam Dow at the American University of Paris invited me to give a keynote at the biennial International James Baldwin Conference. The conference, titled "A Language to Dwell In," featured brilliant talks by a wide range of Baldwin scholars, and other keynotes: by Baldwin biographer James Campbell, and the luminous Robert Reid-Pharr, who spoke movingly about reading Baldwin in the wake of 9/11 and a new globalized racial violence. At that meeting I connected with some of the great Baldwin scholars of our moment—including Magdalena Zaborowska, Monique Wells, Jake Lamar, Ed Pavlic, and Matt Brim. I am grateful to Alice and William for inviting me to their "welcome table" and giving this project a boost.

In the intervening years between 2016 and now, a raft of people have taught me how to try to think and read and see the fullness of James Baldwin's life and work. Many of them are mentioned in the pages of this book. Special appreciation goes to Baldwin's previous biographers; among whom I include James Campbell, David Leeming, Herb Boyd and Magdalena Zaborowska. This book does not exist without their efforts. Though he would probably not characterize it as a biography, Douglas Fields's rigorous political exploration of Baldwin's career in *All Those Strangers: The Art and Lives of James Baldwin*, set me down paths I especially wanted go to, including Baldwin's debt to and relationship to the U.S. left. Similarly, Doug was exceedingly generous in offering space in Volume 5 of the *James Baldwin Review* for an excerpt from Chapter 3 of this book. I also owe a special thanks to *JBR* editorial assistant Justin Joyce for posing exceptionally thoughtful questions that became the basis for an interview published in the same issue of the journal.

At the head, too, of my appreciations is my comrade Paul Le Blanc. Paul has been a mentor and role model for many years for his extraordinary contributions to the history of Marxism and the left. It was he who first invited me to consider writing a biography for Pluto's Revolutionary Lives series, which he co-edits with Sarah Irving. The series is itself a model for what engaged scholarship for a wide political readership can be.

I also owe exceptional debts to scholars in Black Queer Studies who since the late 1990s have made the *whole* of James Baldwin legible. There are innumerable people in the field whose work I've learned from in writing this book, but among them are Matt Brim, Roderick Ferguson, E. Patrick Johnson, Jr., Dwight McBride, Robert Reid-Pharr, Marlon Ross, and Maurice Wallace. Feminist critics, too, like the esteemed Trudier Harris, have been instrumental in shaping my own thinking about Baldwin's work and life.

I've had remarkable assistance from the library staffs at both the Beinecke Library at Yale, which hosts the James Baldwin

Photographs and Papers, and the Schomburg Center for Research in Black Culture in New York, home to a large store of Baldwin's archives, manuscripts and letters. Research to work in these locations was generously supported by Purdue University. Alan Wald, who is himself an invaluable archive of the literary left, was generous in sharing materials in his collection about Baldwin, as well as critical insights from his own scholarship.

Pluto Press has wrapped its arms around this book in ways for which I am very grateful. Thanks to my general editor David Castle. Melanie Patrick designed the knock-out cover for the 2019 hardcover, an homage to the first edition of Baldwin's masterpiece, *The Fire Next Time*. Robert Webb and Dan Harding have been meticulous in getting the manuscript into top shape. Kieran O'Connor and Will Confalone have helped the book reach people.

People closest to me have provided the most important support, both material and emotional. If book-making depends on life-making, I owe my greatest debt to Tithi Bhattacharya. Benjamin Balthaser was a great late-night sparring partner as we talked through Baldwin (and Richard Wright); Benjamin also sharpened many of my arguments about Baldwin and Zionism. My comrade Joe Allen showed great support for this book. Mike Mergenthaler coached me through the writing burn. My Chicago comrades Dennis Kosuth, Kirstin Roberts, Jason Yanowitz and Annie Zirin were welcoming friends as I spent time working on the manuscript in that city. My family out west, my father Jack, sister Jean, their partners, and children, hover as ongoing inspiration in the margins of this book, as does my mother, Lynn, who made me believe I could love my life and my work.

This book is dedicated to the children closest to me: my son Max, and my daughter Shayari. I give them this life of Jimmy

Baldwin because they, too, live in a world on fire, a world they inherited but which was not meant to burn. With them, for them, we can and must do better.

Bill V. Mullen

Revolutionary Lives

Revolutionary Lives is a series of short, critical biographies of radical figures from throughout history. The books are sympathetic but not sycophantic, and the intention is to present a balanced and, where necessary, critical evaluation of the individual's place in their political field, putting their actions and achievements in context and exploring issues raised by their lives, such as the use or rejection of violence, nationalism, or gender in political activism. While individuals are the subject of the books, their personal lives are dealt with lightly except insofar as they mesh with political concerns. The focus is on the contribution these revolutionaries made to history, an examination of how far they achieved their aims in improving the lives of the oppressed and exploited, and how they can continue to be an inspiration for many today.

Series Editors:
Sarah Irving, King's College, London
Professor Paul Le Blanc, La Roche College, Pittsburgh

Also available

Index